Groundwork of
Worship and Preaching

Groundwork of Worship and Preaching

Richard G. Jones

London EPWORTH PRESS

ISBN 7162 0355 3

Enquiries should be addressed to
The Methodist Publishing House
Wellington Road
Wimbledon
London SW19 8EU

Computerset by
MFK Graphic Systems (Typesetting) Ltd.
Saffron Walden, Essex

Printed in Great Britain by
The Garden City Press Limited
Letchworth, Hertfordshire SG6 1JS

Preface

THE Local Preachers' Studies Board and the Local Preachers' Committee of the Methodist Church are grateful to Richard G. Jones for writing *Groundwork of Worship and Preaching*, the text-book authorized by the Methodist Conference for local preachers on trial studying for the Connexional Examination in Worship and Preaching. It is hoped that the book will also be of use to lay preachers in the United Reformed Church, and indeed to anyone with an interest in this field. The author has been advised by the members of the Worship and Preaching Panel of the Local Preachers' Studies Board, to whom thanks are also due.

The Study Scheme for the use of local preachers on trial is at the back of the book.

JOHN STACEY
Connexional Local Preachers' Secretary

Contents

Chapter 1

Christian Worship

As Local or Lay Preachers we are called to lead Christian worship in the life of the Protestant Churches. At once we have to try to be clear about the nature and purpose of our worship. What are we trying to achieve when we meet in a special church building and sing and pray together, listen to sermons and join in simple rituals? What is it all for? How do we begin to plan such an experience? How can we test whether it has been successful or not? We soon find that there is a wide variety of responses to such questions. The easiest way to notice this is to look at the various types of church building in which today's Christians are worshipping. Each type expresses something slightly different about the nature of Christian worship. Imagine then that you are sent to lead worship in five different church buildings, and in each case you ask yourself 'What did people believe about worship when they designed this sort of place?'. We shall soon notice this wide range of views.

First, you go to a typical rectangular building with a high, strong-looking pulpit dominating the central front area. Behind it there is probably a pipe organ; beneath there is a small table and communion rail. There is a cross or possibly the cryptogram 'I.H.S.' woven into the pulpit fall. There is some coloured glass in the major windows and a sombre plaque or two along the walls. Maybe there is a text written over the arch above the organ chamber, behind the preacher. Otherwise there is little formal symbolism anywhere. The pews are built in firm straight lines down through the body of the building, with one or two aisles and a limited amount of space below the pulpit. Perhaps there is a gallery running round three sides, or merely a balcony at the back. The word 'chapel' immediately comes to your mind. When you stand in the pulpit the place looks like a dense regiment of wooden seats.

The design has tried to gather as many people together as possible within an extremely simple shape so that all can clearly see the preacher and hear both preacher and organ. The height of the roof helps the sound of both the speaking and the singing. The structure is the most economical possible for that purpose. There is no waste space and few frills. The place could well have been erected by people who had limited resources and simple tastes. What does it say about Christian worship? In particular this chapel is saying that Christian worship is a matter of meeting together around God's Word as mediated through the Bible and a preacher, and sharing in appropriate singing and praying. There is very little emphasis upon the sacraments, so that a font is probably not apparent anywhere and the communion table is physically insignificant. There is only a slight awareness of aesthetic beauty, so the frontal area may well be a muddle of items not visually satisfying nor carefully planned. It may indeed be somewhat crude to our modern tastes or frankly hideous, as when a choir has been interposed between pulpit and organ and equipped with elaborate rails on which to support music books. Very occasionally however such chapels, if uncluttered, can have a striking and satisfying beauty about them (as with the meticulous balance, simplicity of line and absence of fuss that one notices in a good Queen Anne house).

That chapel was probably built in the last century. It will almost certainly not have been built after 1930, but could conceivably be dated back into the period of the Evangelical Revival. John Wesley must have preached in many such buildings towards the end of his ministry. So there is a sense of tradition about them, a sense that they were part of a very important element in the religious life of the country, that they enshrine the great Bible-preaching emphasis upon which most nonconformist congregations were established.

Secondly, you go to a markedly different building. It is in an area which was once a wealthy middle-class suburb. It has a fine spire, a high nave, and a design like many a parish church.

The ground plan is basically that of a cross, with stubby transepts at either side, steps leading up into the chancel, and at its far end a communion table raised up high. The choir is mounted on either side of the chancel, facing each other, and the pulpit is at one side by the chancel steps and is balanced by a lectern opposite. There are soaring pillars down the sides of the nave and possibly a large stone font in a transept. The organ is not conspicuous. There are perhaps some elaborate stained-glass windows, especially the dominant one over the communion table, and you expect to encounter symbolism everywhere – crosses, the XR sign, the signs of the fish, the ark or the shepherd's crook. When people walk in they instinctively hush their voices (but they don't do that in the chapel).

The place seems to be built to promote a sense of the grandeur of God, to send the eyes soaring up the pillars to the high roof, to create a feeling of being in a rather rare and special part of the world. The far table seems to be surrounded by a sense of mystery and distance. Every feature of the building has some sort of symbolic meaning – the cross for the ground plan of the building, the golden eagle for the lectern, the carvings on the pulpit and table and pew heads, the pictures captured in the stained glass, the insignia on the doors. What does the building say about Christian worship? Here the setting seems to be saying the worship is awe before the otherness of God, that it requires liturgy and stately movement and ceremonial, that it should feature a balance between the preaching and the reading of the Bible, that it should have as its climax the Lord's Supper, which is the final mystery at the highest point in the building.

That church was probably built between 1860 and the turn of the century, when the more wealthy noncomformists were saying that they too saw themselves as needing dignified churches to worship in, and wanted the ceremony and order which the local parish church featured. Since the Church of England had experienced a revival of neo-gothic architecture, a longing to capture great past glories of the medieval church, and a hunger for more sacramental observance, so the chapel began to give way to a place like the parish church. It too might be called 'St Paul's' or 'St John's'. It too would need a well-

11

trained choir to lead the chanting of psalms as well as the singing of hymns; it too might use services derived from the Church of England Prayer Book, even if slightly amended by John Wesley and his followers. It too treasured order, robes and modest ritual.

Thirdly, you go to the city centre, or to the edge of what was, and may still be, a teeming, poor neighbourhood, to a place which everyone calls 'the Hall.' It has a big, wide doorway opening on to a busy pavement. Inside it is more like a small concert hall, with a stage dominating the arena and places for a large choir behind, but overshadowed by a huge organ. The tip-up seats are arranged in a big semi-circle around the stage, which has a small lectern at its centre. Underneath there may be a tiny communion table and rail.

It was probably built between 1880 and 1930, and was part of the great effort of that era to try to reach the poor and those who never went near the traditional churches. Great revivalist crusades had been held to try to win those people, and most Church leaders believed that the best method was to have pleasant 'halls' built on the main streets and easy to enter. There the worship would consist of lively catchy music, led perhaps by an orchestra, and so needing a stage. The centre would be dominated by the preacher, who was supremely an orator with a folksy touch. The worship was designed to enable people estranged from the churches to hear the gospel news in a bright and challenging way, and would probably conclude with an impassioned appeal to come and kneel at the front and be converted. There was no sense here of social class, of people standing on their dignity, of special pews for favoured people. It was 'the people's worship' and you could clap your hands and shout the choruses and laugh loudly at the preacher's jokes and put a penny in the collection if that were all that you had. And on Saturday night next you could come here again for a concert instead of going to the local pub. It offered the poor man's culture as well as the poor man's religion.

The building expresses a notion of worship far removed from that of St John's. Here the emphasis is upon mateyness, on healthy and boisterous emotion and uninhibited singing, on the rousing preacher and the traumatic experience of conversion. There is little symbolism, subtlety or sophistication about it.

Next, you go to the council estate built between the 1930s and 1960s, where there is a rather forlorn dual-purpose hall suffering painfully from vandalism and surrounded by broken fences and wild bits of garden. Inside at the far end a big high cross hangs against the major wall, with a small communion table beneath. There is a simple pulpit on one side within the sanctuary area, and the blue patch of carpet there supplies a hint of warmth despite the general drabness everywhere else. A screen has been drawn midway across the hall, and the people sit in lines on portable seats. There is a sense of the makeshift about it all.

What does the building say about Christian worship? That although we need to focus our attention upon a cross, upon the Word and the sacrament, we can do that in a building designed for lots of other purposes too – for Scout parades and Youth Club sessions, for badminton and five-a-side football, for ,the local concerts and Christmas fairs and jumble sales, for voting at election times, for the Sunday School and the Pensioners Club. Worship is not all that different from these hurly-burly activities, for it too is part of the common life of the local community and tries to offer to God all that bustle and fun and helpfulness. It can perhaps best do that in the same place wherein all those other worthwhile activities happen, thereby demonstrating that religion and communal life are all part of the same endeavour to serve God and man. A church which sets out to serve the world's needs must use its resources so that its buildings can fulfil a whole variety of purposes and be as fully at the community's disposal as possible. Are not the worship of God and the service of man but two sides to the same coin?

Finally you go to a church built in the last ten years. It is not big, but the architect has made the building look quite distinctive and has sloped the roof and designed the windows so that the major wall focuses the eye and is well lit. A long slender, carefully-proportioned cross emphasizes the height. The pulpit is to one side, not very large, and a wide table stands in the centre, backed by rich curtains. A neat font, designed to tone

13

with pulpit and table, stands on the other side. There may not even be a communion rail, but the whole sanctuary space will be slightly raised, offering a long strip of cushion upon which a line of persons can kneel. The seating is moveable but comfortable and colourful. It is arranged around the central area as a big half moon. The whole place is designed with simplicity, relying upon bare plain walls and soaring windows of clear glass reaching up from ground level. The lamp shades and organ console, the flower stands and the hymn numbering boards have all been planned to suit the dominating lines and shapes of the whole. It is aesthetically very satisfying, even if the bare walls and long windows give a slightly chill impression.

What does it express about Christian worship? That worship is a distinctive activity requiring a distinctive, special building; that it centres upon the Font, the Table and the Word; that it is a matter of the whole family of God's people gathering around these focal points and able to see each other's faces whilst doing so; that there must be room for movement, maybe for drama and dancing, so the table and pulpit and font will be moveable; that we should covet colour and symbolism and freshness, even if we can't afford and don't need elaborate and enormous buildings any more.

Those five churches have expressed a wide variety of feelings, assumptions and attitudes about worship. It is the event for God's people to gather round Word and Sacrament; no, it is the happening when those who are not believers can be challenged to accept the gospel, repent and believe. It must centre upon the Table set here amongst us; no, it must centre upon the Table set high and far away in its aura of mystery. It should be in the place where our week-by-week service is offered to God and man; no, it must be in a special place which makes one hushed because it is holy ground. It must eschew the distractions of artists and designers; no, it must harness all those skills to intrigue the people and prompt them to seek the deep meanings only hinted at in symbol and cunning design. It must be conducted with a firm predictable order, led by the skilled people at the front; no, it is our common offering and we all contribute to it together, with the leader acting as our

14

representative, not our mentor nor teacher nor commanding officer. It involves our escaping from the world and its hurly-burly; no, it involves our remembering all that, and bringing it consciously to God. It involves our acknowledging that God is encountered in the everyday; no, God is encountered in a special story, a tradition treasured by his saints down through the ages, maintained only because those people have watched over it with scrupulous care and sometimes at terrible cost. It is marked by a free and easy shouting and clapping and con-viviality; no, it is marked by reverence, stateliness, respect, reserve.

So there is a welter of opinions amongst us as to what Christian worship is intended to be. If you ask the different members of the normal congregation what they come to wor-ship for, there will be another wide range of answers. Some will say that they come to be inspired, to have their faltering faith renewed and revived. Others want to 'feel God's presence', or to receive a helpful message, or to be encouraged by meeting their friends or singing the hymns. If the question is pushed hard, 'What do you hope to get out of attending a church service?' the answers will range freely over concerns such as those. There may be a noticeably subjective element within them. 'I go to worship so that I can get the following benefits for myself. . . .', or 'to charge my spiritual batteries', or some-thing similar.

Perhaps all those principles of church design, and all those unguarded answers from the average members of the average congregation express something of the truth. When they appear to be contradictory perhaps that is because the truth is somewhere between them, and one should not go to extremes either way? Perhaps the worship of God is a special sort of activity not really like the holding of a jumble sale and Youth Club discos and requiring a place that gives one a special sense of occasion? Yet it should not be so extravagantly different that it divorces the worship of God from the everyday service of man? Perhaps the preacher should be the central figure, yet central as the people's representative and not the people's dictator? Perhaps the worship should sometimes lead up to a formal commitment as a result of conversion, but more often

15

lead up to a formal commitment by receiving the bread and wine? Or, if a lay person is conducting the service, prayers and affirmations of commitment and service?

Other Christians

The more you mull over such questions the more necessary it becomes to look around at other Christian bodies and see what they are doing. The Quakers are maintaining their long established principle that worship is a time for quiet meditation together, and that the Spirit can prompt any member to lead the thoughts or to stimulate everyone to sing or pray. For them, there is no need for specially-trained preachers and ministers, but the need is for everyone to be trained in quiet reflection and the occasional sharing of their insights.

The Orthodox hold that Christian worship is by far the most important activity that anyone can conceivably share in, and that in the liturgy the whole great purpose of God is carefully and fully rehearsed, over and over again, week by week, so that if you are regularly caught up in the liturgy you are being totally educated for both life on earth and life in heaven. God's activity in creation and redemption, in human history and beyond it, will all be rehearsed. It doesn't matter if at first you don't understand the meaning of every bit of the stately ritual, because you must come again and again, week in and week out until you die, and still you won't have plumbed its riches of meaning. Every conceivable appeal to the sense will be utilized – gorgeous vestments, ecstatic music, sweet-smelling incense, elaborate imagery and icons and symbols, clapping and full-throated chanting, magnificent pageantry.

The Pentecostalists and black Churches have developed the participation of the whole congregation quite remarkably. You clap, shout out your own praises and 'amens', and lead the prayers and testimonies if the Spirit so takes you. You are an integral part of the ecstasy of the people of God. The music can be led by any sort of instrument that can express praise. The sermon can be interrupted if you so wish. The service can last as long as you want.

16

The Church of England has experienced a whole range of changes in the last few years, most of them aimed at making the communion service the main act of worship, at enabling all the people to share as fully as possible in that service and at stressing the corporate nature of worship. These changes will be studied further in chapter three.

The Roman Catholics have also developed the people's participation. Now the Table is usually brought down into the centre of the church, there is far more hymn-singing, many people are involved both in the reading of lessons and the service of the communion, the priest preaches a longer sermon and builds it more clearly around the Bible readings. Moreover every person is given a sheet setting out the whole service and the Bible lessons for the day. Everything is in plain English. Although enormous changes have happened within the last few years there is an atmosphere about that worship which seems to say 'This is what the Church Catholic has been doing ever since the first apostles. That is the great succession in which we stand. Take heart, we have lasted through many a turbulent and violent century before. We will go on doing this until God ends time altogether.'

Undoubtedly a look at other communions and their worship life helps us to assess what is really important and what is not. It also shows us how much vigour there is about many different forms of Christian worship, and how varied are the forms which Christians from different traditions will find appropriate for their regular use. But ask the question about the nature of Christian worship, what it really is all about, and the most useful concept will turn out to be *celebration*. Christian worship, whatever church it is held in, is God's people celebrating their faith, celebrating the gospel news, celebrating that all worth and truth belong in God. Worship is thus an ascribing of worthship to God, an ascription that leads to praise and thanksgiving and joy.

When a baby is born and the mother is strong enough, it is right and fitting for the family and friends to be called together for a celebration. When a young person comes of age, there should be a celebration. When a couple marry, or have 25 years of marriage to be thankful for, there should be a celebra-

17

tion. When Christians meet together on the first day of the week, the day that points to Jesus' resurrection, there should be a celebration to which all friends are invited. The focus will not be on the needs of the participants, but upon the event which draws them together – the acts of God in Jesus. It is a way of God's people saying that only God matters, only God is of supreme worth, only God can direct us into truth and light and life, only God is worthy of praise. But of such supreme praise! Moreoever, God can be known through the story of his work amongst us, the history of the Jewish people, the events of Jesus the Christ, so that a rehearsing and recalling of those events must be a major feature of the celebration.

Of course, the mood of the nation at present is not particularly favourable to Christian worship. Recent studies suggest that church attendance over the last 150 years has never been very high. It rose until about 20 per cent. of the population attended a Protestant Church fairly regularly during the middle of the nineteenth century, but the figure has dropped steadily ever since and is now in the region of 8 per cent. Within some neighbourhoods the position has always been better than average (e.g. some mining communities or many suburban areas) whereas some areas have been worse (e.g. London has always had an abysmally low rate). Some sections of the population have never been effectively 'churched' and millions of people today have only the haziest notion of Christian belief. This means that anyone who regularly shares in Christian worship is in a minority position, even when we allow for the other 8 per cent. of the population that attends Roman Catholic worship. It means that the gulf between the 'pulpit' and the 'pavement' is wider than ever.

It is worth our while to pause here, asking what are the main factors promoting that gulf and making the task of the churches less and less popular, the activity of a fringe people. Is it necessarily something that is inherently wrong with us, making our worship life so utterly irrelevant or dull, that no sensible person today would want to be associated with it? Is it because the modern world has become progressively more evil and superficial? We cannot dismiss that first question too easily, because we all know of churches where the worship is indeed

18

remarkably dull and pitiably irrelevant, conducted in a funereal atmosphere and using a language and hymnody that were becoming old-fashioned in Victoria's days, and are even more so in our own. But on the other hand there is no essential reason for imagining that Christian worship will ever be a popular activity, that the majority of people will ever become deeply committed Christians, that the Church will ever attract to itself more than a minority. Nowhere in the New Testament is there the slightest hint that it will ever be otherwise than now. So we have a primary responsibility to see that our forms of Christian worship reflect properly the vitality and beliefs of Christianity. But when we have done that, there is no guarantee that the majority of mankind will then become Christian. Indeed, the more some people see of genuine Christianity, the more they may well want to repudiate it.

There could be reasons for nodding assent to the second question posed just now. Perhaps the modern era is an increasingly evil or irreligious one? This is a theme which has attracted a great deal of attention from theologians over the last thirty years. Most of them are reluctant to make simple judgements implying progressively evil tendencies in contemporary culture. Instead, they see many factors at work, many of them having both good and bad features, or aspects which are essentially neutral. Preachers need to understand these issues clearly, so we should give careful attention here. There are at least five factors to consider.

First, we obviously live in a culture which finds less and less need to refer to God when explaining anything. Therefore those institutions which were once very closely linked to the churches and used Christian language now try to shake themselves free – educational ones, legal ones, medical ones. The disciplines involved in the practice of those institutions do not have to be rooted in some sort of faith in God, they are quite autonomous and may even flourish better if properly freed from any sort of religious apron-strings. A doctor does not have to know the Bible in order to be a good surgeon; a politician may be highly competent at managing affairs of government without believing in the Trinity; a scientist may unravel mysteries that bring enormous benefit to mankind, yet

19

may well be an atheist. So, knowledge is no longer tied securely to religious beliefs. The world has become 'secularized' and most functions can be well understood and managed without invoking a religious frame of reference.

This has the effect of pushing religious talk out on to the margins of most people's concerns. The religious way of looking at things becomes one which a few rather unusual people choose to adopt, whereas the vast majority choose not to. When the religious people use their religious words, the others find it hard to connect them up with their own, mainly scientific, pragmatic, functional ways of describing things. Religious words don't seem to relate to everyday experience in an obvious manner. Religious talk becomes something which happens within a small circle of people who understand the 'in' language. Evangelism becomes very much more difficult than before. So does preaching.

There are some advantages however. It puts Christians on their mettle if we no longer live in a world in which religious faith is self-evident. In a sense, it makes *faith* more meaningful, because now it has to be a much more deliberate act of asserting that this is the way the believer is going to look at life despite the easier option of sharing the attitudes which are prevalent all around us. There is an important discussion of this whole question in John Stacey's *Groundwork of Theology*, pp. 127–41.

Secondly, modern societies are much more pluralist than before and have far more authorities to turn to. In many a city today there will be some Christian believers, some Moslems, some Jews, some Hindus, some Sikhs, some humanists, and a great number of people who are agnostic in their world-views. All these different groups will have a slightly different notion about the sort of society we ought to be building, about the sort of laws that ought to apply, about the sort of education system that ought to inculcate the community's values in the young. There may be some areas of general agreement, but also others of sharp disagreement (over abortion, for example). There will no longer be one dominant authority to which all can refer. Instead, there are many authorities, and that of the Church has been knocked off its previous pedestal. The most obvious

20

illustration of this occurs when a problem is discussed on the media. There will be influential persons adopting quite different stances, and maybe none of them will take up a specifically Christian one at all. The whole impression created will be that of many viewpoints, all of them open to challenge or objection, and all having a struggle to justify themselves.

This has an effect upon preachers. Nobody can now assume that someone by standing in the pulpit must be listened to respectfully and without any challenge. The preacher's authority will be under as much question as anyone else's in the modern world. Nor can the preacher refer to the authority of 'the Church' or 'the Bible' as if those sources were simple, easily-defined, universally acknowledged. The age of simple, plain, easily-identifiable authorities is past. The preacher cannot assume that his or her opinion, his or her experience, his or her learning, is to be accepted without cavil by the members of the congregation.

Thirdly, we now live in an era which is so intoxicated by the immediate benefits of technology and the marvellous possibilities for the imminent future that there is far less sense of history within our culture. Modern life does not encourage us to take long views, to consider the whole sweep of events from the primordial past, to treasure the legends and sagas that make up our background and enrich our sense of tradition. Instead, the cults of today centre upon immediate experience, upon being alive now, and of changing everything quickly. We are less interested in roots, more concerned with the latest shoots. We care little about where we have come from, but are fascinated by the point just ahead, toward which we are moving as fast as possible.

That situation has a debilitating effect upon Christian belief, which centres upon the crucial events of the past. Christian believing is largely a matter of taking up a special attitude towards a string of events that are woven into a very particular history, the history viewed by the writers of the Bible. So Christian discipleship involves taking one's bearings from that history and constantly referring to it, over and over again. It is virtually impossible to be a Christian and not be vividly aware of the importance of the past, of events in Palestine centuries ago. That does not mean being nostalgic or longing for that past to return again, but it does mean the constant rehearsal of that past in such a way that it throws light into the present and future. (For a lively discussion of this theme see Harvey Cox: *The Feast of Fools*.)

Fourthly, our culture is less and less one which depends upon the spoken or written word for the communication of ideas. Instead, it utilizes the visual media more and more extensively. This means that people are not trained to listen for long to a speaker, nor to rely upon oratory for stimulus, nor to depend upon books for knowledge. People do not nowadays commit a great deal of information to memory, nor learn things by rote or by catechism. They merely need to know whereabouts data is stored and how to get at it.

This affects preachers greatly. Sermons must not be long nor detailed. The message must be put across in many more ways than merely by the spoken or written word. The worship must aim to grip the whole man, not just to stretch the mind. The major reliance within the Protestant Churches upon the word must be balanced somehow by a reliance upon other ways of enabling God's truth to lay hold upon us.

Finally, there are many who hold that worship is difficult for us today because the warm cohesion of the local community has been disrupted by our present styles of living. Instead of living in intimate groupings of people who know each other extremely well and feel deeply committed to each other's well being, we now live in sprawling neighbourhoods of estates and fast roadways. When we go to church it is not to be alongside the people whose living we all share, but to be gathered into a building with lots of people whom we never normally meet and with whom we have too little in common. Thus the worship of the parish church in the countryside village of a hundred years ago was strong, and drew upon firm bonds of togetherness which the people felt profoundly. Likewise in the small industrial communities, the mining villages, the urban villages, there was the same strong sense of belonging together which made chapel life so rewarding and supportive. It is not the same today. When we can somehow recapture that mysterious feeling of 'community' we shall be on the way to renewing our common worship life too, for the two belong to each other. Fragmented and isolated modern man is being cut off from the chance of worship through being cut off from a proper involvement with his fellows.

This point can be exaggerated, and can easily become a pining for a lost age which becomes idealized in the process. Those intimate neighbourhoods a hundred years ago were sometimes appalling places to live in, and exposed the inhabitants to a dreadful lack of privacy and many outrageous social pressures. But there is some truth here nevertheless. Think of the occasions when an act of worship made the most impact upon you, and they will include times such as week-end conferences when the group came to know itself very well and discovered a deep sense of common purpose. Or it may have been a prayer meeting or communion service in a house group, or a nurses' fellowship or a student gathering. What gave depth and power to the worship experience was the bond of mutual concern which had first welded the people together.

Thus there are many factors within modern life which make it difficult for Christian worship to flourish. To return to a previous issue, does this throw light upon the basic question of the character of Christian worship? Not really. It helps us to shade in the background against which Christian worship takes place today. But it doesn't tell us what that worship is *for*. In the end the answer to that is a statement of our faith. Christian worship is to celebrate the sort of God in whom Christians believe – the God and Father of our Lord Jesus Christ who lives amongst us in the power of the Holy Spirit. We worship him because he is the supreme reality of the universe, the source of all value and truth and character and goodness and beauty. We worship him simply because he *is*. Our worship is a way of putting our faith into songs, affirmations, listenings, prayings and pledges. Its only justification in the end is that God is indeed like that, like the One whom Jesus displayed and the Bible was written about. Otherwise, there is no point in any of it at all.

For this basic reason, we have no business to discuss Christian worship as if it were a device for getting personal benefits. It cannot be justified by those improvements which it undoub-

23

tedly produces in its subjects. Some of them can perhaps be induced in other ways. A sense of peace can, after all, be readily discovered by the judicious use of drugs, and even a bingo hall can give one a sense of mateyness and good cheer. No. Christian worship is good solely because God is good. It is right solely because God is the final truth about all life. It is a celebration because the sort of God shown us in Christ is the most glorious good news anyone could ever hear about or experience. Almost all Christians are agreed here, and there is a growing consensus that this is central to our understanding of Christian worship. Thus we require such buildings as can best enable us to share fully in that celebration. None of the five types cited at the beginning of this chapter may be the ideal, yet each may have something in its favour. The final one may be especially important, reflecting an understanding which is growing upon us and amongst us today. In the next chapter we will take that enquiry a little further.

Chapter 2

Worship in the Early Church
and the Free Churches

THE first Christians were converted Jews. They were accustomed to regular worship in three different places, their homes, the Temple, and the synagogues. The home was especially important, for here the family's meals were often an experience of prayer and praise as well as of eating and drinking, and at the great feasts there would be elaborate rites in which the family would share. The most important of all was, of course, the Passover. There was a precise procedure for each family to follow as it met to remember the great deliverance under Moses whereby their ancestors became a freed people and God was revealed to be a Saving God. It was the high-point of the year. Every other significant moment in the family's experience would also feature customs and meals steeped in religious meaning – when a new baby was circumcised, when a son reached his twelfth birthday and became 'adult' and able to join with the full-grown men in public worship (the *barmitzvah* ceremony), at weddings and funerals. At every occasion there were ceremonies to be enacted, prayers to be offered, hymns to be sung, Jewish history to be recalled. Home life was rich in religious teaching and worship. This may well be the reason why the Jewish people have been able to keep their faith with such tenacity even in the most difficult and antagonistic of settings, because nobody could wholly prevent them worshipping God in the accustomed manner in the privacy of their homes.

Thus it was quite natural for the first Christians to hold meetings, rituals, religious feasts, in their own homes. It was

25

natural for many of the first congregations to be those which met in houses, especially of the more wealthy people, where there was more room. It was natural for 'love feasts' or 'agapes' to be held in large rooms, and for these to be occasions in which Jesus was especially remembered and the events of the Upper Room recalled.

At first, the Christians went regularly to the Temple for the great feasts, for offering special sacrifices, and for the normal opportunity to meet with religious leaders and authorities and debate the great matters of faith. That was because the Temple was the greatest centre for the regular practice of the Jewish sacrificial system and also something like an open university. The outer courts were thronged with teachers and crowds of people listening and debating with them, so that nobody could be abreast of the best theology of the day or the latest interpretations of the Law unless he participated in that discussion (see Luke 2:41ff).

But soon some Christians became convinced that they were no longer to worship according to the old sacrificial system, with its birds and animals for the slaughter, its high moments of Passover and the Day of Atonement, its special order of priests and its illustrious High Priest. Jesus' death and resurrection made all those rituals unnecessary, for the one great offering had been made once and for all; the priesthood was needed no longer, for Jesus had acted as more than a priest on behalf of all men. One can read a very elaborate exposition of this conviction in the Epistle to the Hebrews, but from very early days Christian thinkers like Stephen had grasped it.[1] Jesus had apparently spoken about the Temple being destroyed.[2] It was a major reason for the Jews' distaste of the Christians, even if some of Jesus' disciples were still prepared to make some token appearances in the Temple (as did Paul in the story related in Acts 21). So, very quickly, many Christians stopped regarding the Temple worship as of any significance or obligation to them.

The third place was to have a much more abiding influence upon Christian worship – the synagogue. The synagogue was

[1] See Acts 7.   [2] Mark 13:2; 14:58; John 2:13–22.

one of the most remarkable religious institutions in the ancient world. No other faith had anything quite like it. How it arose is still shrouded in obscurity, but by the time of Jesus it was widespread throughout the Mediterranean world, wherever there were Jewish communities. It was both a worship centre of a most unusual sort, a school, a community centre for its members, even a law court for them. Its sabbath worship consisted mainly of up to seven readings from the Scriptures (our Old Testament) preceded by very brief introductory prayers, then maybe the singing of some psalms, then the sermon expounding one of the previous readings, then the final prayers. There were no special clergy to conduct the service, but a presiding elder who sorted out who was to do what, an attendant to handle the scrolls, the readers, preacher and someone to lead the prayers. Thus normally about 11 men would be involved, so there was a rule that a synagogue could only function if at least 11 families were able to support it. It meant a detailed weekly rehearsal of God's word together with an exposition in which any adult Jew (that is, any male over 12 years of age) could participate.[3]

The school was held during the week, led by a teacher (rabbi), the main purpose of the education being to fit the boys to be able to share in the sabbath service. Thus they learnt the ancient Hebrew, the scriptures and their meaning in such a way that by the age of 12 they too should be able, if called upon, to read any portion from the scroll, or even to preach the sermon. The synagogue thus became a remarkable centre for maintaining love of the Scriptures and a people able to explain them to each other. Girls were not usually involved, nor did women play any part in the simple liturgy on the sabbath – they attended at the back, behind a screen, and were little better than spectators. In the home, however, the women played a very important and sometimes leading role in the liturgies.

Thus wherever there were Jews in sufficient numbers, there were synagogues. Inevitably there were many of them in the bigger cities, and the different ones would attract Jews with common social status or interests. They also attracted the

[3] There is an interesting account of synagogue worship in Luke 4:6–27.

occasional Gentile, drawn by the serious quality of life of the members and the high moral standards inculcated. These became known as the 'God-fearers' and are mentioned in the New Testament.[4] But the sabbath style of worship had immense influence – the 'synaxis' (or 'gathering together') as it was called. (For further information see W. David Stacey: *Groundwork of Biblical Studies*, pp. 301–3.)

Christian worship sprang up, then, within Jewish worship, or side by side with it, and particularly under the influence of the synagogue. In the New Testament one can sense this happening, when Christians began to formulate new creeds (such as 1 Timothy 3:16 or 1 John 4:2), new blessings or cries of praise (Romans 11:36; Ephesians 3:20f; Revelation 22:20 or 7:12), new prayers such as the Lord's Prayer stemming from Jesus, new outlines of the faith such as are preserved in the accounts of the early sermons (as in Acts 2 and 4), new hymns (such as Ephesians 5:14; Revelation 4:8, 11; 5:9f, 12, 13; 15:3f). Thus the New Testament is soaked in the life and thought of a worshipping people, and doubtless owes much of its form to the needs of that worship.

It is clear that from the earliest times the rite of water baptism was practised by the Church (see Acts 2:41). The synoptic gospels do not record Jesus ever baptizing anyone, but John's gospel states that at one stage Jesus' disciples were baptizing, as also was his cousin John (John 4:2). If so it was only a temporary practice, for baptism was at first much more closely linked to John's ministry and there was even a group of Jews in Ephesus who still maintained John's baptism (Acts 18:25). Steadily baptism became closely related to the gift of the Holy Spirit, and the rite whereby converts became incorporated into the believing Church (Romans 6:3f). It is likely that whole families received baptism, including children, because the family acted as a united group in a much more thorough way than we experience in the modern world (see Acts 16:33). (See further John Stacey: *Groundwork of Theology*, pp. 332–6.)

By reading 1 Corinthians 11:17ff we can sense the problems

[4] e.g. Luke 7:1–10; Acts 10.

28

that were arising when the Lord's Supper was combined with an evening meal. Paul was scandalized by the way in which that celebration had become an occasion for some to gorge themselves whilst others starved. The passage is also very useful to us because it shows the tradition which Paul believed to be binding upon his churches. The accounts given in the gospels do not quite tally with each other, as can quickly be seen by comparing Luke 22:14–20 with Mark 14:22–25 and Matthew 26:26–29, the most glaring difference being Luke's mention of Jesus twice taking the cup. All four passages make it clear however that Jesus had given some specific instruction that he was to be remembered by the sharing of bread and wine, the former signifying his body and the latter his blood, thus pointing to a 'new covenant'.

There were other problems arising, especially the everlasting one of the tension between the spontaneous, the words or actions of some immediate inspiration, and the regulated, the prescribed, the formal and ordered. To what extent should Christian worship feature these two elements? Whenever the one is abandoned in favour of the other, something essential is lost, and the result is an imbalance. We can sense Paul wrestling with this problem in the advice given in 1 Corinthians 12, or the wariness in the early Church about those who claimed to be led by the Spirit, to which situation much of 1 John is addressed.

At some fairly early date most Christians had changed their day of worship from the old Jewish Sabbath (our Saturday now) to the following day, our Sunday. The main reason was that this was the day on which the Lord had risen, so it could fittingly be called 'the Lord's day'. It could not have been an easy decision, for it made life hard for young Christian congregations in the Roman empire. Sunday was an ordinary working day, whereas Jews were normally given special exemptions enabling them to utilize Saturday for their sabbath. The result would be that in many a place the Christians would have to worship very early in the morning before the day's labour began.

Early on there were other very important developments. The major weekly act of worship on the Lord's day became a

29

synaxis modelled upon the synagogue, together with a fairly stylized Lord's Supper without the shared meal which had been such a scandal at Corinth. As the early Church grew it struggled hard to hammer out a common faith, a common form of ministry acceptable to all Christians everywhere, a common recognition of which writings were to be regarded as authoritative and which were not, and a common form for the main services and especially the Lord's Supper. All of this was a long and complex process, but despite all the obscurities which defy the best modern scholarship, we can sketch out fairly confidently the shape of the service for the Lord's day.

According to the account in Mark 14:22–25 Jesus did seven things at the Last Supper when dealing with the bread and wine. He took the bread, gave a thanksgiving, broke it, then shared it out; he took the wine, gave a thanksgiving, then shared it out. It is fairly simple to contract these actions into a basic four: He took (bread and wine); he gave thanks; he broke (the bread); he shared out (both bread and wine). The second act (the thanksgiving) was of great importance in Jewish family rituals. When the father 'gave thanks' before, say, the Passover meal it was not simply a brief utterance thanking God for the food, like the grace we say before meals. It was much more important than that. It was an extensive prayer of thanksgiving to God for all his great deeds on behalf of the Jewish people. It could include a thanks for creation, for the covenant with Abraham, for the rescue from Egypt, the gift of the Law, the settlement in the Promised Land, and so on. It was something of a rehearsal of praise, as are some psalms, such as 105 or 106. In the same way the Christians believed that the thanksgiving should be a fitting rehearsal of all the great things God had done for his people.

By about the year 300 we can outline with some confidence the major act of worship on the Lord's day in most of the churches in the west. This excludes those churches which have never been closely linked with the main western body (soon to become the Roman Catholic Church). Thus we are ignoring the Egyptian Coptic Church, the Ethiopian Church, the Syrian and Armenian Churches, and many which looked later to Constantinople and became the Eastern Orthodox Church.

We may too be excluding the Mar Thoma Church of South India, a body which claims to have been founded by the Apostle Thomas. The western service was in two parts, the synaxis and the eucharist (meaning thanksgiving), and would be:

Synaxis

Introductory prayers and biddings
Scripture readings and psalms and hymns
Sermon
Benediction (enabling the catechumens to leave)
Prayers for the world
An expression of peace

Eucharist

The offertory (= Jesus' taking)
The thanksgiving
The breaking or fraction
The sharing or communion

A quick glance will show that the two parts could equally well be termed 'the service of the word' and 'the communion' (or Lord's Supper or Breaking of the Bread). The first part centred upon God's truth as witnessed within the Scriptures; the second was a deliberate remembrance of Jesus through a sacramental meal. The catechumens were those people, not necessarily children, who were under instruction in the faith and had not yet been baptized into the believing community. It was held to be good for them to share in the readings and sermon, which would have contained much teaching for them, as well as for the believers. But they were not yet able to share in the Church's praying and its eucharist. After baptism they would, of course, participate in the whole, but a fairly general custom was to have the baptisms on Easter Day only.

In many parts of the growing Church, during those first three centuries, there were forms of prayer which became more and more treasured by the young congregations. It may well be that the prayer we know as the Gloria goes a long way back into

31

early Christianity. Prayers and hymns had to stand the test of time, of constant usage by the Church. Those which experience showed to be the most useful were the ones to survive and become widely adopted. In the same way those writings which seemed to go back to the first apostles, and which constant usage had shown to be the most valuable, were the ones to be finally endorsed as part of the New Testament canon by the year 382 (see David Stacey: *Groundwork of Biblical Studies*, pp. 173–6).

However, some elements of the Church's worship were dropped, even if mentioned in the New Testament. Thus the special prayer for the sick and the unction with oil mentioned in James 5:14f have only barely survived in the Roman Catholoic Church, and even there somewhat fitfully. The agape meal was abandoned, although later revived during the Evangelical Revival and occasionally used today.

The Evangelical Revival and after

It is a long jump from the early Church to the time of the Evangelical Revival in the eighteenth century. Readers who want to study the story of the development of Christian worship in the West through those intervening centuries should consult the books cited at the end of the chapter. In the eighteenth century, English Christianity was mainly that of the Church of England, then at a low ebb. There were small groups of Roman Catholics and some small but sturdy groups of Noncomformists – Baptists, Congregationalists, Presbyterians (especially in the North where Scottish influence was at its strongest), Quakers and Unitarians. With some notable exceptions the parish church existed on a somewhat dry observance of the Prayer Book of 1661, with an occasional celebration of Holy Communion, an abysmal standard of preaching and singing that was confined mainly to the chanting of the psalms. The clergy were often absent, or indifferent to the needs of the great masses of the people, yet very jealous of their rights within their parishes. Amongst the Noncomformists (referred to as 'Free Churches' in the rest of this book because they are free from control by the State) there was a much stronger

32

tradition of Bible teaching and an educated clergy. A livelier tradition of hymn-singing was most obvious amongst Methodists, and the regular singing of metrical psalms characterized the Presbyterians.

The Evangelical Revival had profound impact upon both the parish church and the Free Churches. Whitefield and Wesley began to preach in the open air in a style that was both evangelical and biblical, and yet simple and plain enough for the common people to appreciate. Preaching was thus revived. Wesley especially emphasized the importance of both baptism and communion, so that the sacraments too were revalued and some parish churches began to hold weekly communion services. In the Methodist societies a thorough system of pastoral care began to be established, so that no Christian was expected to practise the faith on his own, but everyone had a Class Meeting to attend and Class Leader to care about him or her. Hymn singing experienced a major revival under the fertile genius of Charles Wesley (who wrote at least 5,000 hymns) and led to a much wider use both of English hymns, particularly those of Isaac Watts, and of many of the great hymns of the Christian tradition. John Wesley took great pains to translate German hymns such as those of Paul Gerhardt or Count Zinzendorf. Intense personal religion was being experienced by great numbers of people previously outside the Church. A passion for holiness gripped the new converts and a carefully organized system of care encouraged them thereafter.

The worship in the Methodist chapel was built around the reading of scripture, the preaching, the singing of the hymns and the offering of fervent prayer. Although Wesley had expected his followers to attend the parish church for communion, this broke down soon after his death, and the Methodist preachers became ministers who celebrated the sacraments. The orders they used for both baptism and communion were those of the Prayer Book slightly amended by John Wesley. The only new liturgical rite he had introduced was the annual Covenant Service, which he had adapted from an order by Richard Alleine. There had also been a revival of the agape, or love feast, but as the Methodist Church began to become an ordered Church, and less a collection of revivalist societies, this

33

faded. Watchnight services were also an innovation by Methodists.

The renewed vigour which the Evangelical Revival brought into British Christianity was bound to affect other Churches. It released new spiritual forces, enthusiasm and confidence. Sections of the population, hitherto unchurched, began to respond to the new preaching, new singing, new methods of pastoral care. The Free Churches became a much more significant force, both religiously and politically, and saw that they had many interests in common. Inevitably the Presbyterians were the least affected, for Wesley did no work in Scotland. Their more sober singing styles prevailed until comparatively recently, together with the long-established custom of holding communion only once a quarter.

The first half of the nineteenth century was an extremely turbulent one for the revived Free Churches and the new Methodist Church. English society was experiencing the birth of a vast new class of people, the poor working class living in the extended squalor of the expanding cities and growing towns. Their aspirations, pitted against the conservatism of those who held power and money, were convulsing an England deeply frightened by the upheavals in Europe. The Methodists who succeeded Wesley became as autocratic and dictatorial as he had been. Their church life was under the strict control of the ministers. The tendency was for them to become a parallel Church to the Church of England with a similar liturgy but leavened by exuberant hymn singing, expository and forceful preaching, and greater lay involvement. But Church life was rent with controversy, and many new bodies broke away from the parent – the Primitive Methodists, the Bible Christians, the Wesleyan Reform Union, and others. Amongst them there was a general distaste for domineering ministers, for formal liturgies, for the sacraments and all that indicated 'churchiness'. They favoured a much more free-wheeling style of Church life, lively evangelism, the leadership of those who had been thrown to the front and who appeared to be the most inspired. They were much more associated with working-class feelings, yet firmly opposed to violence and revolution and the extremities of political action.

The second half of the century saw an enormous boom in chapel building, and the creation of a large middle class who attended churches and chapels in considerable numbers. England's population grew rapidly, her industry and empire expanded apace, albeit with many a boom and slump. The Free Churches were now well established in the upper layers of the working class and in much middle class life, and were able to build huge chapels and to become a force in the land. Organs became immensely popular as the ideal instruments for leading the singing and music favoured by the big choirs. But despite the steady growth, the enormous energy of the period, the launching of many schemes for social welfare, the prodigious missionary work to every corner of the Empire, the lower working classes were unchurched except in one or two mining or agricultural areas.

At the end of the century Moody and Sankey brought the American-style revivalism to England in a concerted effort to reach the unchurched. They did not succeed, but they let loose a new style in Church life and a new form of simple hymnody set to catchy tunes. The Wesleyans then launched the 'Forward Movement' whereby Central Halls were established in the big cities, and new patterns of social work and evangelism were practised. The Halls were originally intended to be half-way houses between the pavement and the normal church, to be free and easy places in which the masses could be attracted to the gospel preaching, converted, trained in the Christian life and then passed on to the nearby churches. But that never happened. Instead, the Halls became churches and had somehow to introduce sacramental worship into buildings not designed for it and into a style of Church life for which it seemed odd and ill-fitting.

By the time of the Great War (1914) the Forward Movement had begun to falter. But everywhere Church life was in decline, the era of expansion was over, and resources appeared strained. The war had a devastating effect. It involved an unprecedented slaughter which decimated many a family and local community. It shattered morale. It produced an England going through agonies of strikes, social chaos and unrelieved poverty. When the nation got its breath back a second World

35

War was unleashed. Fortunately there was much less slaughter, although more damage.

The various Methodist Churches, excluding the Wesleyan Reform Union and the Independent Methodists, came together in 1932 to form the present Methodist Church. A major problem was that of the forms of worship to be authorized within it. The Wesleyans had retained a regular celebration of the Holy Communion according to John Wesley's amendment of the order in the Prayer Book, together with a respect for the Anglican Mattins (Order of Morning Prayer) and a fairly 'high' view of the ordained ministry and the place of liturgical forms. The other bodies had a much more liberal attitude to liturgies amounting sometimes to a contempt for them, a 'lower' view of the role of the minister, less place for the sacraments and more place for revivalist hymns and methods. The search for a common service book inevitably led to all parties having to compromise. In 1936 the *Methodist Book of Offices* was issued, with both the traditional Wesleyan order for Holy Communion and an alternative one to be used after a normal preaching service, together with a new baptismal order, the traditional Covenant Service, and orders for the other liturgical occasions.

The preface to that book expressed the hope that 'the very best expressions of Christian devotion throughout the ages will be found embedded' in its pages, and denied that there was 'any attempt to disparage the practice of free prayer' since 'there is no conflict between free prayer and liturgical prayer'. It pointed out that in many of the orders in the book there was a specific place for free prayers, and 'fervently hoped that the habit of such prayer will revive amongst us'.

The book was a compromise, however, and it is hard to see how its use could possibly encourage the growth of appropriate 'free prayer'. The inclusion of the shorter Communion Service implied the approval of the denomination for the habit of having short Communion Services after the preaching services, as if the Lords Supper was an additional rite for the especially pious who would not mind spending longer at worship. The order of infant baptism seriously undervalued the significance of the Church and stressed Jesus' willingness to 'receive' chil-

36

dren, making the occasion too sentimental. There was a general tendency to wordiness and to a concentration on the feelings of the worshippers.

The new *Methodist Hymn Book* launched earlier in 1933 by the united Church was much better, and served well for the following 50 years. It was one of the main influences to promote Methodist unity. It was a large collection of 984 hymns, giving ample space for the cream of the hymns of Wesley and Watts (243 by Charles Wesley, 44 by Watts) and for hymns of the revivalist type as well as the great hymns of the whole Christian tradition. It included too a useful selection of 64 psalms which could be either chanted or read. But there were inevitably some weaknesses in the book. Many of Wesley's eucharistic hymns, expressing a high doctrine of that sacrament, were omitted. A great number of sentimental and flowery hymns from the second part of the nineteenth century were included. The sections covering children's hymns and those for overseas missions dated far too quickly. Nevertheless the collection served to justify the claim that the Church of England was characterized by its Book of Common Prayer, but the Methodists by their hymnal. The question of a successor to it is being discussed as this book goes to print.

The reference to the Church of England prompts the reminder that, of all the Free Churches, the Methodists (especially in the Wesleyan tradition) kept the closest to the Book of Common Prayer in their worship life. This conscious link tended to be loosened in the earlier part of the century by the controversies raging within the Church of England over the Prayer Book. By the time that the First World War ended, it was obvious that some sort of revision would have to be made. Several strong groups had arisen to make the regular parish worship much more consciously catholic, some of them appearing to be mere copiers of Rome. Many of their practices were actually illegal, not being permitted by the existing Prayer Book. There was serious danger of discipline breaking down within the Church. But when a revised Book was prepared, to permit new prayers and practices, the House of Commons voted it out twice. By 1928 the Bishops decided to allow their clergy to use the Revised Prayer Book even though Parliament

37

had not approved and such action was technically against the law of the land. The bitterness stirred up by this controversy was to make any other necessary revisions impossible until the 1960s.

Amongst the other major Free Churches there was a great stress upon preaching; upon the preacher as the central actor in worship; a distrust of fixed forms and orders, creeds and liturgies; a concentration upon the moods, feelings and needs of the worshippers rather than the sovereign glory of God; an excessive reliance upon the spontaneous and extempore; a very limited place given to the sacraments, which were mainly justified by the 'help' they could give to the participants rather than by the gospel truths which they expressed. But there had to be some standard forms nevertheless for the major acts of worship. The *Book of Congregational Worship* issued in 1920 showed a close reliance upon the Anglican Prayer Book. It was followed in 1936 by the *Manual for Ministers*, which was far less dependent upon the Prayer Book, but gave way to much sentimentalism, a general devaluing of the sacraments, and at its worst to some sheer banality (e.g. an order for the sanctification of a Church Bazaar!). Many of these faults were being corrected when *A Book of Public Worship* was produced in 1948; this was a forerunner to the work of revision described in the next chapter.

The Congregationalists produced in 1951 a very good hymn-book entitled *Congregational Praise*. It was smaller than the *Methodist Hymn Book*, aimed at high standards in words and music, drew upon wide resources from the whole Christian tradition, and utilized some of the best of the recent Church music. Later in 1962 the Baptists produced the *Baptist Hymn Book*. The Church of England has never had one definitive book, but has used three – *Hymns Ancient and Modern* originating in 1861, revised in 1904 and then again in 1950; *The English Hymnal* of 1906; and *Songs of Praise* issued in 1925 but enlarged in 1931. The first represents the central area of Anglican churchmanship, but the Free Churchman would find far too many hymns devoted to Saints Days and too few to personal religion. The second was more consciously for the Catholic wing of the Church, and lacks exuberance whilst being somewhat narrow in its interests. The third introduced many more contemporary writers and music, but has been criticized for being theologically tepid. These last three books are very much smaller than, say, the *Methodist Hymn Book*, the size of which indicated the great importance of hymnody to the Methodist people.

In the 1930s some groups of Free Churchmen became increasingly concerned about the carelessness of so much of their worship, the casual way in which the sacraments were administered and regarded, the excessive attention being paid to the subjective element (the feelings of the people), and to the shallowness of so much of the theology of the times. Two groups arose to work quietly but steadily for a renewal of worship – the Congregational Church Order Group, and the Methodist Sacramental Fellowship. Amongst Free Churchmen it was probably the Presbyterians who had best retained a strong theological tradition, thanks to their Scottish connection with the great Reformed traditions of churchmanship stemming originally from Calvin's reformation in Geneva. This was expressed nobly in their *Presbyterian Service Book* of 1948. But in that Reformed tradition the Holy Communion was still only celebrated about four times a year, as in many a Scottish church to this day.

The situation by the 1960s

If now you refer back to the beginning of the last chapter, where various church buildings were described, you can surmise from which period and tradition they originated. The 'typical rectangular building' may come from the earliest days of the Evangelical Revival, but in any case will represent that central tradition which held that worship must focus upon the preached word. The second building, copying the parish church in its neo-gothic architecture and style, dates from the second half of the last century and represents the middle class at worship and probably making extensive use of the Book of Common Prayer (in Methodist circles, as amended by Wesley), and of liturgical formality. The third is the product of revivalism and perhaps the Forward Movement (both of which affected the other Free Churches as well as Methodism).

39

The fourth building, the dual purpose hall, represents the period after the 1930s of financial stringency and of desperate efforts to keep up some sort of Free Church 'witness' in the most unchurched groups of people who live in the working class estates that surround all our cities and towns. These often obtained support from the theology current at the time, which stressed that God was most clearly encountered in serving people's needs and helping to create community spirit, rather than in special buildings and ceremonies. Both the building and the theology look a little shabby nowadays, yet they say something important both about our concern to maintain Christian worship in difficult places and also to serve our fellows gladly without an elaborate fuss or a marvellous institution with splendid premises.

There is thus a wide variety of buildings and, more important, of understanding of what Christian worship is like. To many people it seemed too haphazard and untidy, so the 1960s were a time when the Free Churches were in many ways ripe for reforms. That takes us to the substance of the next chapter and the building of the fifth type of church described in chapter one.

Chapter 3

The Liturgical Movement
and many reforms

In the last chapter it was suggested that by the time the Second
World War was over and its immediate ravages repaired, the
Free Churches were actually living by several traditions concerning their worship, none of them fully satisfying. These had
resulted in several types of church building, each expressing
something different about the nature and form of Christian
worship. An institution like the Christian Church cannot live
happily with diversity tending often to be a muddle, so the time
was ripe for a new look at worship. This was provided by a
movement of the Spirit which had been gathering strength
within European Christianity for about a hundred years. It is
called the Liturgical Movement, but this is not a very satisfactory name for it, as may become clear the more it is described.

Amongst the monks of the Benedictine Order in France in
the 1840s there grew up a passion for improving the quality of
the worship in their major monastery at Solesmes, and a hope
that from there a renewed worship life could be passed out to
the nearby parishes. There they effected a revival of chanting
in the haunting simplicity of plain song. They restored a
meticulous sense of discipline to the way in which the worship
was conducted, plus a sense of the mighty mystery which
Christians celebrate through the gospel and particularly in the
Holy Communion or Mass. They tried to recapture what they
thought was the glorious worship of the Middle Ages, with a
sober element of the theatrical about it, of ordered but impressive ceremonial.

The movement developed steadily and was deeply affected

41

by Belgian Benedictines in the early part of this century. One very significant teacher – Dom Beauduin – had been a parish priest in a poor industrial working class area where he had found that the key to the renwal of the parish's life, as well as the key to promoting the dignity of his down-trodden people, lay in a total renewal of the worship-life in his Church. There he centred his work on an extensive programme of teaching his people the meaning of every part of the liturgy. He encouraged them to build up their devotional lives in their homes and with their children, using schemes which linked the family prayers to the Church's prayers. He tried to make the Sunday mass into an occasion when his people were offering to God their normal working lives, so that worship was not divorced from the reality of daily work. In Belgium and later in Germany, a great number of priests and lay people came to the Benedictine centres to discover the new vitality being taught and practised there. Not only was the teaching role of the priest being revived, so too was preaching and the study of the Bible. Thus some features of the Protestant Church at its best began to be rediscovered amongst Roman Catholics, along with the singing of hymns.

By the 1940s this movement had developed an impressive literature, a wealth of scholarship, and considerable experience of the renewal of parish life even in the most difficult areas of Europe. Its teaching began to be noticed by Protestants. One of the first obvious effects in England was the formation of a group known as 'Parish and People', within the Church of England, which promoted the introduction of Parish Communion. This meant abandoning on Sundays the very early Communion services followed later by the Order of Morning Prayer with sermon at 11 o'clock. They were replaced with one major Communion service for everybody, for families with children, which became the focus of the life of the parish church, held perhaps at 9.00 or 9.30. Often this was followed by a Parish Breakfast, which helped greatly to promote a sense of community amongst the worshippers and was, in effect, a type of modern love feast without much formality. By the 1960s this practice had become very popular and was the spur to the use of many new hymns, of much more teaching by the clergy about the nature of the weekly liturgy, of redesigning the interior of many traditional churches, and of a somewhat new style of brief but lively preaching. Moreover it produced a sense of urgency about revising the traditional Orders of Service sanctioned by the Prayer Book. The pressure for revision led to the introduction of entirely new forms of service in the 1960s and 1970s, especially the Series II Communion in 1966 and the shorter Series III in 1973.

It will be helpful if at this point we consider the main convictions of the Liturgical Movement as it had reached the Free Churches in the 1950s and 1960s. It will be simplest to list six main convictions, although it would be inaccurate to imply that there was a set body of teaching which was adhered to rigidly by everyone involved. Instead, it was more like a number of key ideas which gripped different people in slightly different ways, yet ideas which belonged fittingly together.

First, it was widely held that the definitive and normative act of Christian worship is the eucharist, and that therefore this service should be the focal point of the worshipping life of every congregation every Sunday. No other act of worship expresses so adequately the central glory of the Christian faith. No other act expresses the unique distinctiveness of the Christian religion. The early Church knew this, and made it the weekly form of celebrating the resurrection – so should we.

Secondly, as a development of this, the eucharist re-enacts (or rehearses, or memorializes, or represents) the supreme and once-for-all sacrificial offering on behalf of man of the Saviour, Jesus Christ. It both points to this marvel and makes it present again to the person of faith. Further, it both indicates and helps to carry out the linking of us sinful men with the perfect offering, Jesus, and thus works for our sanctification. It both teaches us yet again about the incarnation (Jesus being made one with us sinful humans) and the atonement (our being put right with God in his ultimate holiness). But it does more than teach, it helps to produce that atonement. It is an *effectual* sign. Of course there is room here for a considerable range of views about the incarnation and about the atonement, as is suggested by the various words used above ('re-enacts', 'rehearses', 'memorializes', and represents'). It is not necessary to hold an

43

extremely high 'catholic' doctrine which says that the bread and wine are changed in their substance, but not appearance, to be the body and blood of Jesus. One can hold a much simpler view than that and yet believe that the eucharist is *par excellence* the occasion at which the atonement is most adequately presented and most powerfully grasped by the believer. The point does however become very much diluted if one feels that the eucharist is only a matter of remembering Jesus' words and deeds at the Last Supper.

Thirdly, the eucharist is the occasion for the whole participation of the whole people of God, the body of Christ. It is the supreme act of the Church as a whole, not just of the priest or clergyman. Therefore the meaning of every part of it should be known as fully as possible by everyone, the language should be as plain and helpful as possible, the people should share in everything as fully as possible, and the priest or clergyman should only do those things which are most fittingly done by one representative, ordained person. Especially this would apply to the main acts done in the place of Jesus, the recollection of the four things he himself did at the Last Supper. But in everything else the people can and should be thoroughly involved – prayers, readings, singing, offering and even in preaching – yet when the presiding ordained person acts it is on behalf of all and should therefore be seen and followed by all. This principle meant of course a massive reformation within many a catholic parish. But, when one comes to think carefully about it, it also involves a drastic change about the way Free Churches behave, for they have often lived with a dominance of the minister as serious as the dominance of the catholic priest.

Fourthly, the Church's worship should be built around an observance of the Christian Year. This begins in November with the Sundays of Advent, moves through to the great celebration of Christmas and Our Lord's incarnation, thence to Epiphany and, after an interval which is often devoted to Our Lord's teaching and ministry, to the sombre days of Lent, Palm Sunday, Holy Week and then the glory of Easter. Soon after it leads to the Ascension, Pentecost and the gift of the Holy Spirit, and finally to Trinity Sunday, after which there is a long

44

period of about five months often devoted to many aspects of the Christian's life and the work and witness of the Church, until the next year begins again with Advent. That calender should determine the yearly cycle of worship life, with the great seasons being especial high points of celebration. It should be in itself a means of instruction into the nature of Christian belief.

Fifthly, the eucharist is the means *par excellence* by which we offer to God our normal living, our life of toil and leisure, the stuff of our regular human experience. Especially is this symbolized by the offertory when money, bread and wine are brought up to become the signs both of our common life and of God's transforming deed in Jesus.

Sixthly, the preaching matters profoundly. As the Protestant reformers said so loudly and often, the Word must never be divorced from the Sacrament. So the Bible must be adequately read and its message must be faithfully expounded. The preaching must put into words the meaning of that point in the Christian Year, and must relate those words to the chosen Bible passages. The preaching should not be a homily, a short pious admonition on whatever subject takes the fancy of the parson, nor should it be a commentary upon some item of parish or national news, nor an exercise in fancy rhetoric. It should relate the biblical message to the contemporary life experienced within the parish. So the phrase 'liturgical preaching' was born.

As the full force of these convictions began to grip Free Churchmen in the 1960s a spate of revision began. Almost all the cherished and hallowed orders were examined again and found wanting. The Methodist Church began a wholesale process of revision that was to lead to the Sunday Service in two forms (one culminating in the Eucharist and the other being a service of the Word only), totally new orders for baptism, confirmation, marriage, burial and ordination, and an improving of the Covenant Service. By 1975 these were all completed and published in *The Methodist Service Book*. The only item carried over from the previous 1936 book was the first service of the Lord's Supper (basically as from 1662) on the grounds that where people are attached to old forms they should not be deprived of them. The Service Book does not include the service for the Recognition and Commissioning of Local Preachers. This is printed separately, but carries the same authority of the Methodist Conference as do the other services. None of the orders for the commissioning of lay persons, nor even the Ordination of Deaconesses, is included, because this would make for a much larger and more expensive book. That for the Ordination of Ministers is printed because it perforce expresses the Methodist doctrine of the ministry. This is important and should be readily available to all, because it relates so closely to the doctrine of the Church.

At the same time, other Communions were also revising their liturgies, notably the Church of Rome, the Church of England and the Congregational Church (largely merged into the United Reformed Church in 1973). The *Service Book* of the United Reformed Church, published in 1980, is the first authoritative collection of orders of worship to be used within that new body, and contains a service for the Accreditation of Lay Preachers. It does not, however, print the Collects for each Sunday, a practice which takes up much space in the Methodist book. Furthermore, it is designed to be used by ministers alone whereas *The Methodist Service Book* is essentially for congregational use.

A new interest in liturgy had sprung up everywhere, and a general but loose agreement had occurred about the principles upon which liturgies were to be devised. The result is that the new orders are quite remarkably similar, as can easily be seen by comparing the current Roman Mass, the Anglican Series II and III eucharists, the Methodist Sunday Service and an Order of Holy Communion of the United Reformed Church (published in 1975 in the hymnal *New Church Praise*). All of them have the same shape, and hark back to the rite becoming standardized in the West by the fourth century, which was outlined in the previous chapter.

One other change became almost universally accepted. Previously the Christian had always addressed God in prayer and hymn as 'Thou', and his gifts and attributes were 'thine'. Both these terms had become archaic and awkward by the end of the 1960s. Tentatively at first they were replaced by 'You' and

46

'yours', but quickly this style became both acceptable and favoured by the vast majority of believers in every communion. To make this change into more colloquial language is not really an innovation, since when 'Thee' and 'thou' were used in Elizabethan times they too were the colloquial expressions of the day.

New liturgies for the Lord's Supper in the Free Churches

A. *The Methodist Sunday Service* has the following form:

The Preparation
Hymn
Collect for purity
The commandments
Confession of sin (shared)
Declaration of forgiveness
Collect of the Day
Hymn or Gloria in Excelsis

The Ministry of the Word
O.T. lesson or Epistle or both
Hymn
The Gospel reading
Sermon
Intercessions
The Lord's Prayer
Blessing

The Lord's Supper
The Peace
The Nicene Creed
The setting of the Table: Hymn
                          Offertory
                          Preparation of elements
The Thanksgiving
The Breaking of the Bread: Fraction
                            Silence
The Sharing of Bread and Wine: Prayer
                                Communion

The Final Prayers: Silence
Prayer of thanksgiving
Hymn
Blessings

At a first glance you can see that this order is based upon that which was outlined in the last chapter, the developed rite in the West by about the fourth century. The first two parts (the preparation and the ministry of the Word) correspond closely to the synaxis, the synagogue service. The third part is a faithful and close copy of the eucharist, and it is obvious that after the initial acts (the Peace and the Creed) the four acts of Jesus are reproduced very clearly – he took, blessed, broke and gave. It is clear too that the first two parts, the synaxis, make a service in themselves, one very much like the traditional Free Church service centred upon the Bible readings and sermon. Thus they could form a satisfactory order for a service which was not to culminate in the eucharist.

This is an important point, because all the services which Methodist Local Preachers conduct will not culminate in the Lord's Supper, except in those very rare situations in which a Local Preacher has the appropriate dispensation from the Methodist Conference. In the United Reformed Church the situation is slightly different, of course, since accredited Local Preachers can be appointed by the District Council to preside at the Holy Communion. In other Free Churches the position is less rigid than within Methodism. However, any Local Preacher can conduct a service which is eucharistic in its general structure, by following the first two parts fairly closely and then concluding with prayers of thanksgiving, dedication and intercession as outlined in *The Methodist Service Book*, pp. B18–21. This provides a very satisfactory shape for such a service, and it is assumed throughout the rest of this book that this is the general norm we shall use.

The general directions which precede the service make it clear that it is not to be regarded as an immutably fixed form, but that many variations can be introduced and hymns used in more ways than suggestion. In addition there are, as has been mentioned, four alternative patterns for intercession printed as an appendix, and four alternative forms of thanksgiving when

48

the eucharist is not being celebrated, together with traditional and contemporary versions of the Apostles Creed as alternatives to the Nicene. But as a guide to what is considered as essential, a marker like a small flag indicates the basic elements which should not be omitted.

These form a service which would be:

Collect of the Day
O.T. Lesson or Epistle or both
Gospel
Sermon
Intercessions
The Lord's Prayer
The Peace
Offertory
Preparation of the Table
Thanksgiving
Fraction
Silence
Communion
Silence
Prayer
Blessing

The service is noticeably different from the 1936 order based upon the Prayer Book service of 1662. It is not as long and as wordy. It omits many of the long admonitory speeches and the elaborate quoting of texts. Many of the elements of that service (e.g. the Gloria in Excelsis or the Lord's Prayer) are in a different place, so that the communion itself now comes as a much clearer climax and is followed by very brief prayers and maybe a hymn. But the general tone of the service is different. That of 1662 is decidedly solemn to the point of being miserable, with a constant citing of one's sins and prayers for mercy both before and, at considerable length, after the communion itself. One almost feels that one can never get away from the sense of sin however hard one tries. But the Sunday Service has a different ethos. It is much more exuberant, as befits a celebration of the Lord's resurrection, and focuses one's attention more upon the Lord of glory than upon the Lord dying and suffering upon the Cross. Sins are indeed confessed, but right at the beginning, when they are clearly forgiven and then not harked upon any more.

There is considerable stress upon scripture, with three passages being read, and a sermon being regarded as essential. There is respect for the season of the Christian Year, since the Collect of the Day is regarded as essential too. This is a prayer which captures the meaning of the theme for the day, applies it to the need of the worshipper, and does this in a concise, crisp form (the appropriate Collects and lessons for each Sunday are printed later in the Service Book). There is due respect for prayers and forms which have come to us from centuries of the Christian tradition – the Gloria in Excelsis, the Creed, the expression of peace together before partaking of communion, and the shape and contents of the Thanksgiving. But there is also room for more contemporary material such as the form for confession, or the forms for the intercessions. There is opportunity for the Commandments to be read. This is a feature which the fathers of the Reformation stressed in particular. They held that knowledge of God's moral law as set out in the commandments was a preliminary to sensing one's need of God's grace, as discovered in the gospel news.

Liturgical scholars often devote much scrupulous attention to the Thanksgiving, known as the 'Canon of the Mass' in catholic circles. This is because it is supremely in that part of the service that the minister is expressing the faith of the Church, for it is especially there that God is being thanked and praised for being the sort of God he is, who has done the mighty things which Christians celebrate. As a result, many of the elements that make up the Thanksgiving have acquired technical terms and much care is taken both to express the faith adequately and to give a shape which centuries of Christian worshipping experience have shown to be the most satisfactory. In this case a fairly standard format is used, the sequence being:

The Sursum Corda   ('Lift up your hearts')
Praise to God the Trinity
Sanctus   ('Holy, holy, holy')

Benedictus	('Blessed is he who comes ...')
Institution	(recounting Jesus' acts at the Last Supper)
Praise to Christ	
Anamnesis	('we do this in remembrance')
Epiclesis	(calling upon the Holy Spirit)
Oblation	(offering ourselves to be a living sacrifice)
Praise on behalf of all mankind	

Note that the whole congregation is expected to take part in a great deal of the service, including the prayers, and that the longest portion to be said by the presiding ministerial voice (the thanksgiving) is broken up so that the whole people share in parts of it. It is quite common too for the people to repeat the prayer of humble access immediately before the communion. Furthermore there is explicit instruction for there to be periods of silence, when each worshipper can offer the appropriate personal prayers. Finally the rubrics (that is, the instructions printed within the service order itself at each stage) make it clear that there should be the simplest acts of dramatic power – some form of expressing peace together, then a formal presentation of the offertory (money and bread and wine), a formal breaking of the bread (the fraction) for all to see, as well as the powerful dramatic symbolism of each worshipper taking the bread and wine.

B. The order of Worship for the Lord's Supper, printed in *New Church Praise* and widely used within the United Reformed Church in England and Wales, has the following form:

The Word and the Prayers
The entry of the Bible
Call to worship (scripture sentences)
Prayer of approach
Hymn or Psalm
Confession of sin
Assurance of pardon
The Kyries ('Lord have mercy upon us')

51

The Gloria in Excelsis
Prayer for grace (possibly Collect of the Day)
O.T. Reading
Psalm, Canticle, Hymn or Anthem
N.T. Reading(s)
Sermon
Hymn
(Notices)
Prayers for the Church and the World
(Notices)

The Thanksgiving and the Communion
The Invitation and the Gracious Words
The Peace
Offertory

Offertory prayer
Hymn
The Narrative of the Institution of the Lord's Supper
The Taking of the Bread and Wine
The Thanksgiving
The Lord's Prayer
The Breaking of the Bread
The Sharing of the Bread and Wine
Acclamation
Prayer after Communion
Hymn or Doxology
Dismissal and Blessing

At first sight this looks much longer than the previous order. It is only slightly so, but the effect of having more items cited gives the impression of greater length. Perhaps this reminds us that today we prefer to have services that *look* short when set out on paper. It has the same basic shape as the previous one, the first part focusing upon the Word of God, and the second upon the Eucharist. There is slightly more evidence of the use of scripture, in particular when we come to the eucharist and the narrative of 1 Corinthians 11:23–26 is read.

When we look at the second part, it becomes slightly more difficult to detect the basic four-fold sequence of Jesus' acts (he took, blessed, broke, shared) although that shape is there in the framework. There is a much fuller statement of what we think we are doing in coming to the Lord's table, which is stated as three beliefs, thus:

We celebrate his perfect sacrifice upon the Cross
  and his glorious resurrection and ascension
We declare that he is Lord of all
And we prepare for his coming in his kingdom.

That last statement makes it especially clear that we are worshipping in the interim period between Jesus' ministry on earth and the Great Fulfilment at the end of time, called technically the 'parousia' in the New Testament.[1] The Lord's Prayer is immediately before sharing the communion, as in many of the ancient liturgies. There are also other minor differences between this and the previous service. Nevertheless, it is obvious that this order has been composed on the same principles as the previous one, with the same assumptions about the nature of the service. Thus we can easily see the extensive effect which the Liturgical Movement has been having upon Free Church worship at its most sensitive and important point, the order of communion.

Critique of the Liturgical Movement

The study just made of two service orders which are deeply indebted to the Liturgical Movement, together with the reader's own experience of Christian worship, should help us to be critical of these new developments in the best sense of the word 'critical' – appreciating both the strengths and weaknesses. Let us take a more critical look at the six points cited earlier in the chapter as roughly characterizing the movement.

First, that the eucharist should be the normal Sunday service, since it is the definitive act of Christian worship. A great deal of Free Church experience suggests otherwise, that a service which centres clearly and faithfully upon the Word of

---

[1] For the importance of this, if we are to express our convictions about Jesus Christ adequately, see John Stacey: *Groundwork of Theology*, pp. 293–306

God should be the norm for each Sunday, and that at regular intervals this should culminate in the eucharist. Most Free Churches practise a monthly communion, yet the Presbyterians have a quarterly one. At the far extreme the Salvation Army and the Society of Friends have no sacramental worship, and yet both bodies have manifestly been schools for Christian saints. Moreover those Free Churches which have the highest theology of the Christian ministry and which emphasize that the communion should be celebrated by an ordained minister (or, in the extreme, by someone with a special dispensation to act in lieu of a minister) have not produced a pattern of ordained ministry that could reasonably enable each congregation to share in the eucharist every Sunday. There are not enough ministers to go round, and few signs that those Churches want to have sufficient for such purpose.

Is the pattern which had developed in Rome by the fourth century to be regarded as automatically that which should prevail everywhere in the Christian World in the twentieth? It is not easy to see why. Some argue that it took the early Church over 300 years to sort out its doctrine, especially its understanding of the nature and work of Christ, and to express this in the great creeds. Ever since, those creeds have been held to outline the necessary elements of Christian belief. In the same way, it took the early Church about the same period of time to settle the outline of its worship and this should be regarded as equally binding as, in the realm of belief, the creeds. But to this it can be replied that one cannot make too strict a parallel between belief statements and worship forms. There are essential differences between the two, so that what applies to belief, where one has to draw a hedge around Christian faith and say that anything outside is heresy, and what happens in the formation of worship are separate matters altogether. Worship patterns are always changing, just as words are always changing, so that the history of Christian worship is more like the story of a river always on the move through new territory and being joined by fresh streams. Furthermore, those who object deeply to the use of creeds go on to say that these outlines of early Church belief are of little value today, because they use thought-forms that are quite outmoded and were designed to counteract positions which nobody holds today. They are thus obsolete. Most Christians would not agree, and would find both creeds and worship forms to offer valuable norms.

If one takes another tack altogether, one can argue that worship patterns must reflect the culture, thought-forms, and styles of behaviour, of the time and place. What was appropriate for an illiterate Cornish convert in 1780 is not necessarily appropriate for a highly educated Christian in 1980. Likewise, people vary in their need for sacramental worship, so one cannot assume that Eskimos and Englishmen should all automatically need to have a weekly worship pattern which has the eucharist at its centre. To this point most advocates of the Liturgical Movement would answer 'No, we don't say that every Christian in the universe should go to Communion every Sunday. We argue that the Christian Church – and that means the local congregation – should aim to have the eucharist each Sunday if at all possible, and that it is the eucharist which sets the ideal pattern for our worship. It should be regarded therefore as the norm and standard, even if local conditions make it difficult to have that standard every week.' There we must leave the discussion.

Secondly, the eucharist uniquely sets forth the central glory and mystery of the Christian faith; it demonstrates the atonement. Some reply that good preaching does precisely the same. But does it? Preaching is an attempt to put beliefs into shared words, but in the communion rite much more is happening. One is participating in a shared drama, doing things which are profoundly full of meaning which perhaps no words could ever quite describe. The act of kneeling, for instance, receiving bread and wine as pledges of the Lord's death and life, feeding upon that food, then rising to face life renewed – how can one possibly put the same meaning into mere words? It cannot be done, any more than the incorporation of a person into the Christian community is adequately expressed unless the rite of baptism is involved, with water sprinkled over and hands laid on that person.

Thirdly, the eucharist (and indeed all acts of Christian worship) should mean the participation of all the people as totally as possible. In theory Free Churchmen should not have needed to relearn this, since they have always held 'the priesthood of all believers' as a sort of battle cry and have been deeply suspicious of clergy acting as priests. But in practice much Free Church worship has been wholly dominated by the minister or preacher, with the congregation sharing only in the singing of hymns, an occasional 'amen' after a prayer, the singing or recital of the Lord's Prayer, and the making of the offering. One could get the impression that the worship is that of the supreme leader, which the congregation is invited to attend mainly as listeners. That Christian worship is the worship of the people of God is a lesson most Free Churches urgently need to learn and then practise, so that the congregation is not supine and servile, but much more involved. This point will be emphasized in later chapters.

Fourthly, the observance of the Christian year is obviously needed in many a Free Church congregation to rescue us from the round of special Sundays with which our calendars are often cluttered. Suppose a Church has as its great occasions the following – Women's Sunday, Youth Sunday, Men's Sunday, Choir Sunday, Sunday School Anniversary, Young Wives' Sunday: what does that say about the Church? It says that we want to focus our attention upon different groups of people in our midst, and to construct our worship calendar around them. But if instead the calendar is constructed around the Christian year, the stress then is upon the great acts of God. Which matter most for the worship of Christians? Various groups or interests amongst us, or God's mighty works? If it becomes the former, there is the constant danger of our worship becoming trivialized or made into the worship of humans rather than the worship of God. This peril is most obvious in many an old-fashioned Sunday School Anniversary where the occasion becomes a glorification of children rather than the adoration of the Father.

The fifth point may well seem to many Christians to be decidedly forced. In modern life the bread and wine are not satisfactory tokens or symbols of our everyday lives. Bread is still maybe a staple food for most homes, but wine is not. The money could be held to be symbolic of our work, but it rarely feels like that. Thus the effort to interpret the offertory of

bread, wine and money as an expression of our ongoing working life suffers from insuperable difficulty because the symbolism is not powerful enough. Indeed, it may well be that there is
no effective symbolism for working life in most modern communities. One can sense this if, say, one asks each member of
the congregation to bring up something which expresses working life. The result is a collection of most disparate objects
ranging from typewriters to nappies. To expect the usual offertory to be able to represent our common humanity and then
God's transforming of it, is to stretch our imaginations almost
to the point of sheer pretence.

Sixthly, there has arisen a new stress upon preaching as a
business of expounding God's message for that particular season or day. Of course Protestants rejoice in this – at first sight,
that is. As will be discussed later, this means taking a slightly
different view of preaching than that which has prevailed
within some Free Churchmanship. It also points to a discipline
about preaching which has not always prevailed amongst us. It
has led to a new stress upon the use of a lectionary (that is, a
scheme of themes and bible readings for each Sunday) and a
widespread acceptance of the one which was prepared by the
Joint Liturgical Group in 1967.

But other criticisms have arisen about the influence of the
Liturgical Movement. It has been said to be essentially
backward-looking, harking back to the early Church. On the
other hand, is there not something inevitably backward-
looking about some vital elements in Christian faith, which
devote attention to events in Palestine long ago? It has been
said to be too concerned with details, with the minutiae of
worship, with trivial matters, and to have ignored the weightier
issues of the spirit in which the worship is conducted and the
congregation is involved. Has it indeed been more concerned
with form and letter than with the spirit? Again, the liturgies
are said to be sometimes stilted, to use archaic biblical and
traditional phrases which mean little today. The services are
still minister-dominated. The new forms require fairly elaborate explanation to the average congregation. They sometimes
use Scripture in a very wooden manner. Behind them is the
assumption that every Christian is a literate person who likes

57

worship to be highly ordered and wants it to be as sacramental as possible.

More serious is the criticism about the spirit of worship. There has always been a tension in Christian history between the spontaneous, the ecstatic, the extempore, the immediate response to the inspiration of the moment (and what is loosely called today the 'charismatic') and the need for order, predictability, set forms offering defence against the mere whims of the moment or the imposition of one person's wishes and moods upon everyone else. The tension was very apparent in the Church at Corinth and produced Paul's somewhat sharp words in 1 Corinthians 12–14. Has the recent acceptance of so much liturgical reform been achieved at too great a price, so that too little room has been given to the free moving of the Spirit? Or is the answer to be found in adopting a diet of worship in the local congregation which gives room to both the ordered liturgy and the less structured, flexible style of both the evangelistic rally and the charismatic assembly?

Again there is criticism that the Liturgical Movement, as it has actually affected the Free Churches, has diverted our attention away from the needs of the world and our mission there, and concentrated us upon events and activities within the Church's life far too much. It has made us more concerned about getting the right Collect of the Day than the right help for one-parent families. We have become so bothered about petty details concerning the order of service, or the phrasing of a prayer, or the way the offertory is presented, that we are just as open to rebuke by Jesus as the scrupulous Pharisee. We are more worried about tithing out our liturgical dill and mint and cummin than the weightier matters of the law – justice, mercy and good faith (for which see Matthew 23:23). So it has distorted our discipleship.

There is some justification for that criticism. Undoubtedly some of us have become so obsessed with the finicky details of the ordering of worship that we have been able to ignore our primary obligation to serve mankind in the name of Christ. Yet that has not necessarily been so. The liturgical renewal in the catholic Churches of Europe often went hand in hand with a renewal of service to the parish. That pattern has occurred again and again with other Churches which have found that renewal in mission and in worship rightly belong together. Indeed, many would say that one cannot really have the one renewal without the other. Maybe then this criticism is really to be directed against some Christians who have tried to make liturgical concern an excuse for ignoring the demands of mission. On the other hand we should note that some people who are deeply concerned about mission have also used that as an excuse for ignoring the requirements of high standards in worship, and have become sloppy in their approach to God. Perhaps some liturgical seriousness is precisely what they need?

Finally, do the main concerns of the Movement help the Churches to face up to the peculiar challenges posed by modern secular man, the challenges discussed at the close of chapter one? This is an enormous and complex question, particularly since generalizations about 'modern man' are to be handled with great caution. A few tentative comments can be made. Insofar as our contemporary worship life does enable us to encounter God, then it is enabling the Church to meet the need of modern man. A worship life that is less totally dependent upon the spoken word and can utilize the visual, the symbolic, the aesthetic, the dramatic, is likely to be an asset. Again, a worship life that is less dependent upon one sole authority figure, that of the preacher, is also likely to be an asset. A worship life that stresses the corporate nature of the Church as the family of God's people is an asset to counter the lonely individualism of today and the lack of 'community'. So there are many indications that the Movement may indeed be equipping the Church better to serve the present age. There are no neat conclusive arguments here. Indeed, we are not really engaged in a simple argument between two protagonists, one for and one against a clearly defined policy. We are engaged in a complex discussion about the appropriate style for Christian worship today. We can say with much gratitude that the Liturgical Movement has helped force the Church to reconsider her whole worship life, its forms and purposes. It has thus raised some of the most crucial problems about the nature of the Church and, along with them, questions about her missionary life and the character of the congregation. At the same time it has offered us some strong hints about the ways in which we should be seeking to respond.

Developments in hymnody and family worship

The 1960s and 1970s saw a great explosion in the writing of new hymns, in the use of many new musical forms for Church worship, in the popularity of religious musicals like 'Jesus Christ Superstar', 'God-spell', 'Joseph and his amazing techni-colour Dreamcoat', in the growth of folk music, in the intro-duction of new musical events like 'Come Together', and in the use of a greater range of musical instruments. All of this has meant a boom in the publication of new music for the Churches' use, and many new hymn-books and song books coming on the market.

The major denominations have responded cautiously by publishing supplements to their existing hymn-books. Thus the Baptists published *Praise for Today* in 1974 (it has 104 hymns); the United Reformed Church produced *New Church Praise* in 1975 with 112 items; *Hymns Ancient and Modern* was extended by *100 Hymns for Today* published in 1969 and *More Hymns for Today* in 1980; the Methodists produced *Hymns and Songs* in 1969 containing 77 hymns and 23 songs.

This obliges us to note the difference between a hymn and a religious song. The former is designed to be sung by a great range of Christians for very many years, to express the central convictions in the Christian tradition in a simple but tightly structured manner so that it can be sung to a fairly strict tune not requiring constant variations from verse to verse. Prefer-ably the lines should rhyme closely, so that the hymn is easily memorable as well as easily sung. The latter can be much longer in its construction, but also it can express the particular mood of the moment, as in the peace songs that expressed horror at the Vietnam War, and the concerns of smaller groups of Christians. At times it is hard to tell whether one is dealing with a hymn or song, because there is no sharp dividing line between the two. But clearly the Church needs both hymns and songs for its worship life, so it requires both hymn-books and song books. The former should make available the great riches of the whole Christian tradition together with the best contemporary writing, and should perhaps be intended to last for forty or fifty years. The latter should only be designed to last a short while, to capture the immediate moods in a vivid way and to have a more limited appeal.

The time has now come for the denominations to produce new hymn-books. The standard ones, even when supplemented by recent additional material, need to be revised. Accordingly the Churches of Christ, the Congregational Federation, the Wesleyan Reform Union, the Methodist Church and the United Reformed Church hope to have an entirely new major hymnal available by 1983. One can presume that this will be fairly extensively used by 1990.

But there is one more recent development for us to consider – the growth of Family Worship and Family Communion within the Free Churches. Many factors have been at work to promote this growth, which began mainly within the Congregational Church at the end of the 1950s but was very influential within other Free Churches in the 1960s. The movement began partly as a revolt against the traditional patterns of Sunday School work, in which Sunday School was a different institution from the worshipping Church, meeting maybe at the same time but in a separate building. When one asked the question 'What is a Sunday School for?' one could easily get vague answers about children's need for moral instruction, or of learning about the Bible when young. But if the question is pushed hard enough no Christian can be content with any answer which falls short of a statement such as – 'to rear children within the Christian faith and the worship of the Christian Church, so that they will become believing and practising members of the Church'. One cannot achieve that through an institution which is in any way separated from the worshipping congregation.

Other pressures were at work. The coming of a more secular Sunday and the steady decline in church-going plus the arrival of very popular television programmes on Sunday evenings all caused a general shift in the patterns of church attendance, with the main congregation in most places occurring in the

61

morning instead of in the evening. There was also a minor revolution in the methods of Sunday School work, caused partly by educational research into how children respond to religious ideas. The result was a move away from traditional styles of bible teaching involving the imparting of many facts and somewhat adult religious ideas, to a form of teaching known as the 'experiential' in which the instruction began with experiences of which the children were well aware, and moved from there to biblical and simple doctrinal themes and notions. The experiential approach stressed that children should share with adults in the basic experiences of the Church's worship.

The outcome has been that most Free Churches have given up afternoon Sunday Schools and the habit of having children in the morning service with a 'Childrens' Address' for their benefit. Instead the pattern has become common of having the first part of morning service carefully designed to introduce worship to the whole Church, young and old, after which the children go out to their Sunday School classes, whilst the adults remain for their normal worship and sermon. Many Sunday Schools have changed their title to 'Junior Church' to indicate the new sense of purpose. It has become more and more common for there to be Family Services involving the whole people once a month, or fairly regularly, or at the great Christian festivals. This service has often become the most appropriate one in which the sacrament of infant baptism can be celebrated. It has meant that those who lead worship must now be able to lead this type of Family Service well. Some of the special considerations this involves will be mentioned later.

This development which has done so much to give Sunday Schools clearer and better aims and to make the whole congregation more aware of its responsibilities for children, has also produced several problems. Some people assert that it is impossible to conduct a worship service which will be satisfactory for the needs of both children and adults. Either the general level is reduced to the elementary, with the adults feeling that their maturity is being denied, or else the children are subjected to an adult experience which is beyond their ability. Many, however, would deny that this problem is as stark as this sounds. In practice many Sunday School teachers have found it difficult to share in adult worship life any more, have rarely heard a sermon or attended the Holy Communion.

Another problem has been the growth of a syllabus for the work in the Sunday Schools and Junior Churches which has operated on quite different lines and themes from that in the normal lectionary. The leader has then been bewildered by the opening part of the worship. Should it relate to the Sunday School lesson or the adult lectionary lesson? Moves to combine these two differing lectionaries are now afoot.

The other major problem has been that of introducing children to the Lord's Supper. If this service is for the whole Church, for those in training for membership as well as confirmed believers, then cannot all partake of the elements of bread and wine? Is there some specific age before which one should not partake but after which one should? Is that age always to be identified with the age of confirmation or reception into full membership? Particularly in the case of the children of Christian parents, why should they be barred from what their parents receive, thus dividing the family? Is the bread and wine to be given to those who are mature enough to understand what it is all about? If so, does anybody understand it thoroughly and should there not be tests in understanding before anyone receives?

This last problem has become more acute when one considers the family unit. The great advantage of the new developments has been that a family can come to church together on a Sunday morning, sit together for the first part of the service, then meet together afterwards; ideally all will have been considering the same theme, although at different levels of comprehension. When the Family Service occurs, then all can remain together throughout. But if that service involves the eucharist why should the parents be treated quite differently from their children when they all kneel at the Table? Others have argued that it is unseemly for little children to receive the bread and wine, that they should instead receive some sign of the gospel blessing such as a hand laid upon their heads and a simple grace pronounced over them, and be encouraged to look forward to that day when, their commitment being more mature, they can receive the same elements

63

as their parents. There has to be some time when Christian children begin to receive the bread and wine, after all, since otherwise one would be arguing for them to receive as from babyhood. But where is the dividing line to be drawn? The Methodist Conference debated the issue repeatedly in the early 1970s and finally decided in 1973 that it would have to remain unresolved, and that each congregation should try to sort out its policy clearly without there being a standard denominational practice.

Chapter 4

Handling the Bible

CHRISTIAN worship and preaching use one particular resource in an especially serious and significant way – the Bible. All Protestant Churches have a high doctrine of the Bible and regard it as the 'supreme revelation', or some similar term. Thus the Methodist Church holds it to be the record of that divine revelation which is 'the supreme rule of faith and practice' and would usually hold that any teaching on faith or morals which could not be clearly justified by reference to the Bible could not be validly taught nor preached.

There are enormous problems in assuming that this reference to 'the Bible' can be done easily. To begin with, it is not as simple as making reference to one book, but to a great number. Our present Bible is a minor library of 66 different items, rather than a single one. Secondly, these books come from very different periods and circumstances over a period of approximately 900 years, ranging from the sermons of a prophet like Amos over 700 years before Christ to the sophisticated reflections of an educated leader like the writer of John's gospel, maybe 100 years after Jesus' birth. Thirdly, the books are of widely different types, including collections of detailed laws (like Deuteronomy), love poems (the Song of Songs), historical narrative (such as Kings or Chronicles), collections of sermons or oracles (e.g. Hosea), hymns for use in the Temple worship (the Psalms), visions concerning the future (Daniel or Revelation), collections of pithy sayings about the wise life (Proverbs), accounts of Jesus' life and death (the gospels), letters circulated to the early Church (like Galatians), letters to certain individuals (Philemon), the history of a period in the Church's life (Acts), and so on. The Bible is not just a library, but a library containing many very different sorts of books about a wide range of matters.

This would nevertheless raise few major problems if the books were all generally agreed concerning the basic religious doctrines. But, fourthly, this is manifestly not so. To take two simple examples; there is considerable difference in the teachings concerning the nature of evil, or the nature of the afterlife. In the earlier books evil is mysterious, but generally assigned to God, who has 'hardened man's heart' (as happens to Pharaoh in the early chapters of Exodus); Satan is a general investigator of man's life, as in the book of Job. In the New Testament, however, sin is a force which grasps man's total personality and is centred within (as in Mark's record of Jesus' teaching in Mark 7:20–23), and over which Satan acts as supreme king. There is a big difference between these views. In most of the Old Testament period there was no clear picture of a life after death. One's shade went down to the murky pit of Sheol, deep under the earth, but one's personality lived on through one's sons. In contrast, in 1 Corinthians 15 Paul envisages the believer living on through a new type of body in an existence dominated by Jesus Christ as Lord. Again, there are big differences.

These differences would not be so difficult to handle if one could say that there is a steady progression of ideas, from the more primitive ones encountered in the earlier books up to the more advanced ones found in the later. But that is not so. Often two sets of competing ideas lie side by side with each other in books coming from the same period. Thus the book of Deuteronomy sets out a very humane code of laws governing the life of God's holy people, offering a lofty picture of both the required worship and communal life. The prophets of the time appear to have searching doubts as to whether or not this teaching is what God wants. Micah protests, in the famous cry of 6:8, that God only wants justice, mercy and humility. Many scholars feel that much of Jeremiah's teaching springs from disillusionment as to whether or not God's people ever should or could follow out Deuteronomy properly. Again, there is fundamental difference concerning the sort of future God wants to offer his people. The prophet Ezekiel sees it as one in which a magnificent new Temple completely dominates the whole scene. The second and third Isaiah have pictures in which the Temple does not feature at all.

We do not escape such problems when we look at the New Testament. At one point Christians are bidden to respect the teaching, but not the practice, of the Jewish leaders and Pharisees because they sit in 'Moses' seat' (Matthew 23:2), yet elsewhere they are described as the children of the Devil and as total liars (John 8:44). More importantly, there is considerable confusion about the coming of the Kingdom. Has it come in the person and work of Jesus? Or in his cross and resurrection? Or ascension? Or in the experience of the Holy Spirit at Pentecost? Or will the Kingdom come very soon, so soon that we should not bother about normal worldly responsibilities and planning? Might its coming usher in a thousand special years of peace (as in Revelation 20) before the Final End? Will it mean that in the end all men will be saved, or most men, or a few? On all these matters there is no clear answer. One unfortunate result is that cranks of all sorts can burrow around in the Bible and find some sort of ground for holding the most weird notions. Further if one asks whether or not there is a clear teaching on matters vital to Christian ethics and behaviour, there is again no absolute unanimity. Paul teaches us, for example, to regard the State as having been instituted by God (Romans 13); the writer of Revelation sees it as the great enemy of God, the Beast, the Scarlet Woman, the Great Whore.

For these reasons it is extremely doubtful if anyone can go to the Bible and find a neat simple answer to any question about its teaching. In many cases, to be true, the teaching of the Bible acts somewhat like the many faces of a diamond, offering us a brilliant range of ways in which to picture or understand something. Thus there are many different ways of picturing the role of Jesus' death and self-offering upon the Cross. It is like the greatest act of the High Priest each year and yet even more

67

marvellous since Jesus is both Priest and sacrificial Lamb (Epistle to the Hebrews); it is like the payment of a ransom to free many slaves (Mark 10:45); it is like the process of adopting children (Galatians 4:5); it is like a battle at which the evil powers are destroyed (Colossians 2:14f), and so on. These many pictures all give us a richer understanding of the supreme mystery at the heart of the faith. They don't contradict each other. They are complementary, all working together to produce a bigger range of vision for us. But on other matters, the many facets of biblical teaching do not so complement each other as to give a richer picture, for they represent fundamentally *different* ways of looking at some matter.

In the period 1935–65 there were many scholars who taught that flowing through the Bible there is a steady stream of agreement about the major themes of Christian doctrine. This gave rise to what was termed 'biblical theology'. It was held that one could, with care, produce the stream of teaching about all significant matters – the biblical view of society, of law, of morals, of salvation, of the future, etc. This would have enabled a preacher to say 'The Bible says ...' and then (provided he or she had grasped the full extent of the biblical teaching) give the presumed biblical view. It is now clear that we cannot do this with anything like the confidence that was then presumed. The biblical teaching is too diverse, too difficult to sum up in any concise body of teaching, too rich for us to master by one set of affirmations or pictures or theories. Thus we should *not* presume that the Bible is a compendium of religious teaching in which the same basic ideas are developed and set out. In some cases, yes; in other cases there are strong tensions which are never resolved. For that reason 'biblical theology' has had to be greatly modified. For that reason it is arrogant for any person to stand up and say 'The Bible says ...' and then propound a doctrine which purports to be the total view of all the writers of all the books in the Bible. The more we know about it, the less we should dare to do such a thing.

Finally, there is the major difficulty which has already been hinted at, that the biblical books were written for societies and cultures in which a very different style of thinking prevailed. There is a vast difference between the ways in which an ordinary Englishman thinks in 1980, and the ways in which the ordinary Jew thought in 800 BC, or the ordinary Christian in AD 80. This gap has been increasing at a great pace in modern times, ever since the explosion of new ideas which began with the Renaissance in Europe 500 years ago. It has recently accelerated rapidly as a result of the scientific and industrial revolutions and now the development of the mass media and the instant transmission of ideas across the globe. We notice this in the gap – sometimes the gulf – between the outlooks of the modern teenagers and their parents, which is a gap of only about 30 years. Multiply that gap many times over and we begin to sense what a huge gulf it is between us and medieval man, and an even more enormous one between us and biblical man.

Examples are very easy to see. Biblical man thought that the world was a large disc curving slightly upwards at the rims, with an inverted basin mounted on top of it and coloured blue (hence the sky). It had windows which would be opened to let through the waters stored above (hence the rain). It was mounted on huge pillars to stop it rocking in those all-encompassing waters. For the last 400 years it has been impossible for European man to think like that. Or again, up until fairly recently Christians thought of a vast unseen world full of spirits and devils and demons and angels, all affecting our lives. Modern man has almost, but not quite, abandoned this whole way of looking at things, and Christians have realized that one can believe fervently in the power and danger of evil without having any of those more primitive ways of picturing it. Again, ancient man thought that a baby was produced solely from a man's seed, with the woman's womb acting as an incubator. Modern man knows that every baby is equally the product of the man and the woman who each contribute half the necessary genes and chromosomes. Thus, if a marriage is infertile, it may be due to something lacking in either the male or female, but until the last 100 years or so it was assumed to be a major fault which could only exist in the woman. Thus infertility in the Bible was regarded as a shame to the woman, but never to the man. We now know better.

This huge gulf means that modern man has to exercise a

69

great effort of his imagination to try to picture how men in the biblical periods were thinking when they wrote what they did, or when they sent their messages to their fellows. It requires an enormous effort of imagination to try to think like an eighth-century BC peasant listening to the oratory of an Amos or Isaiah. Indeed, some scholars suggest today that it is well nigh impossible for us to get anywhere near the thought-world of the New Testament times and societies, let alone those of ancient Israel. However, that may appear to be too extreme a verdict, especially because those who live within the Christian Church live within a unique society that has always been trying to remember those early periods and what the Bible then meant to those who first heard it.

Many Christians hold that the gulf is not too great, because human nature has not changed. People are equally sinful, and the essential character of sin has not changed. People are as much in need of salvation as they ever were, and the character of that salvation which is offered in Jesus Christ has not changed either. But we have to be wary about that argument. Of course it has an obvious but limited truth, in that man's basic needs for food, security, belonging and rightness with God have not fundamentally changed. Yet our total way of thinking about ourselves, our setting within the world of the natural order, our relation to God, has changed dramatically. We don't and can't talk, think, write or pray like even medieval man did, so that in a very profound sense human nature itself has altered. It has not necessarily altered for the good, nor for the bad; there are probably both benefits and snags about the changes. Thus modern life is freed from many of the superstitions and wracking fears of the mysterious spirit world that terrorized our fairly recent ancestors. That is obviously good. On the other hand modern man doesn't fit so harmoniously into the world of nature, and has become a ruthless tyrant over it. That is bad.

To sum up, the Bible is not an easy authority to refer to, although all our Churches do so in an important manner. It is a collection of many different types of book from many different cultures, and does not have a plainly unified view of religious faith and theology unfolding neatly within it. The gulf between the thought-world of its many writers and ours today is col-ossal. The preacher must be a very careful person indeed.

Different views of the Bible

Some readers will have felt uneasy at many of the comments above. They will have felt that the case has been pressed too hard, and that the difficulties are greatly exaggerated. With help from background scholarship, they will hold that it is fairly easy to sense what the writer was getting at, and that in any case the Holy Spirit is promised as our supernatural aid in precisely this task. They will feel that the Spirit was the primal inspira-tion behind the writings in the first place, and has been ever with us since to guide us into all the truth of God so written. With this help we can be assured of being able to get to the 'plain meaning' of the scriptures, despite the hundreds of years that separate us from the original writers. Others will, how-ever, feel that the case is much worse than indicated above, that we only ought to refer to the New Testament, because it is nearer to us in time, and that only the most general of ideas can be gleaned from it with much certainty.

This diversity of opinion within virtually every congregation is not a depressing feature of the Church, unless people at either end start violent quarrels with each other and fall into active mistrust. It is a constant feature of the Christian Church, and always has been from the very beginning. It is perhaps only with the hard-liners at the far extremes that major worry emerges. Those who assert that every word of scripture is to be equated with the express and dictated Word of God are main-taining a particularly dogmatic position, for they must hold that God inspired the original writers infallibly, who wrote per-fectly what they were directed to do, that we now have in-fallible access to the original writings, and that our translators have conveyed the meaning infallibly into current English. Otherwise we cannot equate the written words of scripture with the Word of God. On the other extreme are Christians who do not see the Bible as any more valuable than many other religious books, and are equally glad to refer to current Christ-ian writings as to the New Testament. For them, the only thing

71

that is special about the latter is that it gets us fairly close to Jesus, but we can never be certain that we actually encounter any of his precise words or even themes. The major difficulty with that extreme view is to explain how it has transpired, nevertheless, that the Bible has had such a tremendous significance for the Church, and why so many people in our own day have had a transforming experience of God and his Word through reading the Bible or hearing it explained.

The great majority of today's Christians adopt a position somewhere between these two extremes. We believe that the Word of God is indeed mediated to us through the words that are written in the Bible and through reflecting about them, followed by obedience to them. It is impossible however to equate that Word with the words that are written down on the pages of our Bibles. We must use our wits to sense that Word, and can be assured that as we do so along with other Christians the Holy Spirit will be helping us. We believe that the supreme test as to what that Word will be like is to be found in Jesus Christ. That which exalts him and is clearly of the same character and spirit as we encounter in him, is true for us. This is what really makes the Bible authoritative, that it bears witness to Jesus and, in the New Testament, that witness is close to the person and events which we believe to be the key.

The preacher should normally presume that the majority of the congregation will hold a central position in this range of possible views. Therefore the preacher will not speak or behave or preach or pray as if every word of scripture is the unmediated voice of God himself, of absolute truth and authority. At the other extreme the preacher will not regard scripture as an interesting historical relic, of similar value to any other ancient writing on religious subjects or, for that matter, as any modern writing by Christians. The truth lies between those extremes.

There may, however, be especial heart-searching from many members of the congregation concerning the place of the Old Testament in Christian worship. Many will argue that it should hardly ever be used, for a number of reasons including the following: (1) The picture of God it conveys is pre-Christian and sometimes appallingly crude, cruel and primitive and generally abhorrent to the Christian conscience. Thus there is a shudder at the thought of the God who orders Samuel to hack a defenceless enemy king to pieces (as in the story of Agag in 1 Samuel 15), or whose special servants can summon up bears to devour any little boys who torment them (as in the story of Elisha in 2 Kings 2). (2) The Old Testament, when honoured religiously, leads to Jewish faith, not Christian. It produces a people who expect God's will to be found in a mighty series of commandments written down for all time in the Torah (the law usually identified with the first five books of the Old Testament) and who hope for a final Messiah who will vindicate them against all the other peoples of the world. (3) Much of it is utterly irrelevant to life today, including the religious and spiritual life. Thus the long genealogies, the monotonous regulations concerning the Temple and its worship, the accounts of all the kings who had ever ruled over either kingdom of Judah or Israel, the thunderings of the prophets against petty enemy nations of their times, all this is only of antiquarian interest to us today and not able to feed us spiritually.

Nevertheless, the Christian Church accepts the Old Testament as an essential part of its Bible. There are three main reasons for this. (1) The Old Testament is the record of how the God of Israel came to be known amongst his chosen people. But the God of Israel is the one true God, the God whom Christians worship, and who is supremely the God and Father of our Lord Jesus Christ. We are not talking about two 'gods' here, the God of Israel and the Father of Jesus, but the one same glorious God. (2) The writers of the New Testament assume that every reader believes in the God of Israel. Thus there are no more accounts of how God establishes the universe as its creator, maintains it through his providential care, works to bring salvation to a people he has chosen and called, reveals his moral will and offers his promises for the future. All of that is presupposed in the New Testament. (3) Jesus assumes the Old Testament in all his work, and is inexplicable without it. It provides the setting for his whole ministry. Almost all the titles, explanations, comments and pictures which are employed to bear witness to Jesus are derived from it.

For these overwhelmingly good reasons, the Old Testament is an integral element in the Christian scriptures. It is impossible to express the heritage which is ours, the extraordinary story which has made us the sort of people we are, without giving those books a major place in our tradition. They lead up to Christ and act as preparation for him. But we are of course to use our sense when handling the Old Testament. There are indeed great portions which are irrelevant for us, together with portions which do not lead nor point to Christ. Since Christ is judge of scripture, its Lord, those portions have the less authority for Christian believers. This makes us into discriminating users of the Old Testament. Yet we should not forget that likewise we must be discriminating users of the New, for there too there are occasional passages which jar against the supreme revelation in Jesus (as in parts of the book of Revelation?) and others which appear tame in the light of the grace and truth which is in Christ (as many hold the epistle of James to be).

The preacher's problem

The task of the preacher is to bridge that enormous gulf between the culture and thought-world of the biblical periods, and our life and world today. The preacher is commissioned to help people today hear the Word of God, but that Word has to be discerned in those events and ideas and dreams and teachings that were expressed in that vastly different setting centuries ago. The preacher must therefore be thoroughly aware of the nature of the biblical literature, the character of the times in which it was first formulated, and then be peculiarly gifted in showing how that Word can be related to today's scene, so vastly different from the one in which it was first uttered or heard. It is very hard indeed to say precisely how the preacher must perform this difficult but essential task. It is clear however that there are various devices and tricks which must *not* be used. We can regard them as the preacher's pet mistakes, to be shunned like the plague. Unfortunately all preachers tend to slip into these errors willy-nilly, including the most skilled and effective ones. Nevertheless, the fact that these faults are common does not mean that we accept them with a shrug of the shoulders. We must guard against them at every stage of our preaching. They do not clarify that precious Word: they distort it.

The preacher's common errors with the Bible

(1) Assuming that the 'biblical view' is expressed within one passage. The danger of assuming that there is one biblical viewpoint has already been cited. How does the preacher come up against it? Consider two examples. First, a preacher decides to tackle the theme of judgment as it is introduced in the famous parable of the sheep and goats in Matthew 25. There the final judgement acts as a complete surprise for all the persons involved. It is a surprise for those gathered at God's right hand, the 'sheep'; it is a shock for the 'goats' gathered at his left and finally sent into eternal punishment. The basis of the judgement is whether or not they fed the hungry, gave drink to the thirsty, clothed the naked, visited the sick and the prisoner. In all these instances they were ministering to Christ himself. The preacher is tempted to announce, on the strength of this passage, that the final judgement of all persons is made by God on the basis of whether or not we have cared for human need.

But the parable in Matthew 25 is not the last and definitive word in the Bible upon the theme of judgment. It is one of the pictures offered. In the first part of the selfsame chapter from verse 14 there is a noticeably different sort of parable to illustrate the way God judges us, the parable of the 'talents'. In this story three people are given different amounts of money by a master going away on a journey. In his absence they work and trade with that money and on his return they render account. The one who took no risks whatever with the money is condemned and thrown out to 'the outer darkness'. The implication is that judgement depends upon our willingness to take risks and pioneer new work for God. It is thus very different from the first parable cited above. But it is also very different from the carefully constructed theology of Paul, who affirms that ultimately we are judged by our faith in Christ, or of John

75

who sees our response to Christ as the essence of the judgement. Yet maybe John and Paul are not all that removed from the parable of the sheep and goats, for a careful look will show that the judgement is based on our care for the least needy 'of my brethren', which means those of the Christian Church and not all needy men in general. However, the initial warning still holds. One cannot build a doctrine of judgement, or anything else, out of one passage, even if it is one of Jesus' parables.

For a second example, consider the usual preaching at Pentecost. The key passage will be Acts 2 which describes how, fifty days after the Passover Feast (our Easter) the Spirit was released amongst the waiting disciples who then preached openly, and the Christian Church was born. This is the account which Luke, the probable author of Acts, provides. It assumes this sequence of events – crucifixion, resurrection, ascension, experience of the Spirit at the feast of Pentecost, birth of the Church. Most people's theology is grounded in this picture of the order of events. The Church is born several days after the resurrection, as a separate event. But this is not the only way of looking at this matter. The writer of John's gospel, probably working later than Luke, has a subtly different way of looking at it. For him, there was the crucifixion and, merged into it as one great act of 'glorifying the Son' there is resurrection and ascension and the imparting of the Spirit and creation of the Church. With this approach, Jesus breathes the Spirit upon the disciples as part of his initial resurrection (see John 20:22f). This means that neither passage – Acts 2 or John 20 – can be used as the final word on when the Church was established in the giving of the Spirit. No preacher can base a great argument on either passage without being aware of the other.

(2) Building a theological case or moral position on one passage. This is a development of the previous warning. Just as doctrine cannot be constructed from one passage in isolation, nor can theories about the way the Church should be ordered, moral principles for Christian conduct, nor rules for the spiritual or devotional life. Thus the parable of the Unjust Judge and the Importunate Widow (Luke 18:1–7) cannot be used to justify the assertion that we must be lengthy in our

prayers, for there are stern warnings elsewhere (e.g. Matthew 6:5–13) that we should be brief and to the point. Hence the model prayer which we know as the Lord's Prayer is startlingly short, a mere 50 or 60 words. Again, it is notorious that almost every existing form of ordained ministry can find some sort of justification in some passage or other in the New Testament, so that a famous biblical scholar surveyed the claims of all the traditions and exclaimed, in words borrowed from *Alice in Wonderland*, 'All have won, and all shall receive prizes!'.

Or take the fine list of the Christian virtues, gifts of the Spirit, which Paul sets out in Galatians 5:22–24. It is preceded by a contrasting list of vices. The informed preacher should not assume that these lists have a classic character, so that they are perfect and complete and the last word of the apostle upon the subject. Paul suggests a different list of vices in Romans 1:28–32 and another in 1 Corinthians 6:9f and another in Colossians 3:5–9. There seems to be a different list of virtues in Colossians 3:12–17, and a slightly different pair of lists lying behind Ephesians 4 and 5. If one tried to construct two such lists, of vices and virtues, from the Epistle of James, the result would be different again. The moral is clear. Don't build a total picture of the form of the moral life from any one biblical passage.

However surprising it may seem, we should not do this with the Ten Commandments either. It is a common practice to assume that they represent the quintessence of the Old Testament revelation of God's moral will and that, since his moral law does not fluctuate with the passage of time, they have a permanent validity for us too. That assumption needs questioning. There were later moral codes set out in the Old Testament (e.g. much of Deuteronomy). The Ten Commandments are never presented in the New Testament as the complete expression of God's moral will (although a few of them are cited in passages such as Mark 10:19). Instead, the royal way of love is presented by Paul as the grand summary of God's moral command (as in Romans 13:8–10 or Galatians 5:14) and described movingly in 1 Corinthians 13. The writer of John's gospel obviously holds the same view. For him, the moral life is that of 'doing the truth', obeying Jesus' commandments, and

77

that means loving as Jesus has loved (for which see especially John 13:12–17).

Finally, to make this point at an absurd level, one should not build a moral position out of one text or passage. One cannot legitimately go to Isaiah 11 and the vision there of the lion and the lamb lying down together in peace, and deduce that God does not will any creature to feed on another's flesh, and that therefore vegetarianism is mandatory upon us all. Nor can one deduce the opposite moral from Genesis 4 where God accepts Abel's offering of a sheep and rejects Cain's of vegetables. The earnest musician cannot go to the glorious hymns that echo through the book of Revelation and argue that hymn-singing is the best possible preparation for the after-life. The story of Ruth and Boaz should not be made into an apologia for sex relations outside marriage, nor is the command in 2 Thessalonian 3:10 that 'If anyone will not work, let him not eat' to be construed as a denunciation of the Welfare State ...

(3) Utilizing allegory or typology. An allegory is a normal story, but every detail is a hidden reference to some other reality. Thus I once heard an ardent allegorist in the pulpit tackling the story of the ark. He saw it as an allegory of the Church, into which all *nations* and *sorts of people* were invited. Thus the ark gave refuge for sheep (those who need leadership), elephants (big people), snakes (bad people). In no time one's fancy can run riot. Perhaps the bulldogs represented the British and the bears were the Russians? Again, the story of the man let down through the roof before Jesus, told in Mark 2, has been interpreted as an allegory of the Church (the house), with the crowd in the way (the congregation) and the scribes arguing (church leaders, perhaps the Church Council or the Board of Elders?). The man can only be healed by breaking through them all, and the preacher turns the story into an attack upon whatever he chooses. Allegory is a menace, because it enables a preacher to escape the plain meaning and construct a device for attacking or pillorying whatever he wants to have a crack at.

Despite this warning, it is clear that some allegories are used in the Bible itself, plainly and openly. Isaiah 5 is built upon the

78

allegory of Israel as a vineyard, and probably Mark 12 is similar. The dream of Nebuchadnezzar recorded in Daniel 2 features a golden image, which Daniel interprets as an allegory of the kingdoms of that time. In the same manner, Joseph had understood the Pharoah's dream in Genesis 41 as an allegory of future years of plenty and scarcity. Jonah is probably an allegory for those in Israel who wanted an exclusive policy towards foreigners. Further, there appears to be an explanation by Jesus in Mark 4:13–20 concerning the parable of the sower, and it is an allegorical one. Each type of soil represents a type of person, the seed represents the gospel word, and so on. In Matthew 13:36–43 another such explanation is given of the parable of the wheat and tares. Does this mean that Jesus specifically used and encouraged allegory? Probably not, but undoubtedly the early Church practised it extensively. The ark was often seen as an allegory for the Christian Church, for example. But in time the perils of this approach became clearer and clearer – that is, after several centuries. Today we are well advised to avoid allegory unless it is the plain meaning intrinsic to the passage, as with Isaiah 5.

Typology is very close to this. It sees key figures and events recorded, say, in the New Testament as being a repetition of similar events and figures in the past. The later events are then modelled upon (or 'typed' by) the former. Thus Matthew's gospel records in chapters 5–7 the way in which Jesus stands upon a mount and delivers a new moral law called by us the Sermon on the Mount. The typologist suggests that Matthew sees Jesus as a new Moses, for Moses too stood upon a mount (Sinai) and had revealed to him the moral law (the Commandments). In a similar manner the typologist could argue that the transfiguration story is typed upon Moses' view of the Promised Land just before he died, or the feeding of the five thousand is typed upon the feeding of Israel by manna in the desert. There are obvious traces of this sort of idea within the New Testament. Thus apparently the writer of John's gospel understands the crucifixion as a 'type' of Moses lifting up the serpent in Numbers 7, hence the comment in John 3:14. Again, Paul argues that Christian life today is 'typed' upon the wanderings of Israel in the wilderness (see 1 Corinthians

79

10:1–14). Sometimes undoubtedly this way of interpreting New Testament passages can suddenly provide a great flash of illumination. Nevertheless we are well advised to beware of it, or the carefree preacher can find himself indulging in all sorts of crazy fancies of his own invention.

(4) Spiritualizing. This is one of the easiest known ways of trying to relate an awkward passage to contemporary life. The story in 2 Kings 5 describes how Naaman of Syria comes to Elisha for a cure for leprosy and is ordered to wash seven times in the Jordan. Then he is cured, even though he reckoned that there were far better rivers back home to wash in. A preacher may spiritualize this story by saying that it represents a typical man seeking salvation but not wanting to be humiliated, wanting instead to find other less demanding and more congenial ways of securing it. The story has been changed from a specific one of a man existing in one definite historical moment finding physical healing, to a far more general one about all men at all times seeking spiritual healing. Or again, there is a vivid account in the Gospels of Jesus being asleep in a boat caught in a sudden violent squall and liable to capsize. Jesus is woken, and he rebukes and calms the storm. The boat and all in it are then safe. The preacher spiritualizes this by saying that it is a story designed to show that when Jesus is present with you and life's storms buffet you, he can be bidden to rebuke the storms and bring you to calm conditions.

It is difficult at first to quarrel with such interpretations, because it is indeed true that we seek congenial and undemanding ways of trying to effect our salvation from God; it is true that an awareness of Jesus present in stormy circumstances does indeed contribute an inner tranquility and calm. But these interpretations avoid facing some of the very awkward issues which otherwise the stories raise, issues like the place of miraculous healing, or the action of Jesus in working a miracle over the natural order when his life and that of his friends is threatened. Did he not resolve to avoid miracle-working, according to the accounts of his early temptations in the desert? To spiritualize these stories is therefore a dubious way of evading very awkward problems.

80

As soon as you have recognized this it becomes clear that spiritualizing is to be suspect. If you ask the question 'What did the original writers probably intend by that passage?' such interpretations become even more suspect. In the first example, you would be bound to answer something like this – the original writer intended to say that a Syrian foreigner experienced the power of the God of Israel by coming to the prophet for a cure from leprosy and, despite his pride, obeying the humiliating command to bathe seven times in the dirty little river of Jordan. He was cured, thanks be to God! Thus the writer was almost certainly not intending to set out some lofty spiritual principle for men of all time. In the second example, the writer was almost certainly trying to recount a vivid story treasured by the early Church, a story which showed how marvellous was Jesus of Nazareth, how much more than an outstanding human being, so much so that even the winds and waves obeyed him. He too was probably not trying mainly to set out a noble spiritual principle which would bring comfort to persons in every subsequent period of history.

We can therefore formulate two rough and ready rules. It is not legitimate to produce such a passage and then say that the 'spiritualized' meaning is the plain meaning of the passage. Manifestly that is not so. You cannot preach on 2 Kings 5 by saying that the more general spiritual truth is what the passage is intended to be about. But, on the other hand, our second rule is that it *is* legitimate to be preaching about a general spiritual truth (such as, that to call upon Jesus in the midst of tumultuous storms is to find a great resource of calm) and to use the story of Mark 4:35–41 as *an illustration* of an event like such a spiritual experience. Or again, you might be preaching about our natural human tendency to make salvation and our rightness with God come about in as easy a manner as possible, and say 'It is all a bit like the story of Naaman in the Old Testament, who also wanted to be healed without any indignity'. In this instance you are using the biblical passage as a likeness to the spiritual truth you want to talk about, so the story can be utilized as a form of *illustration*. This is clearly different from saying that such a way of looking at the passage is the one true way, expressing the plain and original meaning.

Yet those two simple rules may be regarded as too restrictive. A further word is necessary. The spiritual or theological genius need not be bound by them. Thus Charles Wesley can get away with seeing the story of Jacob wrestling with a curious angel at the place called Peniel described in Genesis 32:22–32, as an account of typical Christian experience. The believer wrestles and wrestles with God through the dark night and at last yields and finds disclosed to him the amazing mystery of God's being, the 'pure universal love' of God. Wesley puts it into one of the most remarkable of his hymns (339 in M.H.B.):

> Come, O thou traveller unknown
> Whom still I hold but cannot see!
> My company before is gone
> And I am left alone with Thee;
> With Thee all night I mean to stay
> And wrestle till the break of day.

Wesley could achieve that feat of spiritualizing the Jacob story because he was a spiritual and poetic genius of rare originality and depth. We do not have Wesley's vivid imagination and power in poetry. We lesser mortals should therefore avoid spiritualizing, or we merely trivialize the text of the Bible, and are not as convincing as we could be.

(5) Regarding biblical characters as representative of all men at all time. The preacher asserts that every true prophet is called in a way such as Isaiah describes in chapter 6, with a call from God 'Whom shall I send, and who will go for me?'; every sinner hears the word of God saying as in 2 Samuel 12 'Thou art the man!'; every rich man is commanded by Jesus to sell everything he has, as with the young ruler in Mark 10; everyone must be 'born again' as Nicodemus is told in John 3; everyone has an experience of inner struggle such as Paul describes in Romans 7; and so on. The preacher has assumed in these instances that the persons being described in the Bible are representative persons, and that there must therefore be an immediate linkage between us and them. If Isaiah is called in that manner, so are we. If Nicodemus is given that word, so are we.

82

But it is not legitimate to assume that those specific persons who feature in those biblical stories are in some way representing all mankind, and that therefore something important about our own personalities and spiritual histories is necessarily being expressed through them. A moment's reflection soon clarifies this point. Not every prophet is called in a manner akin to Isaiah's, with his overwhelming vision during the dramatic sacrificial worship in the Temple. Apparently Amos was called whilst tending his sheep, whereas Jeremiah had always been so strongly convinced of his calling that he attributed this to God having chosen him whilst in his mother's womb. Not every sinner is confronted by a man of marvellous courage such as Nathan who can make us furious with someone's arrogant sin and then make us convict ourselves out of our own mouths, as he did with David. Not every rich man is ordered to sell everything and give to the poor. Zaccheus was not so ordered, for example. Nicodemus was an enquiring Jew of the old school, and not many of us have a religious background remotely like his, so that the command to be 'born again' is not necessarily appropriate to us. Again, not many of us have had the inner struggle with the presumed moral law of God that Paul agonized over, so that we cannot necessarily identify ourselves with Romans 7. We were not brought up as Pharisees, after all.

Not only does this rule out our drawing too straight a line from the experience of Paul to that of English Christians in the twentieth century, it also rules out many links that preachers too readily assume between us and the characters described in the Bible. Very few members of today's congregations are actually likely to have much in common with Elijah, Ahab, or Jeremiah, or Simon Peter, or Stephen, or Cornelius. Indeed there are only two totally representative characters in the whole of the Bible—Adam who represents us all in our sin, and Jesus Christ who represents man redeemed. Every other person or character featured in any Bible story, or in the history of the Church, has only very partial traits, experience, character, in common with us. Those biblical persons were not described, nor their experience set forth, because the first writers saw them as representative characters, but because they were

83

obviously important persons in the whole multi-coloured story of how God has dealt with his people. That is why Agag and Saul and Samson and Ezekiel and Thomas and Pilate and King Herod and Elymas appear in the narratives, because they are caught up in that amazing history, sometimes for good and sometimes for ill. They are not cited because they somehow illustrate the essence of all human nature. After all, one could equally well go to Greek mythology if that were what one was wanting.

(6) Making simple parallels between biblical situations and today's. The children of Israel escape from slavery and trek through the desert, to be fed by the mysterious manna sent specially by God. Does that mean that some small nation which is freed from the colonial yoke in our era and is desperately poor and starving can expect some miraculous food supply to suddenly appear in its own desert condition today? The walls of Jericho fall down after the final march round them and the blast of the trumpet. Does that mean that the Church which encounters formidable opponents blocking its progress can parade its strength to them and utter a great shout and then find that the opposition is simply shattered by God? Micaiah (in 1 Kings 22) sees the rebellious alliance between Jehoshaphat and Ahab as fatal, despite the fawning of all the other prophets. Does that mean that a concerted foreign policy between, say, Britain and America which is acclaimed by most superficial observers but doubted by one great religious leader, is to be regarded as fatal? Isaiah tells King Hezekiah to lie low despite the siege by the Assyrians, for God will save the city of Jerusalem. Isaiah 36–38 describes the amazing deliverance. Does this mean that if Britain refuses to be stampeded by the unions, or the Common Market countries, or the Russians, but sticks doggedly and carefully to its past policies, God will suddenly whisk the trouble away? Of course not. We cannot simply strike up a few superficial parallels between the Old Testament era and today and assume that we can transfer the biblical message across the intervening two or three thousand years and that it will emerge plain and clear for our time. The instances just quoted show how absurd a procedure that can

become. Yet preachers are always trying to do this, always trying to find the parallels between the situation described in the Bible and those of today. Indeed, many would hold that the purpose of great preaching is to be able to do this. Be warned. This art can only be done tentatively, and then by people who have both thoroughly grasped the ancient setting and the present situation. Those parallels which can rightly be held to exist will never be as crude as those outlined above and will require the most sensitive handling.

What about parallels with the New Testament? Is not that a much more obvious possibility? Maybe, yet again every preacher needs to be warned about jumping into those quick and neat assertions about the similarities between the early Church and its setting and the situation today. Think of a few commonly practised parallels. A preacher is declaiming upon the opposition to Jesus in his ministry. It came from the most highly-trained religious authorities and from their leadership, as well as from some common people. 'Right,' says the preacher, 'so it came from people like the Archbishop of Canterbury, the President of the Methodist Conference, the theologians, they are the people who hound out the Christ.' The statement makes the congregation sit up. It brings the whole issue into the present day. It sounds startling and vivid. But it implies an easy line from the Sanhedrin and the Pharisees up into today's world of the Christian Church and its leadership. Is it legitimate?

The preacher notes that Jesus had within his band of disciples one, Simon of Cana, who was a Zealot, the ancient Jewish counterpart of the revolutionary freedom fighters of our day. The preacher then says that Jesus gladly accepts freedom fighters into his company, and maybe regards himself as the leader of them all. Can we actually build *any* sort of conclusions regarding today's revolutionaries and guerrilla fighters from such a tiny reference to Simon of Cana? The preacher notices that in his ministry Jesus normally avoided going through Samaria, as did most Jews travelling down to Jerusalem from Galilee. He then tells us that the Church of today ought therefore to avoid places which are traditionally hostile to it, such as the big slum clearance estates on the edges

85

of most of our major cities. Can we draw that parallel? The preacher is expounding the parable of the labourers in the vineyard (Mark 12), and how the master will finally punish those rebellious tenants. He then refers to today's world and the many efforts made by certain Christian bodies to smuggle Bibles and tracts into communist countries, and how the messengers have been repeatedly caught and imprisoned. But soon God will punish those atheistic governments and bring them crashing down. Can we equate those two situations so easily?

A preacher notices that in Acts 8 the apostle Philip opens up the fulfilment of the Old Testament to the Chancellor of the Exchequer in the Kingdom of Ethiopia. The Chancellor becomes a believer in Jesus. He is straightaway baptized, by the roadside. Does this mean that the contemporary evangelist should baptize every convert there and then, whatever the setting? Or that Christians ought to make a special attempt to discuss spiritual matters with those who work for the Treasury? If any preacher were to assert such things we would faintly smile, and feel sorry for such naïveté. A preacher points out that in Ephesians 4:11 five different types of ministry are mentioned, the order being apostles, prophets, evangelists, pastors and teachers, then says that our Church life today is faltering because we do not have those types, nor in that order of priority. We are content with just pastors and teachers. But again, can we draw such a simple straight line between a list of ministerial gifts, which may not have been designed in the first place to outline how Christian ministry ought to be shaped down through all time, and the current situation of the Christian Church?

We could go on and on raising such queries about many of the common parallels which preachers expound regularly. The constant fault is to suggest that the similarities between the ancient situation and that of today are so great as to make the situations easily comparable. To sum up, because we have to be constantly on the alert for all six of these possible blunders in our handling of scripture, we are able to gather together six awkward questions which we must ask about our handling of the biblical material. They are:

(1) Have I assumed that there is only one 'biblical view' on the

matter I am preaching about, and should I be aware of a greater range of biblical teaching?

(2) Have I built a conclusion too firmly from just one passage?

(3) Have I resorted to allegory or typology?

(4) Have I spiritualized a passage so as to distort its original meaning and weaken the case?

(5) Have I regarded persons in the biblical accounts to be representative of persons today in too extensive a manner?

(6) Have I drawn simple parallels between the biblical setting and the world of today and thereby obscured the differences, and distorted the plain meaning of scripture?

In a later chapter we shall return to these questions, and their usefulness as a check upon our preaching. Let us remind ourselves that we do not honour God by handling scripture in a naïve way. It is not the mark of an obedient believing Christian to take hold of the Bible reverently and then commit all the blundering listed above. It is a sign of irresponsibility and thus of unfaith. Those who are led by the Holy Spirit have a passion for so handling the Bible, that it sheds a bright light upon our discipleship today. They do not want it to be used to by-pass hard thinking, careful study, thorough tussling with the problems, for that means that its light will be blotched and uncertain and deceptive.

Maybe, these six questions make the task of preaching seem to you to be impossible, or a superficial first reading of the chapter may make you feel that you can do nothing useful with the Bible except use it as a store of illustration. There is, however, a strong continuity between us today and the people of bilbical times, a most powerful linkage between us and them with which the preacher works. It is not to be seen mainly in the unchanging character of human nature, a notion which was queried earlier. It is to be seen in the constant character and purpose of God, the God seen to be Father of our Lord, Jesus Christ. He it is to whom the whole Bible bears witness, even though some dimensions of his glory are missing in much of the Old Testament record and even though we cannot assign infallibility to any passage anywhere. The God who is creator, sustainer, saviour and perfecter is the God who has been dealing graciously with mankind from primeval times to today. Throughout the long panorama of human history, he has been constant. As the Psalmist so frequently puts it: 'His mercies endure for ever.' This is what makes preaching from the whole corpus of scripture to be gloriously possible. The God whose purposes are outlined, sometimes allusively in myths from long ago, in sagas and legends, in stirring accounts of a remarkable people experiencing a remarkable history, in the passionate protest and vision of the prophets, is the same God who is made manifest in Jesus and the young Christian Church. He is the same God who calls to us today, who meets us as creator, sustainer, saviour and sanctifier. Therein lies the strong continuity with the biblical testimony upon which Christian preaching is constructed.

Finally, it will be helpful at this stage to study or re-read the discussion concerning the authority of the Bible in John Stacey: *Groundwork of Theology*, pp. 53–7, the account of the formation of the canon in W. David Stacey: *Groundwork of Biblical Studies*, pp. 162–76, and the concluding passage in Morna Hooker: *Studying the New Testament*, pp. 212–15, in which she discusses the diversity within the New Testament.

Chapter 5

Preaching and the Bible

PREACHING is one of the most important activities that happens within Church worship. It normally occupies a central place within the service. The preacher is almost always placed in a prominent position and the pulpit is one of the most obvious items of furniture in the building. By a long-standing convention, preachers are hardly ever interrupted or questioned during the sermon. There is an ethos of considerable authority about the preaching, verging in some quarters on awe. Yet it is only too obvious that preaching is intensely difficult, does not have the same place in English society that it had in, say, Victorian times, and that it is often the sermon which is criticized today as being the most boring and unhelpful part of many a service. The last chapter dwelt at length on some crass mistakes which preachers can make when handling the Bible. It must be all too easy to be a bad preacher!

There seem then to be contradictory judgments within most Church life about the place and value of preaching. On the one hand the Protestant traditions especially see it as of supreme importance. It is through the preaching that we are all arrested by the Word of God. Put in another manner, God chooses to address men today through the spoken words of his servants, the preachers. Therefore the pulpit ought to be the most significant place in the church, raised high and eminent. But on the other hand, modern culture tends to devalue all forms of oratory, including preaching, as was noted at the end of Chapter One. Older people in the congregation will often lament the poor quality of the preaching today in comparison with what they knew in their youth, but this is partly a lament about the way modern life features other more exciting (and effective?) means of communication.

89

These comments certainly remind us that in some respects preaching may have to use different styles and forms from those adopted in the Victorian or Edwardian periods. But the essential nature of preaching has not changed, the task that sermons must attempt, their role within the worship of the Christian Church. Let us attempt a brief definition. Preaching is that speech in the context of Christian worship in which the great resources of the Christian tradition, especially the witness of the Bible, are related to the practice of Christian discipleship today. Preaching has two main areas of concern then – the Christian tradition and heritage of faith stretching down through the centuries and treasuring within it the witness expressed by the Bible on the one hand, and the tasks of being Christians in today's world on the other. It is something like a bridging exercise in which one support is set down firmly in the Christian tradition and the other is located equally firmly in today's world. The traffic going backward and forward over that bridge is the preaching, the constant interchange of ideas, perspectives, insights, ways of looking at things, accumulated experience, sets of convictions, questions, problems, challenges.

Supposing someone stands up in a pulpit and gives a most illuminating account of how the Epistle to the Galatians came to be written. That is not Christian preaching, unless the account then goes on to show how our discipleship is affected. Otherwise it is an admirable lecture about the biblical literature, but it is not preaching, because (to use again the analogy of the bridge) it is all set on one side of that bridge and there is no traffic going backward and forward. Someone else stands up in the pulpit and gives a clear outline of the doctrine of creation. Very good, and doubtless valuable to those whose greatest need is a clearer theology of creation. But it is not *preaching* unless that sermon grasps the listeners with a conviction of what God wills for us as a result of his creative activity. Otherwise it remains as a useful theological discourse. Again, it is all set on one side of the bridge.

The 'preaching' can also fail because it is set too restrictively within the area of modern issues. Someone declaims from the pulpit about the plight of the third world, the massive injustice

90

whereby the rich nations grow steadily richer whilst the poor ones are crippled by the present world economic systems and inevitably grow poorer and more wretched. The case is stated with great clarity, urgency, accuracy. But this is not preaching, unless it is clearly linked with the great perspectives of the Christian faith and tradition. Without that linkage it is a relaying of information, which is very desirable and commendable, but it is *not* preaching because we have all remained at one end of that bridge and there has been no adequate traffic to and fro. Someone gives us a fascinating account of mission work overseas, or in a deprived area of a great city, or in prisons or some other setting. Unless that is linked clearly to God's constant call to mission it is not *preaching*, it is description. It may be done extremely well, but unless the same God who has always been calling his people to bear witness to him is also heard calling us today to bear witness, no preaching whatever has happened.

Preaching is basically the same sort of activity as theology, but whereas one can practise theology by writing books or getting into ardent discussion in any conceivable setting where people are meeting, or singing Christian hymns, one practises preaching by speaking within the context of Christian worship. Of course preaching can be exercised outside church buildings and in the open air, but again if it is *preaching* it will be set within a general framework of Christian worship and will, in effect, be a sign of the Church at worship outside the ecclesiastical building. If the occasion be one in which a Christian speaker is trying to produce an apologia for the Christian faith, with a lot of questions and answers being bandied backwards and forwards, that may be Christian speaking (which is highly commendable) but not, strictly speaking, Christian preaching. Preaching implies the Christian congregation for its setting, and for that reason this book will not contain any specific hints on open-air speaking or the general presentation of the Christian faith amongst those who are questioning it.

Preaching appears to be somewhat presumptuous. The preacher stands in a prominent place and takes command of the congregation for perhaps twenty minutes. There is an obvious note of authority about the exercise. Some people have credited it with so much that it has almost been equated with the speech of God himself. But what is the authority that is being exercised here? First, it is the authority of the Church. The preacher has been authorized to speak on behalf of the Church, as its accredited representative or spokesman. That is why the preacher must first satisfy the appropriate Church authorities concerning knowledge of the scriptures and Christian tradition, general competence in theology and ability to conduct worship and proclaim the living relevance of the faith. That is why the preacher needs some controlling agency to keep a check upon his or her handling of that authority. All preaching is by virtue of the authority granted by the Church, not by virtue of personal visions or convictions (or indeed hunches) which the individual may be aware of.

Secondly, it is the authority of personal conviction that Jesus Christ, the Lord of the Church, requires this work. Persons vary enormously in the manner in which this conviction arises and the form in which it is expressed. Some Christians have a very vivid sense that Christ has called to this task, a sense so vivid that they feel under mighty constraint and will cry 'Woe is me if I preach not the gospel'. For them, to talk of 'calling' seems highly appropriate. Others may not have such a powerful sense of being grasped by God and compelled to do this particular task. Instead, they may have become aware of the need for the Church to have many more preachers, and may be conscious that there is no good reason why they should not do this as an element in their personal commitment to Jesus Christ. They will be slightly abashed or embarrassed by profound talk of 'calling', yet in reality their calling is as geniune as those in the first group. Every person who has come to a responsible Christian decision to preach and has had this decision ratified by the Church after the necessary training is in the fullest sense 'called', and rightly holds sufficient authority.

Obviously there are many things which that authority is not. It is not an authority enabling us to make final or infallible pronouncements upon matters of faith or discipleship. It does not justify us in telling everyone in the congregation what they all should do in all matters of the Christian life. It does not equip us to give the absolutely correct interpretation of passages of scripture. It is authority to act as one of the Church's interpreters of its faith, but not as a supreme know-all. It is an authority therefore which should humble us, making us feel 'Who is worthy for such a task as this?' rather than 'I'll tell that congregation what God wants them to do', which smacks of arrogance.

But, more than this, it is an authority which has a special relationship to Jesus Christ. He is the Head of the Church. Every authority which is exercised within the Church should be in conformity to Christ. This is why there are occasions when an individual must actually oppose the prevalent authorities within the Church, if these are plainly contrary to the mind of Christ. This happened in the life of the German Churches, for example, when Hitler attempted to enforce a policy of pure 'Aryan' membership upon them, and some Church authorities submitted to it. But the basic assertion that authority should be in conformity to Christ has more far-reaching implications. It means that our authority, when properly exercised, is always that of service. Christ came not to be ministered unto, but to minister. A preacher's authority is of that character. It is not for personal gain, for the opportunity for adulation from others or for having to be listened to. It is rooted and grounded in the picture of self-abandonment and service that we encounter in Jesus. It means too that as Jesus conducted his ministry by respecting people's freedom and personal dignity, and by appealing to all that was best within them, so should Christian preachers. We deny our rightful authority whenever we treat others in the Church with scant respect, or attempt to by-pass their intelligence or try to make decisions for them. Christ's authority never involves belittling people, trampling upon them, scorning them. It always involves exalting them.

It is important for us to be regularly reminded of this fundamental grounding of authority within the life of the Church and according to Christ. It is a constant check upon our temptation to over-stress some special personal interests which may not represent the convictions of the whole Church. You may feel that every Christian should be a non-smoker, or meticulous about keeping to speed limits, or an aggressive teetotaller, but it is not fitting to parade such minority viewpoints in the pulpit

93

as being the will of God. That is an abuse of your authority, just as it would be if you were to assert that nowadays no Christian ought to believe in the Virgin Birth or the existence of angels or the substitutionary view of the atonement. Again if you were to assert that every Christian should be a Socialist, or a Conservative, or a Communist, that too would be an abuse of authority. We should have the sense to see that the believing, thinking and acting of the Church is much wider than that of any one individual, and temper our pulpit speech accordingly.

It is important in other ways. It is easy for preachers to become depressed or bewildered by what they actually achieve. You go many miles out into the country one Sunday and conduct a service in a tiny little chapel attended by a handful of elderly people. Hours of preparation went into the service, but one or two of the congregation fall asleep in the sermon, others shuffle about during the prayers, the singing is dreary and the people do not seem especially grateful at the end. You go away wondering what has been achieved, and whether it is all worthwhile or not. The question about what has been achieved is unanswerable. Nobody can ever quite know. But you can ask 'What have I been doing?' and receive a clear answer. You have been representing the whole great catholic Church to and with that little struggling company of Christian people in that scattered rural community. It is worthwhile, if it is worthwhile for there to be believing Christians in that village or hamlet. If Christian believing and worshipping is not worthwhile there, it cannot really be 'worthwhile' anywhere else either. This is not to argue that it is always appropriate to have a chapel in every hamlet, but to assert that Christian worship is fundamentally right, worthwhile, our bounden duty and joy, in every place under the sun. Therefore it is worthwhile for the persons authorized to lead worship and preach to do this even with tiny companies of believers, whether or not you always come away with a sense of achievement.

Using the lectionary

Recently more and more Free Church ministers and lay preachers have used the bible readings and sermon themes set

94

out in the lectionary drawn up by the Joint Liturgical Group in 1967 and published as *The Calendar and Lectionary* (Oxford 1967). There is nothing novel about the use of a lectionary to decide what scripture readings should be used on Sundays in public worship, or for personal devotion (a need which is met by *The Daily Office*, produced by the same Group and published by SPCK and Epworth in 1968). The Jews used one for their synagogue worship. The Christian Church was slower to evolve one, and did not do so until the form of the Christian Year had taken clear shape in the fourth century. The subsequent lectionaries used in different Christian traditions have varied greatly, but the 1967 form has won wide acceptance in Britain. The Methodist Church had previously had its own lectionary, not widely used, with readings for both morning and evening worship. It soon abandoned that and took this form as normative for Sunday mornings, another one of its own for Sunday evenings. These are all set out in the central section C of *The Methodist Service Book* of 1975. The United Reformed Church's *Service Book*, published in 1980, includes the 1967 lectionary slightly adapted.

This most widely used lectionary is designed for Sunday mornings. It consists of three lessons and a psalm for every Sunday, and for some special feast days (e.g. Christmas Day, Maundy Thursday, Good Friday, etc.). One lesson is from the Old Testament, one from the gospels, and the other from the rest of the New Testament. One lesson is selected as being the 'controlling' one. This expresses the major theme for the day, and the other two are intended to be supportive and a means of gaining a fuller understanding of the theme. The scheme is constructed out of two major cycles of Christian celebration, plus a long period in between in which no major celebration falls. In the history of the Church, the Easter and Pentecost cycle was the first to become widespread, and much later Christians started to celebrate Christ's birth on December 25th and a second cycle was created, even though it is highly doubtful that this date is accurate. There is better reason for supporting a date later in February. However, in the Christian Year which we now celebrate the birth cycle comes first. Each cycle consists of a period of preparation, the major festival or festi-

95

vals, and a sequel. There are minor complications because the date of Easter varies each year (being determined by the sun) and thus the period between the two major points in the cycle varies. In addition, the special feast of Christmas Day may sometimes fall on a Sunday, sometimes not.

The readings begin nine Sundays before Christmas (i.e. near the end of October) with five Sundays of preparation followed by the four Sundays of Advent. The Old Testament provides the controlling lessons throughout this period. From Christmas onwards the emphasis is upon Jesus and his ministry, beginning with the manifestation to the Gentiles (i.e. the Wise Men), called Epiphany. The sequel will last for six or five Sundays before the next cycle begins, nine Sundays before Easter. This will generally be in early February. The controlling lesson is usually from the gospels. After three Sundays the traditional period of fasting and preparation (Lent) begins, and lasts forty days to correspond with the period Jesus spent in the desert preparing for his own ministry. This comes to its great climax in Palm Sunday, Holy Week and then the glory of Easter Day itself. The controlling lessons are from the gospels, mainly that of John, for forty days until Ascension Day. Since Pentecost is fifty days after Easter there are ten days between Ascension and Pentecost, then the controlling lesson is Acts 2. After this there is a long period of about five months stretching right through our summer and well into the autumn. The themes are mainly those concerning the nature of the Christian Church and our own discipleship. The rest of the New Testament provides most of the controlling lessons. Thus during the course of the lectionary year these follow a rough pattern akin to that of the Bible – Old Testament, gospels, then Acts and the epistles.

The lectionary is designed to last for two years, after which you start again. The separate evening scheme of lessons suggested for the Methodist Church is likewise constructed to last for two years. You can work out which year of the two-year cycle applies by reckoning that the Easter of the 'first year' cycle will fall in calendar years that are odd numerically, and the 'second year' falls in even years. Thus Easter in 1985 will involve the first year readings, and in 1986 it will involve the second year ones. You can easily then calculate backward or forward from the Easter period. During the two years of the readings almost all the important Gospel readings will have been handled, and a fair proportion of the epistles. The Old Testament is of course very long indeed (it takes up about 74 per cent. of our Bibles), so that the effect of having one lesson from it every Sunday is that in two years one has still only read about 1 per cent. of the material. That is unavoidable if the individual lessons are not to become too long.

Most experienced preachers suggest that you should not be too strictly governed by the suggested theme for the day. The controlling lesson may well suggest another theme to the preacher brooding over it, and the supporting lessons may well justify such other ideas. On the other hand you may find it difficult to see why some supporting lessons are advocated, and need not feel particularly constrained by them. This reminds us that the lectionary and its themes are not a straight-jacket to preachers, but a clear guide. There may always be occasions when it is fitting to abandon the lectionary readings, theme and collect of the day, and use some other theme and readings. Obviously this applies when there is some especial event to be celebrated in the local church (e.g. its anniversary), and acknowledgement for such exceptions is made by the suggested readings on pages C65–C67 in *The Methodist Service Book*. Other significant events can occur (e.g. as when there are baptisms, or confirmations, or an honoured member of the congregation has just died) and so, for many good reasons, the lectionary should be regarded as our guide and not our taskmaster to be slavishly followed.

This leads us to consider the advantages and disadvantages of the use of the lectionary. Many of the advantages will have become apparent already. Using the lectionary gives a shape and plan to one's whole preaching and conduct of worship, a shape which is determined by the character of the Christian Year. The great festivals of that year will become the high points for the worship and preaching. In practice, a far wider range of themes will be utilized than if you rely solely upon personal 'inspiration', for that is itself restricted by the mental disposition of the preacher concerned. Someone who has no

97

'feel' for nature never feels the Holy Spirit's inspiration to deal with the doctrine of creation. Someone with a vivid conversion experience is constantly feeling that the Spirit is inspiring to sermons on the need for, or nature of, conversion. Someone who enjoys overseas travel is more often inspired to preach on the world Church, and so on. It is all too easy for us to interpret our own favourite inclinations as the promptings of the Holy Spirit, and thus to find a sanctimonious excuse for being narrow in the scope of our preaching. To be guided by the lectionary is a constant protection from narrowness, and a challenge to think and move and preach on a bigger map than before. Our preaching can become less arbitrary, less subject to the moods of the moment.

There are other advantages. The congregation can know what themes are going to be handled, what passages are to be read. Thus the Sunday worship can be used as the central focus for a Christian education programme in the local church, whereby fellowship and study groups consider the themes and lessons either immediately before, or immediately after, the Sunday worship. Similarly, a programme for personal devotion and Bible reading can be worked out to link with the Sunday worship. Of course, this can also be done using schemes other than the lectionary one, but such schemes are not likely to be better related to the Christian Year. Finally, preachers who use the lectionary scheme can have access to many helps and guides such as *The Methodist Service Book* (providing the collects of the day), commentaries (e.g. John Gunstone's *Commentary on the New Lectionary* published in two volumes by SPCK in 1973 and 1974), prayers (e.g. *New Prayers in Worship* edited by Alan Gaunt and published by the St Paul Press in loose-leaf bind format, or Susan Williams' *Lord of our World* published by Falcon in 1973) or introductory remarks about the readings (e.g. David Cooke's *Headings for the Scripture Readings*, Mowbrays, 1972). But the most thorough help is obtainable from the liturgical notes and preaching notes published systematically in the magazine *Worship and Preaching* (published by the Methodist Publishing House). (See also Geoffrey Cuming: *The Ministry of the Word*, Oxford University Press, 1979.)

Nevertheless there are disadvantages, and some have already come to our notice. Some special Sundays are not even catered for in the extra table in the Service Book, including such important ones as the Covenant Service, which often coincides with Epiphany. Other major services in the normal life of the Church are not considered (e.g. Young Peoples Day), yet every preacher must have respect for them. The morning Sunday Schools will almost certainly be using a scheme of lesson material which bears no close relationship to the lectionary, although it is hoped that the British Lessons Council will collaborate with the Joint Liturgical Group in constructing a common lectionary in the future.

More seriously, there are major passages of scripture which are absent from the two-year reading cycle. Thus the lectionary does not include such significant material as the myths of Babel or the Flood, Abraham's appeal to the justice of God (Genesis 18), anything whatever from Numbers, Judges and large sections of Israelite history; there are only 9 verses from both the books of Samuel, and only 12 from such an important source as the prophecy of Amos. The New Testament material likewise omits some highly important accounts, such as the establishment of deacons (Acts 6), the sermon of Stephen (Acts 7), St Paul's conversion (Acts 9) and the first Council of the Church in Jerusalem (Acts 15); such a major argument as Paul advances in Romans 1–3 is ignored. Many themes are missing too, from doctrinal ones like the humanity of Jesus to more practical ones like the necessity for us to be forgiving, or the character of worship, or the life of prayer. These omissions are of course inevitable in any system which is bound to limit the scripture readings to three on 56 days of the year, but their absence could well be an argument for having lectionaries working on a three- or four-year cycle rather than the present two-year system. Further, you return to the same set of readings three times within five years on the two-year cycle, and this can become too repetitive and the sermon topics too predictable unless you are very careful. Thus, if you are going to have a lectionary as guide, should it be merely a two-year cycle? The Roman Church uses a three-year cycle, and this may have advantages.

There is another problem lurking beneath the surface of the discussion. Does reliance upon the lectionary stifle the freedom of the Spirit and tie you down to predetermined themes in a way which denies the freshness of life in the Spirit? Most of us would probably refuse to accept this argument too easily, believing that the Spirit is not that of utter unpredictability and freakishness, but that the Spirit can work even better through predictable channels than otherwise. After all, the Spirit does not encourage us to believe anything we fancy, but operates through the tested strength of the Church's doctrines and creeds so as to reinforce those convictions within the believer. He is not the Spirit of the passing whim, but of the matured experience of the Church catholic, so he is more likely to be at work through a tested scheme of scripture reading than through personal preference and the hunches of the week.

There is a more serious and fundamental problem than this. It concerns the nature of preaching. Earlier in the chapter an analogy was used to describe preaching as like the traffic on a bridge, one end being today's experience of the Christian life and the other being the great Christian tradition within which the scriptural witness is central. If you use the lectionary themes and passages there is a marked tendency to make the preaching have one normal design – to start from the scriptural basis, and then use it to shed light upon the current scene and today's Christian living. But it is equally legitimate in Christian preaching to begin with immediate issues that are known to be vital ones to us today and, with the sermon determined by such an issue, to then let Christian tradition throw light upon it. Someone tied too closely to the lectionary will rarely be doing this, because lectionary themes are not designed for that purpose. In the past such preaching as described here has been classed 'topical', often with some scorn. We have no business to be derogatory about it. It is important that every preacher who wishes to respond faithfully to the urgent concerns of the Church (either local or national or world-wide) should set out to engage in this type of preaching, as well as that which begins with the Bible or tradition and works the other way at their connections. To summarize, too rigid a dependence upon the lectionary may actually limit the styles of our preaching far too much. Thus each of us must work out carefully our degree of dependence upon such a scheme, and be ready to give good reason for it.

Which translation?

The 1960s and 1970s have been rich in the provision of many sorts of Bible version to suit subtly different purposes in the life of the Church. There is now such a wide range that most preachers are bothered by the choice before them, and uncertain which will be provided or known within different congregations. There are roughly four sorts of translation. First, there is that which aims to get as near as possible to the best known text, whilst keeping an eye on the need for it to be intelligible to the reader. Secondly, there are translations which aim first and foremost to be clear and arresting when read in public worship, with the need for strict accuracy coming second. Thirdly, there are versions which aim to draw out the rich meaning of scripture as fully as possible and have the individual Christian's personal devotional life mainly in mind, with accuracy being less important. Fourthly, there are translations which have acquired a unique place in our culture through the way in which they capture the English language at a peculiarly rich period of its development, when its cadences and general sound were especially magnificent.

Examples of the first are not hard to come by. The *American Revised Standard Version* is an obvious one, the *Jerusalem Bible* is near it, so is the *New International Text*. Of the second type one immediately thinks of the *New English Bible*, now being surpassed by *Today's English Version* (otherwise known as the 'Good News Bible'). One should probably include in this area the highly imaginative translations done by Alan Dale for use with children, and therefore very valuable in Family Services – the *New World* and *Winding Quest*. In the third category one would place J. B. Phillips' inspired *Letters to Young Churches* and subsequent translations of the rest of the New Testament, or *The Way* (Tyndale 1972) or *The Living Bible* and the work of writers like David Kossof. Here one becomes most aware of the theological preferences and presumptions of the translator, so one must handle with especial caution.

101

Finally the *Authorized Version* is the obvious case in point, and such extracts as occur in publications like *The Bible Designed to be Read as Literature*.

Sometimes it may be difficult to categorize a translation neatly into one of these four, the *Jerusalem Bible* being a case in point, yet for our general purpose this is helpful. The preachers should normally use category one for Bible study and sermon preparation, categories one or two for public reading in the worship of the Church, category three only for private devotion or interest, and category four for those rare occasions when sheer stateliness matters more than anything else (e.g. possibly at a Cenotaph service or school Speech Day). What is especially important is for the preacher to be aware of the nature of the translation being used, of its strengths and weaknesses and the intentions of those who prepared it. Not all Bibles were designed for public worship, nor all for private devotion, nor all for stateliness, nor all for intelligibility, nor all for accuracy. The wise preacher must appreciate this and choose accordingly. Further reference should be made to David Stacey: *Groundwork of Biblical Studies*, pp. 39–59, and to Roger Tomes: *Consumers Guide to the Bible* (United Reformed Church) and the leaflet: *The Local Preacher reads his lessons* (Local Preacher's Office).

Preaching from biblical passages

Supposing you are preaching from a specific biblical passage, as may well happen if the theme is being determined by the lectionary and the controlling lesson for the day. In that case the sermon has to begin in the Bible and the Christian tradition, and to involve all sorts of reflection concerning our Christian living today, drawn in the first place from that biblical source. What questions do you ask during the first stages of preparation, when brooding over the passage(s)? These vary with the section of the Bible concerned. We will consider four different cases. When reading the Old Testament, the first question to be asked is 'What type of material is this passage?'. It may be myth, poetry, historical narrative, preaching and oracles, proverbial wisdom, laws concerning social life or the practice of worship, reflection about current events, a part of

102

something like a play (e.g. Job), a stylized story (e.g. Jonah) or even a love song. Before anything else, determine the nature of the passage.

Example one – myth
First we consider the instance of *myth*. Do not be afraid of that term, even if it has been bandied about amidst much controversy in recent biblical scholarship and has been frequently misunderstood. A myth is a moral or spiritual truth expressed in the form of a dramatic narrative. Or a myth is 'the Hebrew faith in narrative form' as David Stacey puts it (see the discussion in *Groundwork of Biblical Studies*, pp. 251f). Its meaning lies not in the details of the story involved, but in the truths which the story enshrines. It is thus very close to parable and to poetry. There are many profound religious ideas and convictions best expressed in myth; indeed, many theologians go so far as to say that many major Christian affirmations and doctrines can only be expressed through myth. Suppose then the passage concerned is of this nature. It means that it will in all likelihood be a passage of great profundity and depth, a passage that is full of power for the congregation. Thus myth should never be shunned by the preacher. Instead you tackle it by a series of questions and stages, but working at first from the most accurate text available. The questions are as follows, although there is nothing absolute about the order suggested here.

(1) Has the text been conflated from one or two sources, so that different strands need to be untangled? Here a good commentary is essential, and will remind you that, for example, the highly important myth of the Flood recorded for us in Genesis 6–9 is put together from two basic sources. One seems to have envisaged seven pairs of clean animals and one of unclean ones, going into the ark. The other describes one pair of all creatures. There are other minor differences. It is important to be aware of these minor differences because they are indeed *minor*, and you should not try to lay great stress upon them. Thus it does not really matter a whit whether there were one or seven pairs of clean animals involved. The num-

bers simply don't matter, since the meaning does not lie there at all.

(2) In the light of current belief, what were the writer (or writers) trying primarily to express? This is perhaps the most important question to be wrestling with. The commentaries are invaluable. They may show that the myth had origins in other religions or nations, which does not matter much for the purposes of preaching. What matters is what the people of Israel made out of it, what they saw expressed there. Similarly it does not matter very much what quarry one gets stones from, but what sort of building you construct with them. So here. To take a simple example, Eastern myths of creation sometimes describe the world as having been born like a baby from a God-mother. Genesis does nothing of the sort, but in its myths emphasizes the distinction between God and his creation (otherwise one could easily end up worshipping the creation rather than the creator, as almost happens in some sentimental modern views of the natural order). Thus the writers of Genesis may have culled some elements from many current Babylonian and other myths, but made of them something that was unique to Israel. It is that uniqueness of meaning which we want to draw out. In this process do not be diverted by minor matters which often occur in myths to explain things that puzzled people of the time. Why do women experience such pain in childbirth? That puzzled people greatly, and still does. An answer is worked into the myth in Genesis 3:16, whereby the pain is punishment for having helped in the Fall. It is not the major point of the myth, but a minor detail which should be relegated to a very secondary place.

(3) Does the teaching within the myth represent an odd view adopted by that particular writer only, or is it confirmed generally by the rest of the Old Testament teaching? The myth of Cain and Abel sees murder as a heinous offence against both man and God. Is that view supported elsewhere? Obviously it is. Again, the Flood myth affirms very strongly that God will preserve the earth even though man's sin is so outrageous that it deserves devastating punishment. That view is sustained throughout the Old Testament, with the possible exception of some late apocalyptic work. In contrast to these two examples,

woman was created by extracting a spare rib from man (Genesis 2), but this is not sustained by Genesis 1, which sees man and woman being created together and in the image of God. The view of Genesis 2, then, is something of an odd view, and one cannot make from it a major theory concerning the relationship between males and females. One must be restrained by other material in the Bible.

(4) Does the major theme of the myth find fulfilment and confirmation in Jesus Christ, or does it find repudiation in the light of the New Testament? For example, the opening of Genesis 6 makes curious references to the angels marrying women, and this leads into a statement of the universal evil of mankind. In the light of the New Testament such a story is relegated to the outer fanciful circles of religious speculation, for God is uniquely incarnate in Jesus for man's salvation, and nothing remotely like it occurred before. Therefore Genesis 6:1–4 can only have very marginal value for the preacher. Again, in the myth of the Tower of Babel are we actually to assume that God got worried about men's abilities and confounded their speech to preserve his own security? In the light of Christ that looks absurd, but yet it is amply confirmed by the New Testament that men are inherently quarrelsome and that sin makes us mutually destructive and incapable of communicating properly with each other. It is therefore these latter themes that would have to be developed in any preaching from this myth.

(5) What then does the central meaning of the myth mean for us today? How can it best be put across to a congregation, especially since a clear understanding of 'myth' may not exist amongst many of the people?

Example two – historical narrative
Second, consider the difficulties of preaching from a section of historical narrative. As always, start with an accurate text. Have good resource books and/or commentaries available. Then ask the searching questions.

(1) Are there other accounts of the same incidents? If so,

105

what happens when one compares this account with a parallel one? Does it reveal something vital about the perspectives from which the writer was working? Thus, for example, you may well be making reference to an incident in the books of Kings. If so, compare with the equivalent passage in the books of Chronicles (and vice versa). This is because the writer or writers of Kings worked with a particular view of history which was an extremely simple but moral one. To them, people who were good would flourish, and bad or ungodly people would perish. One can divide people fairly easily into either good or bad, and especially is this true of kings. The good ones reigned for longer and brought much benefit to their people. The bad ones were very bad indeed, and brought chaos. It was a view of history not unlike that illustrated in Westerns. The good men always come out on top in the end; the bad men are usually very very bad and come to grief. There is little difficulty in dividing people up into either baddies or goodies, because people are either one or the other. There are few shades of grey in between. Any preacher using the books of Kings must be aware of this tendency to oversimplify the way good and evil work out in practice. There is a very valuable discussion of this Deuteronomic theology in Henry McKeating: *Studying the Old Testament,* section 2. This is not to rule out preaching from Chronicles or Kings. For example, 2 Chronicles 26 (which is not adequately paralleled in Kings) tells a vivid story of King Uzziah, highly successful and a great leader. Finally he becomes conceited, decides that he can act as High Priest for himself, and is struck with leprosy. It is something of a classic story of how pride comes before a fall, or of how power that is not held in check becomes fatally corrupting. In its way it is a gem which repays a good deal of brooding over, and maybe cries out for the vivid preacher to get to grips with it.

(2) What were the circumstances and the context? In 1 Samuel 15 there is a horrific story of how Samuel hacks a poor defenceless king to pieces 'before the Lord' (Agag, king of Amalek). He does this because the terrible *holem* (ban) had been pronounced, requiring total annihilation of enemies, yet the soldiers had not kept it faithfully but had taken some prisoners and booty. Without knowing the beliefs held by the

participants you could be misled by such a revolting story. At the time, Israel believed that false 'gods' could be killed off if all the people who served them were killed off. The way to assert that the God of Israel was the supreme God of the universe was to wipe out all supporters of 'gods' which somehow set themselves up in opposition. The horrid 'ban' was as much an act of praise to the God of Israel as a means for venting hatred against enemies. The story is not, then, wholly degrading when seen in its original cultural setting.

(3) Was the situation one from which a permanently valid understanding of the way God deals with us can be read off? Or was the situation a specific one not likely to be paralleled at all in the modern world and not therefore of great value to us? 1 Kings 22 tells how the kings Ahab and Jehoshaphat decide to join together and rebel against Syria. It is a risky business and they are both worried about it, so call in the prophets who all say nice pleasant things to encourage them. Micaiah, an old critic of Ahab, is finally summoned and persuaded to tell what the Lord has indeed shown him. He foretells disaster, and says that the other prophets had been duped by a lying spirit. The battle is indeed a tragedy. Ahab is killed. Can you use this story to assert that whenever some religious people predict smooth pleasant things, but just one rugged soul sees a gloomy future, that God is indeed speaking through the latter? Maybe Micaiah was actually the shrewdest military strategist around, who could see that a newly combined army from the two little kingdoms could never be a match for a well-tested Syrian force? Maybe he had suffered so much from Ahab that he wanted the king to be killed? Maybe. We could go on speculating about it. What becomes clear is that this is no classic statement telling us how God works through prophets, so it should not be approached as if it were. But Isaiah 10 is a sharp contrast. Here is a rumination on recent history in which the prophet sees how God is at work through foreign nations even when they are not aware of it, with the prophet drawing out some of the implications of that outlook of faith. It is much more valid to use that passage in relation to great events of history, whereas 1 Kings 22 is far too tricky for such an exercise. This is because Isaiah 10 is rooted in a doctrine of God, of

107

his sovereign rule in his universe, whereas the Ahab story is not so grounded.

(4) If there is the strong feel of God's permanent truth in the passage, how does this look in the light of the revelation which is in Christ? The story of how David kills Goliath (1 Samuel 17) looks like the story of a war hero, positively unsavoury in the light of Christ. On the other hand the story of how the Israelites are fed with manna (Exodus 16 and Numbers 11) is very powerful. If God has called people into a struggling situation, he will provide somehow for their needs. Paul himself uses the similar story of the rock at Meribah, which is struck by Moses with his rod to release water, as an allegory about Christ (1 Corinthians 10:4). Is this story then to be spiritualized or allegorized into one which says that Christ's hidden food (perhaps the eucharist?) will always sustain his people? Despite the strictures on spiritualizing which occur in the previous chapter, this story *may* be an exception to that rule. Maybe the power in the story can only be appropriated for us today if we adopt such a tactic, from which we should usually shy away? If so, we ought usually to avoid preaching from it.

Or take the story of how Isaiah urges Hezekiah to keep cool when the Assyrians besiege Jerusalem (Isaiah 36–38 also 2 Kings 18–20 and 2 Chronicles 32). Isaiah is utterly sure that God will keep Jerusalem safe, and so it turns out. The Assyrians depart, and the king's calmness is vindicated. But does that always apply? Is God always going to keep Jerusalem safe? Manifestly not. Jews who felt like that in Jesus' day were a menace. Jesus saw the city being ruined, with no protective hand from God to give it a charmed security. The narrative cannot be taken then as a permanent truth, to be confirmed through Jesus. Instead Jesus seems to tell us to go on trusting in God and his ultimate purposes even if the heavens fall in upon us. Thus if you preach on this Isaiah passage you must take the issue very much further and deeper if you are to be faithful to Jesus Christ.

(5) Again, ask the question how the insight contained within the passage can best be communicated today, and what

108

are its implications for our own living and the life of the
Church.

Example three – a Gospel passage
For a third example, let us consider the particular questions to
be asked if you are preaching from a gospel passage. Again,
begin with an accurate text. Then look at parallel passages if
they exist. This is very important, because it shows up the
special interests and concerns of the gospel writer, usually
known in modern scholarship as the 'redactor' because he has
done mainly an editorial task on the materials supplied to him
through the tradition of the early Church (see David Stacey,
pp. 208ff.). This comparison can throw up a whole range of
problems for the interpreter, but can save you from some
elementary blunders. For instance, you want to start from
Matthew 20:29–34, the story of two blind beggars being cured
by Jesus just outside Jericho. You fancy making a point out of
the fact that Jesus does not just heal persons in isolation,
sometimes he heals us along with our friends. Perhaps sometimes he can only heal us along with our friends. But look at the
equivalent passage in Mark 10:46–52. There one meets only
one blind beggar, Bartimaeus. The point about friends then
collapses. Instead it looks as if Mark has told the incident in a
simple manner and Matthew has elaborated it. This is often
done by Matthew, not because he is wanting to exaggerate but
because to the Jew *two* witnesses made a testimony valid. Thus
in all likelihood Matthew wanted to stress that Jesus' power to
heal is well attested and is reliable. That understandable intention makes the wise preacher very careful before jumping to
any conclusions regarding the true meaning of passages in
Matthew which involve two people together.

Or consider another possibility. You are concerned about
the poor, and decide to preach on Luke 6:20 where apparently
Jesus proclaims the poor to be blessed. But a check on the
parallel passage in Matthew 5:3 shows a different version of
the saying, with Jesus stating that the poor *in spirit* are blessed,
a version which causes the commentators considerable difficulty. What does 'poor in spirit' mean? You realize that you
must tread carefully. Perhaps 'the poor' is a somewhat techni-

109

cal term whose meaning requires further investigation before rushing into any declamation about it from the pulpit? Or again, you are going to tackle Luke 19:11–27, the story of the nobleman who gives ten pounds to ten servants, goes off to be crowned king, then demands an account of their stewardship. The more you look at the passage, the more difficult it becomes. It is partly a story about someone being crowned king, then returning to avenge himself on opponents who had petitioned against him. It is also a story about these ten servants of whom only three get a later mention – the two who did well with ten and five pounds gained, and the one who merely kept the original pound safely. What about the other seven? We don't know. You then look up the parallel version in Matthew 25:14–29. Here there are no complications about the nobleman being crowned king and being opposed, so maybe that was a separate story, whereas the number of servants involved is three and they receive various amounts (five, two and one pounds). The outcome for all three is carefully described and there are no loose ends. Clearly you are wiser to work from Matthew's version where the story is much simpler and the major point comes across much more directly.

(2) Next, ask to whom the original saying was directed and for what purpose. This means referring to commentaries and background books, otherwise the most innocently simple passage can be sadly misunderstood. Consider one example. You want to use the vivid parable of the rich man and poor man both dying, usually referred to as Dives and Lazarus. At first sight it is a straightforward moral tale. The poor starving beggar goes to heaven, the indifferent rich man to hell, and thus a rough justice is obtained in eternity. But there seems to be more to it. A thorough look at Luke 16:19–31 shows that as Luke understood it, it had to do with whether or not people who have been resurrected will be able to convince hard-hearted rich people. Why should such an issue occur in a simple moral tale? The commentators soon open the whole thing up, and the parable begins to look totally different. The rich man is probably a typical Sadducee, dressing in purple and living sumptuously, accustomed to having servants waiting upon him, and somewhat renowned for being haughty and close-

110

fisted. Sadducees did not believe in resurrection, although Pharisees did; Sadducees took the first two great sections of the scriptures – the law and the prophets – as authoritative for them, whereas the Pharisees added the third great section (the writings). The parable is addressed to the Sadducees primarily. Jesus says, in effect, 'Can you not see your duty to the poor amply set out in the law and prophets? If you can't see it there, poor blinded soul, you won't be able to see it even when you find to your surprise that there is indeed life after the grave, and even if someone was resurrected to tell you about it'. It is then a parable about our duty to the poor, and the way this is set out with stark clarity in the bulk of the Old Testament, so that Sadducees should have got the point, and lived differently. How essential is that background knowledge!

(3) Next, ask whether or not Jesus is laying down legislation which is permanently binding upon all disciples, or giving moral direction by the use of vivid illustration. There is a huge difference between the two, and woe betide anyone who confuses them. It is the difference between a law and someone saying 'In every situation you keep looking about you for persons in need whom you can help. They may be amongst people from whom your own nation has been traditionally estranged, but that makes no odds. Help them. Meet their urgent needs' and telling the story of the Good Samaritan and ending up with the challenge 'Go and live like that'. The latter way is Jesus' normal way. It is not to be interpreted woodenly (as if it is only travellers we must help), but to be a permanent stimulant to us to feel for other people's distress, and then to put ourselves out to help. Traditionally almost every Church has slipped into the error of taking many of Jesus' sayings as if they were precise laws for our behaviour. The classic example is Mark 10: 1–12. Is Jesus here condemning all divorce as far as Christians are concerned? Or giving a plain account of the ideal intention of God concerning marriage? Many Churches in the past saw it as legislation and forbad all divorce despite the awkwardness of the Matthew version (in 19: 1–9) which apparently makes an exception in the case of a partner having committed adultery. Maybe the passage simply should not be taken as moral legislation at all, and it is a profound mercy that

111

more and more Churches are recognizing this in our day. Preachers beware! Don't turn Jesus' sayings about marriage into laws for today, nor his sayings about the use of the sword, nor about the payment of tax, nor any other moral matter. Jesus was not a legalist, which is one reason why the Jewish leaders of the day were pitted against him. Preachers today should not fall into the easy trap of becoming legalists in his name, for this would distort Christian preaching profoundly.

(4) Then as before ask the question 'If that is how this passage must have addressed the people of that time, how does it address us now?'.

Example four – from the Epistles
Fourthly, supposing you are preaching from a passage in the epistles. What questions do you wrestle with? First, ascertain the most accurate text. Then enquire from the background books and other resources about the original setting of the letter in the life of that church at that time. Try to answer the question 'What was the writer trying to say for those people at that period?'. Struggle to elucidate the meaning of difficult phrases or words in the passage. Then look at that passage and its teaching in relation to the rest of that epistle and the thought and teaching of the writer. Does it represent his final thinking on the matter, or a stage in the development of it? This is an obvious question to ask, because everyone, without exception, develops and matures his thought and teaching as time goes on. The biblical writers are no exception to this. What is said at a very early stage is often improved and enriched and maybe altered in the light of further experience. For example, in 1 Corinthians 7 Paul gives some important teaching concerning marriage. The general gist is that Christians should avoid entering into marriage if possible because it involves a whole series of obligations that may impede one's freedom for the Lord's service, but also because the times are short and the *parousia* is at hand. The advice is coloured by this conviction of the imminent return of Jesus. But as time goes on this sense of the imminence of the *parousia* subsides, Paul looks more to the long-term mission of the Church, and his writing about marriage changes noticeably. Thus by the time he writes Ephesians

112

5:21–33 he regards the marriage state, not as a concession to those who cannot contain their sexual passions, but as a mystery like that which binds together Christ and his Church. You cannot imagine a more positive teaching about marriage than that. So you should not regard 1 Corinthians 7 as the definitive word of Paul about marriage. This point still holds if you do not regard Paul as the author of Ephesians, but believe that someone in the circle of Paul's thinking has written it. Again, the apostle and those who think and teach alongside him have moved their teaching about marriage forward clearly and significantly. Therefore preachers who go to 1 Corinthians 7 should be especially careful how they tread. They are wiser to preach from Ephesians 5 if the theme is to be the Christian understanding of marriage.

Take another instance, the development of doctrine. In the earliest period of the young Church's life the teaching on the Holy Spirit was rudimentary and not fully fashioned, and so there was no clear formulation of a doctrine of the Trinity. That was to take about 300 years of hard thinking and discussion before it acquired an accepted form. To this day it is an area of considerable befuddlement to most theologians. The doctrine of the Holy Spirit is also capable of very considerable misunderstanding. In the gospels there is very little teaching about the Spirit. Go to a verse like Romans 8:9 and you can see how the thinking about the Spirit is still in a very formative stage. The Spirit=the Spirit of God=the Spirit of Christ, but the term Holy Spirit is not adopted here, although it is used in Romans 5:5 and later, so no consistent usage has yet been developed. Nor is the thinking behind the use of the term yet fully developed. That is noticeable in Colossians and Philippians, where the term is rarely used, even though both of those letters are dealing with Christian conduct and its motivation. Preachers should therefore handle the epistles not as finalized statements about theology or morals or Church order, but as letters written in the midst of the swirl of history, as all these matters are being hammered out and Christian thinking is developing.

This leads us to a further essential question. What does the teaching in the passage look like when held up against the

113

matured reflection of the Church concerning Jesus Christ? You are to expound this matured reflection, and should not be surprised if some portions of the epistles seem to fall short of this, and appear immature in the light of it. As is well known, Luther thought the Epistle of James to be downright feeble in the light of Christ; others find the Epistle of Jude to be rather a vicious tract; others see a passage like Hebrews 6:4–8 as being highly objectionable because it says that apostasy is unforgiveable and irredeemable; others see a passage like Revelation 20 which talks about the thousand years when the saints rule on earth with Christ as being fanciful speculation not borne out by the general teaching of the New Testament concerning the future and the role of Christ in shaping it; others see the teaching on love set out in 1 John to be a narrowing down of what is taught in the gospels, because here Christian love has become love for the brethren rather than love for all mankind; and so we could go on.

The final question then becomes, as before, how can the insights and truth enshrined within this passage be related to today's Christian experience? If we summarize these questions, then, which every honest preacher must wrestle with, they are these:

In the case of myth
(1) Have I an accurate text, and is there a conflation between different sources? If so, can it be untangled easily?
(2) In the light of the belief at that time what was the writer trying to express?
(3) Is that teaching confirmed generally in the Old Testament?
(4) How does that teaching look in the light of Jesus Christ? Is it confirmed or repudiated?
(5) What then does its confirmed meaning hold for us today?

In the case of historical narrative in the Old Testament
(1) Have I an accurate text, and are there other accounts of this incident?
(2) What were the circumstances and the context for the story?

114

(3) Did the situation indicate something permanently valid about the way God deals with men?

(4) How does this look in the light of Jesus Christ?

(5) What then does its confirmed meaning hold for us today?

In the case of a gospel passage

(1) Have I an accurate text and what are the parallels (if any)?

(2) To whom was the original saying addressed and for what purpose?

(3) Was Jesus here laying down permanent legislation or command, or was he giving vivid illustration?

(4) What then does this mean for us today?

In the case of the epistles

(1) Have I an accurate text? What was the writer saying to those people in that situation?

(2) Does this represent the final thinking of the writer on that matter, or an early stage in the writer's development?

(3) How does that teaching look in the light of the matured reflection of the Church concerning Jesus Christ?

(4) Then what does this mean for us today?

These questions are immensely hard and sometimes we are so daunted by them that there is a mighty temptation to give up. We shouldn't. We should assume that it will take everything we have – our brains, our time, our constant reflection, our reading, our praying, our worshipping in the Church, our sharing with other Christians on every conceivable opportunity – in order to keep struggling with those gritty questions, and that the Holy Spirit is all the time quietly and mysteriously at work to support us, whether or not we are vividly aware of him.

Only four cases have been cited. There are of course many other types of passages, particularly in the Old Testament, but the sort of questions suggested above will still apply. Finally, we have given scant attention here to the most crucial and awkward question of them all, which is the last one in each case. How does such a truth or meaning apply to us in our very different situation? The previous chapter closed with a string of warnings about how not to answer such a question. We should not assume that the 'biblical view' is expressed within one

115

passage, not build a theological case from one passage alone, not utilize allegory nor typology except under the most stringent scrutiny, not spriritualize unless we are rare genuises like Charles Wesley, not treat biblical characters as representative of all men, and not make simplistic parallels between the biblical times and our own. Then there was a paragraph about the basis of the continuity. The next chapter will try to be more positive and inevitably will be looking yet again at this primary question about the nature of preaching.

Chapter 6

Preparing the sermon

SOON you are to preach a new sermon. You sit down many days beforehand to begin planning it. You perhaps take out a rough piece of paper and scribble all sorts of thoughts down, everything that comes into your head upon reading the passage you have chosen to expound or the theme that is gripping you and must somehow be preached upon. When you have done that there may be a healthy muddle of ideas and comments there. Or, of course, there may be very little . . . we have all had that experience.

It needs to be put into some sort of shape. So start a fresh sheet, write in bold letters at the top: AIM. Then try to put into one crisp sentence what you intend to achieve in that sermon, before you go any further. It is quite astonishingly difficult. Maybe it is the most difficult part of the whole process. You have to try several times. 'To expound the Christian understanding of the place of pain and suffering in life.' Well, you say to yourself, that sounds very splendid. You will of course utilize Job, and Isaiah 53, and 1 Peter 4, and you add a further clause to that effect. It then occurs to you that you are tackling a rather big issue.

So you think again. Maybe you ought to simplify somewhat by aiming to expound what the book of Job says about suffering? No, that won't do, because there are aspects of Christian understanding that never occur in Job. So you start again and cross everything else out and write 'To expound the Christian understanding of suffering and pain in the light of 1 Peter 4'. That seems better. But then you remember that that passage talks of Jesus' suffering, and of the suffering of persecution, but not about the sort of suffering which most members of the

117

congregation are involved in. And do you not want to utilize that recent incident of a tragedy that you witnessed, and how a Christian family coped with it? Yes, that's it! So you cross out the previous 'aim' and write 'To show how Christians can respond creatively to pain and tragedy'.

That's much better, you say to yourself. You want to encourage all those persons so that when they too are baffled or suddenly assaulted by some tragic event they will have a positive attitude towards it, they will not get swamped by bitterness and defeatism. Yes, you want to change their attitudes; if there are depressed people present, to lift them out of their depression; if there are people who do not know what Christian resources are available to them, to introduce them to the strengths of patience, acceptance, prayer, renewal that we find in Christian life; if there are persons for whom life has been grim and cruel, to show them that in Christ it is nevertheless wholesome and good. But then a little voice inside reminds you that perhaps you are still aiming very high. Can sermons do that much?

No, they cannot. We begin our preparation or our preaching quite unrealistically if we have not first asked ourselves what sermons can and cannot achieve. Unrealism at that point can make the unwary preacher very cynical after a few years, when it suddenly becomes obvious that all those marvellous sermons, prepared with such zeal and effort and expectation, had actually produced few of the desired effects. So let's consider three things that sermons cannot do well – and five things that, under certain conditions, they can be rightly expected to achieve.

What sermons cannot do well

First, sermons are not a good way of promoting a good grasp of a complex matter or a sustained argument. It is extremely easy to check this, asking people what they remember after they have listened to a sermon. They hardly ever recall the drift of an argument, or the stages by which somebody tried to arrive at a conclusion. Sermons are a means of creating a series of impressions rather than a means of enabling people to work forward from one assertion, or text, or problem stated, to some

118

'conclusion' at the end of a sustained process of reasoning. This is because *people do not listen to every word*. Research suggests that most people actually listen to about 30 per cent. of a speech or sermon. In between, their minds flit off onto all sorts of other sidelines that may have been suggested to them by a remark during the sermon, or they fall asleep even momentarily, or they get lost in their own reveries. If then you are developing a sustained argument, the average listener misses lots of the connecting threads and soon gives it up as a bad job. Preachers must never expect otherwise, nor for that matter must lecturers. The latter have one advantage: their listeners are probably taking notes, and this device helps greatly in following the drift of an argument and helps hold the mind to the subject. Congregations do not normally take notes. Their minds wander.

Secondly, sermons are not a good way of inspiring people to action. Many seasoned preachers will raise their eyebrows at this statement. Sermons are not effective in producing *action*. Suppose, for example, that you want to get something done for the world's poor. A hundred dynamic, pleading sermons will get almost nothing done. They will probably be counter-productive and make the listeners weary of the whole matter. But start a small World Development Group, get lots of discussion going, start a small campaign for a particular project, ask people to join in fund raising. Then things begin to get done. A sermon may help to legitimize such activity, to reassure participants that it is indeed a worthy and Christian enterprise, but the sermon will not inspire the original action nor be an effective recruiting tool. Sermons don't usually do those things well, if at all.

Preachers who want to get people to pray more fervently should realize this. Don't expect sermons to produce a people who pray more adequately or regularly. If that is what you wish to achieve, start a few small and simple prayer groups and get its members to invite others to join. That is likely to produce a more disciplined and enjoyable prayer life for those people. Any sort of Christian action is more likely to be produced by the small task group than by preaching.

Thirdly, sermons are not useful for changing people's

119

attitudes. There is a very straightforward reason. People absorb from the sermon *what they want to hear*. What they dislike, or don't want to hear, or find uncongenial, they dismiss. It is easy to check this. Make a slighting reference to a Socialist government or council and the Conservative voters will remember it with momentary glee, the Labour ones will forget it or remember it with anger. In neither case will it make a scrap of difference to how they vote next time. Or again, suppose you want to eliminate racial prejudice from the congregation. You may thunder away at this evil until you are blue in the face, but nobody's attitudes will be changed by it. Such attitudes are too deeply formed for them to be changed by your oratory. Instead, you must arrange for black people to meet with white, to do things together, to share a common meal, to discover a sense of belonging towards each other, and over the course of time attitudes will change. They *cannot* be dramatically altered by a sermon.

At this point many readers will fidget and want to raise the whole issue of the conversion experience. Are not sermons one of the most effective means of promoting conversion? And is not conversion the most radical and extensive change of attitude within the total personality structure? Yes, indeed conversion is a radical change. But, in line with what has been said just now, the sermon is not the best means of securing that deep-down change of attitude. Note that many preachers who are wanting to effect conversion are driven to adopt all sorts of emotional conditioning devices such as dreamy music in the background, constant repetition of the appeal to come forward, fervent singing, extravagant promises, so that in practice preaching gives way to the techniques of crowd psychology. This reinforces the basic point being made here. Preaching is not a good way of changing people's attitudes, although methods of crowd manipulation may be a means of effecting some apparent but temporary changes.

What sermons can achieve

To begin with, sermons can promote a congregation's confidence in the preacher, or the preacher's Christian faith and integrity. People will come away from a service and say 'He (or

120

she) is a fine person'. The sermon has, if you like, established the credentials of the preacher, shown him or her to be a person who is genuinely trying to live the Christian life and is willing to say so in public. In many situations this is valuable. If the congregation has been dwindling, young people have abandoned the Church, and then a young person preaches with competence and sincerity one Sunday, the effect is to reassure the aged listeners that not all young people have deserted the Church. One could almost say that what the young person preached about is not all that important: what really matters is the fact that it is a young person preaching. Or again, suppose that a Trade Union leader preaches to a middle-class congregation reared on the *Daily Express*, for whom a Trade Unionist is the nearest thing in English society to a violent, block-headed anarchist. The sermon, provided that it is competent and manifestly Christian, will achieve something very useful indeed, the awareness that a Trade Union leader can be a dedicated, sensitive and obedient Christian. It will have established the credentials of that person within that congregation, even if few listeners can afterwards remember a word that was said.

Secondly, sermons can convey useful information to the congregation *if they already want to know it*. If the listeners want to know all the facts about world poverty, the sermon is one possible way of conveying them. A discussion group is a better one, for the simple reason that in the latter setting people can interrupt, ask further questions, tease out data that has not been supplied, and contribute much more actively to the learning process. Yet the sermon is not useless. It has the defect that the preacher has to decide beforehand what information the listeners will be wanting, and may well be wrong. The preacher may pass quickly over some information which the people want in greater detail, or may unnecessarily dwell on other matters which everyone knows already. But (like the lecture) it can inform, to the benefit of those who wish to be informed.

Thirdly, sermons can provide memorable jokes, aphorisms, tit-bits of information, vivid sayings, illustrations, stories, hints and tips. People remember such things, and often carry them away and keep turning them over in their minds long after-

121

wards. Some preachers get dismayed at this. They have preached a carefully-prepared exposition of a difficult biblical passage, and all that people remember afterwards is a joke that was thrown in casually on the spur of the moment, or a minor reference to some TV programme. But the good preacher will accept this as inevitable, and will try to make sure that such odd little scraps, that stick like burrs in the memory, will be as valuable as possible.

Fourthly, sermons can substantially reinforce what people already believe, or attitudes which they already hold. Perhaps this is the most important thing sermons achieve. For example, persons in the congregations may know with the top of the mind only that God rules his earth, or that he is forgiveness. A good sermon on one of those themes does not really tell the congregation anything essentially new, but it reinforces that original conviction and may be able to do so in such a way that it becomes more and more a total conviction of those persons. Afterwards it is held both by the top of the mind and, in a deeper sense, by the whole personality. It becomes *belief.* Because this is one of the major functions of the sermon it is important that you should not see yourself as the purveyor of bright new truths which have only been revealed to you. As stated in the previous chapter, the preacher is speaking with the strange servant-like authority of Christ, on behalf of the total Christian tradition and community, on behalf of the Church catholic, and out of the resources of theology and faith which the whole Church treasures. Preaching is not the job of the eccentric, or the self-opinionated, but of the one who is willing to act as the Church's representative. Of course, preaching operates through the individual personality, with the unique combination of gifts and graces that characterize each individual, but it is on behalf of the whole Church, and the preacher is one of the most important *reinforcers* in the life of the whole Church.

Fifthly, and as an extension of the previous point, preaching can confirm and clarify what people have wanted to believe, but which they have not yet been able to articulate adequately or think coherently about. Thus a person has been trying for years to sort out in his own mind how it is that providence

122

works in this muddled sort of world. He wants somehow to believe in providence, yet there are all sorts of awkward experiences and facts which cannot properly be reconciled with what he had previously thought to be Christian understanding. Then he hears a preacher who expounds the doctrine of providence in such a way as to make it clear that God's care does not operate in any simplistic or automatic manner, does not ride roughshod over our own personalities, does not guarantee safety or a glibly happy ending. And suddenly something begins to click together in the listener's mind. He can identify himself with that preacher's exposition. He feels that he has been groping towards it for years. At last it becomes clearer, and maybe becomes his faith too.

It is in this way that some so-called 'conversions' happen as a result of listening to a sermon. It is when someone has already wanted to be committed to the Christian way that the classic evangelical sermon has been able to help. It has been able to express that wanting very clearly, and to provide a public and accepted method of witnessing to that desire (e.g. through going to the front, or some such public act). Thus the sermon may have appeared to have been the agency effecting conversion, but it is more accurate to say that the sermon and any provision for public response to it have provided the means for the converted persons to express something that was already latent within them. The sermon did not create the desire, but provided the setting for an act of commitment.

All this brings us back to where we started, the aim of the sermon. It needs to be expressed in one simple sentence at the top of that preparatory piece of paper. Do not aim to present a complex argument, to inspire to new action, nor to change people's basic attitudes. Those things will not happen. But aim to reinforce what people already believe or attitudes already held, and to promote Christian growth by offering persons the next stage in their understanding, that which they are already groping towards. You may be able to provide some fresh information, if the hearers want it. You will be able to reassure and reinforce. Incidentally, you will be able to provide little morsels that catch in the memory and can be nourishing for days afterwards.

123

But we need also to remember what preaching is. In a previous chapter it was defined as 'speech in the context of Christian worship in which the great resources of the Christian tradition, especially the witness of the Bible, are related to the practice of Christian discipleship today'. It was likened to the traffic going to and fro on a bridge. How does all this affect the aim of the sermon? It means that this sense of dialogue, of traffic to and fro, must be implicit in that first short sentence put at the top of the page. If it is not, then rub it out and start again. There are many pitfalls to be avoided in constructing that dialogue, but meanwhile we are still back at that early stage of preparation. There is one sheet of paper carrying a jumble of ideas and another which is still headed 'Aim' and where the following sentence has been crossed out many times, altered and adjusted until at last it represents something possible for a sermon to do, and something inherently right as a valid preaching exercise. It is now not going to be a chat about modern life, nor a study of problems in the Bible or the creeds, but *preaching*, spoken theology.

It is most likely to be at this point that you go through the preparatory work with the biblical passages that was outlined in the previous chapter, asking the awkward questions listed there and hunting around in the commentaries and background books. That hunt will produce all sorts of notes jotted down on the 'ideas sheet'. But at this stage too you remember the sombre warnings set out in chapter four concerning ways in which we should not handle scripture. If we don't bear them constantly in mind we readily slither into all those errors; indeed, it is sobering to discover that the commentators themselves are frequently doing so, especially those claiming to be 'expository', so that their work has to be handled with care and not venerated as if they were infallible. Some of the most famous commentators and preachers can be guilty of misusing scripture in the ways indicated, so they must not be slavishly imitated nor automatically accepted.

Now you go to that first page of jumbled notes and look at the balance between the two areas of concern cited in our definition of preaching. Are they both well represented there? If not, then the next task is to see that they are. And at this

124

point, the preacher becomes a great scrounger, borrowing ideas, anecdotes, stories from any conceivable source. Everything is fair game, for you are not meant to be someone who can produce a multitude of highly original thoughts from one well-stocked and creative mind. Instead, you are to be a person who is all the time on the look out for everything that helps make sense of life, or that illuminates life, whether it comes from the daily newspaper, the patter of a comic on the television, the yarn a colleague was repeating yesterday, a book which someone at home was reading last week, or the profound meditation of some Christian which you read before going to sleep last night. It is quite legitimate to add notes about a remark heard from some other preacher as long as the source is acknowledged. If you want to become a preacher, learn how to scrounge.

We have doubtless all heard the standard remark that the preacher must be a man who reads two things regularly – Bible and newspaper. It is too simplistic, of course, but it is a useful snippet of wisdom nevertheless. To prepare for preaching means knowing one's way around the Bible and within the structure of Christian doctrine. It also means a sharp alertness to the modern world and the feel of discipleship within it. But beyond this, it means being the sort of person who is for ever struggling to relate the two. A good exercise for intending preachers is to take the day's paper, select the five most significant items of news, and attempt to construct a theological commentary upon them, showing where they demonstrate, say, the doctrine of man; but asking too where God is at work in justice and mercy, grace and wrath, promise and denial. That is an exercise in producing living theology, and that is of the essence of Christian preaching.

Thus the page of jumbled notes, ideas and related comments, becomes fuller and maybe expands on to more pages. The aim has become formulated clearly. Now the structure must be designed.

Types of sermon, types of structure

The structure is like the skeleton of a body – not particularly noticeable, but essential unless the whole is to fall. Or again, it

125

is like the steelwork of a large building without which there would be no basic strength and upon which the builders later add all the outer cladding until the frame can hardly be noticed. Sermons without a proper structure are so much verbal jelly, wobbling about shapelessly; or like a pile of building materials heaped higgledy-piggledy on the ground. So in the preparation you need to go back to the sheet which is headed by the aim, and then to set out in simple form what structure is to be used.

There are no standard rules to be followed here, no ideal structures to which all should conform. There are as many varieties as there are styles of architecture. The structure for a small town house is totally different from that for a fire station, and even with the house the architect has to bear in mind the setting, the surrounding styles, the size requirements, the nature of the soil, and many other variables. So with sermons. Some structures are more satisfactory for some types and some settings, but less adequate for others. There are some general rules about structure, it is true, but those will be left to the end of this chapter. Meanwhile, we will consider some of the different types of sermon and the many varieties of structure that are appropriate for each.

One obvious preliminary consideration is the setting, and the congregation amongst whom the sermon is to be preached. If you are preaching in a small village chapel to a handful of elderly people do not have a long sermon with a subtle or complex development; if there are going to be several young people not well conversant with the Christian tradition do not attempt a detailed exposition of some knotty biblical passage; if you will be preaching from a high pulpit in a large building and using a microphone do not attempt a sermon that requires a profound sense of rapport with the people. If there are going to be several children present that again raises very special considerations.

The expository
To begin with, consider what is loosely called the 'expository' sermon. This aims primarily to develop a passage or saying in the Bible, exploring its meaning and reflecting upon its significance for contemporary life, remembering that if it fails to do

126

this last task it is not really a *sermon*, but possibly a lecture. Then, in many cases the obvious structure is suggested by the basic form of the passage or sentence concerned. For example, if your aim is to explore the activity of God as portrayed in Genesis 1, there is a recurring structure of God saying 'Let there be ...', God seeing 'that it was good' and, finally, God *blessing*, 'Be fruitful and multiply ...'. You can easily sense being presented with the simplest and perhaps most widely-used structure, that of an introduction, three points that together draw out the meat of the passage, and then perhaps a conclusion (e.g. that this leads to the sort of 'rest' of which Sunday is the sign).

If your aim is to see what the passage tells about the creation of man and what place he has in the universe, then again there is a straightforward scheme already apparent in the account – God makes man in his own image, God gives him dominion, God orders him to be fruitful and multiply, God finds it all to be good. Here the preacher is already presented with a four-fold structure. But if you begin to ask more difficult questions and to have less straightforward aims, the possibilities for many different types of structure immediately arise. Ask of the passage 'How should we respect the natural order?', which is a very pertinent question in our own day with the conscience about ecology stirring everywhere, and you might feel that a great variety of structures is possible. You could start by posing the urgent question in terms widely understood today, and then proceed by making a series of affirmations followed by consequences thus:

(1) Each feature in the natural order is dependent upon others.

Consequence: tamper with one, and there are immediate repercussions in every other sphere.

(2) The myth stresses God's pleasure in variety, in many kinds.

Consequence: we should not exterminate whole species through carelessness or by design.

(3) The universe is created for fruitfulness.

Consequence: we should not let any element (e.g. streams) become toxic or unfruitful.

But note that this is becoming more complicated, more difficult for people to remember, and also that many of the 'consequences' outlined above are questionable, especially to anyone with a technical training in ecology. You could, of course, choose to make far more than three such affirmations, but the more you do this the longer the sermon becomes, the more debatable its arguments, and the more difficult to remember and possibly to benefit from.

Let's try again! Supposing you aim to construct a meditation upon creation, so that at the end the congregation can join in a great act of praise (the occasion could be a harvest festival, of course). In that event the method may be to take some sections of the passage in turn, and the structure becomes:

Introduction

God creates out of nothing (reference mainly to verses 1 and 2)

God creates by calling forth 'Let there be!'

God creates by introducing extraordinary variety

God creates by putting each element in its own place or orbit, so that there is a natural *order*

God creates man as a king over everything else

God orders man to share in creative fruitfulness

Conclusion: Praise be to God!

Suppose we now turn to a totally different passage, the parable of the Pharisee and the Publican in Luke 18. By its nature, this is most likely to give us a two-fold structure. Suppose your aim is to show how this is a parable about ourselves, then the structure would probably be:

Introduction: we are all two people contained in one personality

1A   What the Pharisee was like
 B   In what respects we too are like him
2A   What the tax collector was like
 B   In what respect we too are like him

Conclusion: develop that second nature by God's grace.

If the aim is to show what prayer should be like, you would again derive a basically two-fold structure, because it would probably be:

Introduction: not all prayer is good
1   Bad prayers (those of the Pharisee)
2   Good prayers (those of the tax-collector)
Conclusion

or if you elaborated upon this there would still be a basically two-fold format, e.g.:

Introduction
Bad Prayers   –   Self-centred ones
                  Blind ones
Good Prayers –   Humble ones
                  Non-bargaining ones
Conclusion

Still referring to expository sermons, if you aim to draw out the meaning of a particular text, then again the structure is mainly indicated by the verse itself. If the text is Romans 6:5 – 'If we have been united with him in a death like his, we shall certainly be united with him in a resurrection like his' – there is bound to be a basically two-fold structure to a proper exposition, because that is how the thought within the verse is ordered. If the text is Micah 6:8 – '. . . And what does the Lord require of you but to do justice, and to love kindness, and to walk humbly with your God?' – then a three-fold structure is inevitable. If the aim is to expound the marks of the early Church as set out in Acts 2:42 – 'and they devoted themselves to the apostles' teaching and fellowship, to the breaking of bread and the prayers' – then it must of necessity be a four-fold construction.

However, it is often difficult to see at first just how the thought of a text is constructed. It may include a repetition. Take a good long look at it. For instance, the oft-preached text in John 3:16 is a major introductory affirmation followed by (a) a negative and (b) a positive. This cries out for a structure like:

Introduction: The amazing quality of God's love in the incarnation so that
                  (a) believers do not perish
                  (b) but possess eternal life.

Or again, look at 2 Corinthians 5:17 – 'If anyone is in Christ, he is a new creation: the old has passed away, behold the new has

129

come'. This is a great comment upon 'being in Christ' (the introduction) which again makes the contrasting statements thus: the old has passed away, the new has indeed come. But it complicates this basic shape by stating *twice* that the new has come. If a preacher were to follow the thought slavishly then there would be an inherent and unnecessary repetitiveness in the sermon.

This leads to a final point about expository preaching. Beware of building everything round one small text! Of course, that would be regarded by our fore-fathers as a most monstrous thing to write, nevertheless it is a warning that is demanded by the character of scripture. We must not assume, as our fore-fathers often unwittingly did, that scripture was constructed so that every little verse of it makes adequate sense and conveys an adequate meaning all on its own, abstracted from its context. Such an assumption is highly likely to distort scripture and it is much more akin to rabbinic scholarship of the first century than to Christian theology of the twentieth. It is normally much more satisfactory to work from a passage than a verse, although there are indeed key verses which in themselves capture the essence of a passage and which are therefore exceptions to the above rule (e.g. in John 11:25 the great saying 'I am the resurrection and the life' captures the meaning of the whole chapter, and is thus most highly appropriate to be preached upon).

Many of the comments above apply also to preaching from famous Christian statements or verses or lines from hymns, or well-known prayers. If someone wishes, say, to preach from Reinhold Niebuhr's famous prayer (and why shouldn't one?) then the sermon simply must respect its essential three-fold structure:

O God, give us
serenity to accept what cannot be changed
courage to change what should be changed
and wisdom to distinguish the one from the other.

The argument
There are many other sorts of preaching. Most of the standard textbooks suggest that there are at least five types, and many of

130

them suggest at least five different sorts of structure. I want to simplify matters by referring here to only three other general types of structure. Thus there is the 'Argument', for want of a better term. This is where the preacher develops a case and usually concludes with an appeal to the listeners to take the appropriate action. It could go like this:

Everybody admits that the world is in a mess
But we are all dependent upon one another
So every individual is partly to blame
So *you* are partly responsible
So *you* must seek some source of strength and reform
There is only one such source – Jesus Christ
So you must seek reform from him
So you must repent, believe, be renewed, etc.

The basic ground-rules for the structure of such a sermon are those of logic since it is, after all, a reasoned case, an argument. You must avoid the classic faults of illogicality (don't argue from the particular to the general, etc., etc.). You must see that each stage of the argument follows from the previous one, as do the first four statements outlined above. You must ensure that the connecting links between one stage and the next are properly fitted in. You must make clear the basis, or premise, of the argument, and so on. But this takes us back to the beginning of this chapter. The sermon is *not* a good means of arguing a case. People can't concentrate all that hard upon each stage of a tightly constructed argument, whereas if it is not tightly constructed then it can be faulted as being unreasonable. Preaching is not primarily an appeal to people's sweet reasonableness anyway. It is an attempt to use words to reinforce everybody's faith, so that its conclusion is not a matter of putting 'Q.E.D.' (it is proved) at the end of a brilliantly-argued peroration, but a matter of being able to say and sing together 'now we see Christ a bit better and will serve him afresh'. So we will deliberately *not* spend more time outlining the possibilities of such structures for sermons. The preacher is not the sacred equivalent of the secular professor attempting to argue a thesis before a class. The preacher, must of course, be reasonable and eschew the silly and the illogical, but you should usually not construct the sermon as one prolonged argument or thesis.

131

The issue or doctrine

That leads to a third possibility – the type of sermon which aims to draw out the significance of a doctrine or basic Christian affirmation, or to construct an outline of how we should respond to some problem or issue. These sermons are not aiming to be expository, for there the main attention is first directed to the biblical material and then an attempt is made to translate its insights into the current scene. Instead in these sermons you begin with the doctrinal matter or the current scene or an urgent problem, and try to throw all sorts of light upon it so that at the end the hearers are helped to live with that problem themselves. This is what used to be called 'topical' preaching. Thus the problem may be that of marriage breaking down, of people's sense of anonymity in modern culture, of the constant highlighting of violence today, of the sort of compromises the Christian is constantly having to make, or of the difficulty of exercising forgiveness. The doctrinal sermon may be on the meaning of the ascension, the doctrine of the fall, the phrase in the Apostles Creed about the resurrection of the body, or any such subject.

In many cases you may be thinking about this matter in such a way as to provide a simple structure at once. Thus to take the first suggestion, the problem of marriages breaking down may present itself to you in the following form, which automatically gives a basic structure:

Many marriages today (including those of Christians) break down

But the Lord appears to rule divorce out absolutely

It appears harsh and quite unrealistic to impose such a law upon Christians

But there were exceptions made in the early Church and have been ever since, and Jesus puts concern for persons above the demands of 'law'

Conclusion: there are exceptions to the general rule of the inviolability of marriage between Christians.

Or again, your thinking about the doctrine of the fall may present itself in this simple format right from the beginning:

All men are made in God's image

All men fail to live up to that image

All aspects of our existence are affected by that failure. In such a case it is important to prepare a lively, arresting introduction and to ensure that the whole builds up to an adequate and satisfying conclusion (e.g. the doctrine of the fall is not the last word in Christian experience – Christ is the Last Word). There is also a reasonable development in three stages outlined above, giving it a satisfying progression of ideas.

Faceting, and the 'negative–positive'
But such clear progression may not be possible. Instead you find that when the matter is turned over in your mind many aspects of the issue crop up, and they do not necessarily fit themselves into some neat format. Dr Sangster coined a pet word for this – 'faceting' – because it is like looking at the many different faces or facets of a diamond or precious stone. They are distinctly different, and yet all are needed to build up the picture of the whole. They do not hang together in the way that a string of logical statements hangs together, yet they all pertain to the same matter, the same gem. So you can construct a sermon that is a whole series of looks at a particular issue from slightly different points of view. The sermon on forgiveness may become structured thus:

The difficulty if you know that you often commit this wrong yourself

The difficulty if you have never had the slightest desire to commit such wrong and cannot sympathise at all with the offender

The difficulty if you often forgive the offender for this offence and both of you thought it would never happen again

The difficulty if sometimes this offence causes little harm; but by chance it could be terribly dangerous.

There is no progression in strict logic here, yet all these glances at the matter help to build up the picture. What is going to matter most of all is that there will be a convincing and adequate conclusion. Here we should note that, just as a gem often has one facet which seems dominant, so one particular aspect of this issue will begin to stand out in your mind. In that case the sermon should lead up to that aspect, and the conclusion should be worked from it. To take a different example, suppose one is reflecting upon the ascension, the material might be structured in the following way:

Introduction (perhaps relating to the difficulty of believing the picture given in Acts 1 literally)

The ascension as an affirmation about Jesus (not merely a great teacher nor even a great prophet, but Lord)

The ascension as an affirmation about God's commitment to mankind (He has taken human nature 'up into heaven')

The ascension as an affirmation about the Church (a universal body ultimately indestructible)

The ascension as an affirmation about the universe (it is held together by sacrificial love)

Conclusion (perhaps stressing what a mighty affirmation is made in the whole ascension myth).

Here you are 'faceting' upon a doctrinal theme. No one facet may necessarily depend logically upon another, yet all of them cohere. There are dangers in this method, and these may be apparent if you look again at the above example. It tries to do and say too much. You can imagine someone coming away with the general notion that the preacher is in favour of the ascension, which is not a bad result, yet the final effect would be one of indigestion. There are too many notions, too much material. So if you attempt to use this sort of structure (which is very common) be on your guard against overwhelming the hearer's capacity. Remember that this style is also applicable to the expository sermon, and a glance back at the structure suggested for a meditation on Genesis 1 shows that it was really six 'facets', though they could be presented in roughly the same order as they occur in that chapter. Again the difficulty with this outline was that it hinted at a sermon trying to say too much. You can imagine it lasting far too long and ending up as something of a bore. So if you choose to use about six facets, be extremely crisp with each one.

There is another common structure which is helpful when considering doctrinal themes or current issues and which can occasionally be utilized in expository preaching. It is psychologically a very good structure and, for want of a better term, one can label it the 'negative-positive'. Supposing you

134

want to preach upon the Christian hope and one is aware of many popular notions which are nearly right, yet slightly distorted. Cite these first, showing that none is quite satisfactory, and then lead up to a conclusion which expresses the hope in the clearest and most positive way. The structure would then be something like this:

Introduction: everyone has to live by some sort of hope
Christian hope

is *not* that:	the world will steadily get better
	everyone will be converted
	believers will go to heaven
but that:	God will effect his Great Completion of
	his purposes in his chosen time,
	and heaven be the reality for all men.

Or again, suppose you are wanting to expound the question of forgiveness between persons, you might use the structure:

Introduction: we are constantly having to forgive and being forgiven
Forgiveness is

not:	saying that the offence didn't matter
	offering to forget the whole business
	a bargain (don't do it again and I won't raise the matter)
but:	we will begin again with a wholly accepting and creative relationship between us

Conclusion: to live with Christ is to learn best how to do this.

It is time to recollect the various structures suggested in this chapter. They are not exhaustive, but I have cited the most common ones and tried to indicate strengths and weaknesses. Never stick to one structure, or you can become like an architect who can only design buildings of one standard shape. How dull and predictable his work soon becomes! There are some general rules one needs to bear in mind. Aim for simplicity. If the outline cannot be put on to a sheet of paper with 'Aim' at the top and up to ten sentences beneath, then there is something wrong with it. It should be simple enough for it to be in your mind, so that if the notes are suddenly blown off the pulpit and out of the window you can still say something brief which outlines the sermon properly. Aim for consistency rather than logic, so that the material obviously relates together, the preaching is not going to go shooting off at a tangent, it all pertains properly to the subject. Aim for a build-up of interest and concentration towards the end, so that the conclusion is indeed the summit, the climax, the point at which the listener wants to say 'hear hear' or to shout 'hallelujah!'. In particular, Christian preaching builds up to affirmations about, or challenges from, Jesus the Christ. The conclusion should be the point where Jesus Christ becomes most manifest.

Texts and pretexts

The argument of the chapter so far has been that we must have a clear, crisp, manageable aim for the sermon. That is the first indispensible necessity. Then we must have a clear, easily memorable structure. But what about the text at the beginning? Is it an absolute necessity, as our fore-fathers appeared to believe? The plain answer to this question is no. A sermon does not have to have a text, but some types of sermon operate better with one than without, and always some device is needed to make the general theme of the sermon memorable. If you take it as an inviolable rule that every sermon must have a text, the result will be that you will often start off with this required morsel of scripture but then, because the theme of the sermon cannot be held within it, go wandering off into the area required by the theme. The text is merely a pretext, and the result is a badly constructed sermon. Indeed, the major reason for the bad structure may be the notion that every sermon ought somehow to begin with a verse from scripture.

Many of the sermon outlines suggested earlier in this chapter were ones which handled whole passages of scripture. The only way in which they could be related to a text was when the whole tenor of the discourse led up to some major point indicated in the passage. In that case, that point could be the 'text' and should, perhaps, appear only at the end of the sermon. Thus the meditation on Genesis 1 could end up on the text 'Be fruitful and multiply, and fill the earth and subdue it' (Genesis 1:28). The suggested sermons on the parable of the Pharisee and the Publican could end up with the text 'I tell you, this man went down to his house justified rather than the other' (Luke 18:14). Here we encounter one of the consequences of the view of the Bible which was outlined in chapter four. If now we are convinced that the view of the biblical passage must be considered as some sort of whole, set within a story or important context, then it necessarily becomes more difficult to assume that the whole gist is encapsulated in one isolated verse. Therefore, preaching from isolated texts is less and less practicable as one acquires a more developed view of the character of the biblical documents.

There are however some honourable exceptions, and these have already been suggested. Sometimes a verse does indeed express in summary form a profound statement of truth for which the rest of the passage is supportive. Romans 6:5 or John 3:16 are cases in point. Sometimes a particular verse acts as a valuable summary concerning some aspect of the Christian life, in which case that verse is highly suitable as a text. Acts 2:42 or Micah 6:8 are obvious examples. Sometimes a particular statement may be the crucial one towards which a whole story or block of teaching moves. Examples are Luke 2:49, which is the climax of the story of Jesus staying behind in the Temple as described in the final portion of Luke 2; or the voice of God: 'This is my beloved son, in whom I am well pleased; listen to him' (Matthew 17:5) which is the high point of the Transfiguration story; or 'What God has cleansed you must not call common' (Acts 10:15) which is the crucial statement to explain Peter's vision of the sheet let down from heaven with all sorts of creatures and foods upon it. Those verses are naturally the key ones in the biblical account, and cry out to be the texts for sermons upon those passages.

If, however, you do not feel that a text is the most helpful way of beginning the sermon, or ending it, some other means must be found of making the theme and aim of the sermon easily memorable. In most cases that single definitive crisp sentence which is used in the sermon's preparation should be the one now used for the benefit of the people's memory. Just as a text is constantly cited during the course of a sermon dependent upon it, so this sentence should be regularly cited during the sermon. This recitation helps both to hold the

137

sermon together and keep it from wandering off from its theme, and to remind the people listening. It gets steadily etched into the memory. However this should not be over-done, or it becomes irritating.

Texts then are not essential, but a clear aim and an obvious plain theme and structure are. We should concentrate on these, rather than on being able to peg the sermon on to a verse or verses from the Bible. If the aim and theme obviously revolve around one text, then of course you must use this in the traditional formal way as the introduction and controlling statement of the sermon. But if you wish to begin at the other end, with issues or problems that emerge immediately out of current life, then it is unlikely though not impossible for a text to be the appropriate beginning and control for the sermon. No preacher should feel that a sermon is ill-conceived if it does not use a text, but every preacher should reckon a sermon to be a failure if it does not hold together our current experience and the Christian tradition, in which the Bible plays a central role.

Illustrations

Now we come to the matter of supplying the material with adequate illustrations so that all the major ideas are illumi-nated and clarified. In what might be called the 'Grand Age of the Sermon', the period from about 1850 until 1925 in which sermon oratory reached great heights and became the major skill of the minister, the practitioner was expected to have made a special study of 'illustrations' and even to have elabo-rate filing systems from which the necessary gems could be extracted. Those days have gone, for neither good nor ill, and sermons should not now have to carry the weight they did earlier. But so have styles changed, and we cannot treat the necessity for illustration in the same way. So the filing systems have probably all gone as well, and if you are the sort of person who has begun to keep one going and failed, take heart. You are probably better off without such apparatus. This is because the art of illustration is not a special and separate art, a skilled technique that has to be grafted into that of sermon prepara-tion. It is instead one very important aspect of the whole skill of communication, and one aspect of the basic task of making the sermon relate properly to contemporary experience. It is part of the whole exercise of both making a sermon clear and its ideas and themes applicable to modern life. It is thus an aspect of making the service attuned to today's world and practice, of making the sermon *live*. It is a matter of translating any abstract ideas into everyday occurrence, of taking major affirmations and making them sharp and memorable by expressing them through a story. It requires from the preacher an imaginative awareness of what today's human experience is like, rather than a particular set of techniques with words. Here let us pause a moment. Another definition of preaching is 'Good story-telling controlled by good Christian theology'. It is not a bad definition. Preaching is largely story-telling. Because some preachers regard it as primarily a matter of articulating good religious ideas or notions or affirmations, preaching becomes dull. When preaching is mainly narrative it is likely to become much more memorable, interesting, and therefore useful. After all, the central corpus of books in the Christian religion – the Bible – is not a long discussion on the major Christian beliefs. It is a *story*, the story of how God has been handling his people down through the centuries and into the remarkable era of Jesus Christ. Preaching too is 'Good story-telling controlled by good Christian theology'.

So the main requirement is not that filing cabinet, but a fascination in all life experience, and an absorbing interest in telling others. You need to be a good observer and reporter and raconteur, and to have a memory stocked up with all sorts of vivid recollections. So, on the rough sheet of paper being used as the basic stuff for the sermon, jot down all those recollections and insights and ways in which for you the points of the sermon have been noticed to impinge upon ordinary life, and think of stories galore.

Here we should note that such illustration can be of two main types, each with its strengths and weaknesses. It can be (a) an analogy, or (b) an instance.

(a) To take the analogy first, consider the following examples. 'The Church is like a big family, and you should be able to manage to sort out quarrels there just as at home' . . . 'Just as a pigeon finds its way back home finally, so everybody comes

139

back to God in the end' ... 'Take a glowing ember out of the fire and it soon fades: take a Christian out of the fellowship and his faith soon grows weaker' ... 'Just as every living organism relies upon breathing oxygen all the time, whether it understands that process or not, so everyone depends upon God all the time, whether we believe in him or not'.

The analogy takes a known fact from one sphere of life experience and links it up with another sphere in which the preacher is interested. It uses terms such as 'like', 'just as', 'in the same manner as', 'as ... so', to provide the linkage. Thus it can often help the listener's mind to travel from the well-known (e.g. the ember being taken from the fire) to the less well-known, or the more difficult. It is a device for transferring an idea from a proven or widely accepted matter over to another matter which might be more debatable, less well-known, less widely attested or less widely believed. 'Just as you know the sun will rise tomorrow, even if it is hidden by clouds from your sight, so you can know that God will surround you with love even if your life is full of doubts and problems.' The thought moves from the unarguable (the sun will rise tomorrow) to the sphere in which the listener is in need of constant reassurance (God loves you). The linkage comes from the tell-tale little phrase 'just as'. The *analogy* is doing its work. Scripture is full of analogies, of course. 'I am the good shepherd; the good shepherd lays down his life for the sheep' ... 'As a father has compassion on his children, so has the Lord compassion on all who fear him' ... 'Can I not deal with you, Israel, as the potter deals with his clay?' ... 'For like the lightning-flash that lights up the earth from end to end, will the Son of Man be when his day comes'. All our talking about God is really analogical, for we refer to God as 'Father' or 'King' or some similar term that we use with people. We have good reason to believe that such linked use of language is appropriate.

That brings us to the snag when analogies are being used. Is it fair to assume that there is the sort of linkage between the two sets of ideas? Yes, we say, Jesus *can* indeed be fairly likened to a good shepherd who will if necessary risk his life for his flock; God *is* indeed like a forgiving father; a potter *does* master his clay as God handles his people; the *parousia will* be all-revealing as a lightning flash; the Church *is* like a big family; the homing instinct in the pigeon *is* like man's instinct for God; the glowing coal *is* like the glowing Christian; the living organism's need for oxygen *is* akin to our need for God.

Perhaps your feeling of aptness for such analogies was at its strongest when you looked at the first of the examples above (the good shepherd) and at its most problematic when you considered the last (the living organism). So we must beware. Only use analogies when there is indeed an appropriate linkage between the two sets of ideas being brought together. Especially is this true when trying to make clever scientific ones. If you used the one cited above (the organism) you might afterwards get somebody sidling up and saying 'Oh, by the way, I'm a micro-biologist, and I was very interested in your reference to needing oxygen. It isn't true, you know ...' and you then realize that the whole point you were trying to make cannot stand up, and that the one thing that that particular hearer will take away will be the conviction that that preacher today is a duffer when it comes to anything scientific. Of course we use analogies – is not scripture replete with them? – but we must use them with the utmost care, and not try to be over clever or highly specialized in the ideas from which we build.

(b) The other kind is the 'instance', or example. It is the bread and butter of the sermon, if you will pardon that analogy and accept that it is right to link the two sets of ideas in such a way. It is an essential window, to use yet another analogy. Supposing you are arguing that the act of forgiving requires much more strength of character than that of maintaining a grudge. Then you tell the story of someone who finally summoned up the courage to forgive someone else, and found themselves a bigger person as a result. That *instance* illuminates the point better than all sorts of persuasive arguments ever could, for this issue is not one you can appreciate by the use of sweet reason, but one which you need to experience for yourself, and then it rings true. So you need to be pointing to just that experience, if possible by citing it. A story needs to be told.

Consider another example. You want to convince the

141

listeners that genuine love takes risks and allows freedom to the beloved. So you say: 'Near to us there is a couple who dote on their little girl. The mother never lets her out of her sight. She wraps her up whenever a breeze blows, rushes her inside whenever a drop of rain falls, won't let her have toys with the slightest danger in them, supervises her when she plays with her friends, worries like mad when she goes to school, and pesters the teachers endlessly. But right opposite is another mother with a girl the same age. She takes care, but lets her experiment all over the garden, come in filthy if she wants to, romp around with all sorts of toys and friends. She expects her to look after herself when at school, but is always there in the background when she's needed. Who really loves her child better? The one who smothers, or the one who risks giving her child some freedom? You and I know that the second one is better at real loving than the first, because real love tries to help people become mature, not dependent and sheltered.' You have used an instance. If the next stage in the sermon was the statement 'God loves like that too', then we are back again of course into the use of an analogy, and a wholly proper one.

Again, you want to stress that in many settings the obedient Christian life is bound to be one involving suffering. Then of course the modern world is all too full of instances where the Church discovers this, and the daily newspaper can probably provide all the instances necessary, from Korea to Chile, Russia to Rhodesia. Again, you are pointing to the need for life to have its rhythms, waking and sleeping, being still and being busy, being on one's own and being in company. Having just come back from a holiday, the obvious instances are all to hand. Finally, you want to show how our lives need a framework or order, or a person to whom we are answerable, if they are to hold together properly. Being a teacher you had a superb instance of this only this week when a disturbed child who has given endless trouble in the school happened to confide in you and say how he has nobody at home who cares what he does, nobody to tell him off or to praise him. The instance is right there, in your experience that week.

But there are dangers in using 'instances', and you may well have sensed them already from those quoted. They may reflect too much on the preacher's own life; they may become a string of anecdotes which show off the preacher; they may be unfair on some persons being referred to (e.g. someone in the congregation may know that woman living near you and spoiling her little girl). They may be so obscure or bizarre that they do not actually relate the subject matter to the everyday experience of the congregation – as when, say, someone refers to his time in a prisoner-of-war camp in 1944 as if it were a common lot which the congregation knows intimately about. Sometimes references to Christians in far away lands doing all sorts of wonderful things have the same effect. What on earth has that got to do with us? Or the preacher indulges in some extravagant and possibly exaggerated story of the marvellous success of some group of Christians in Togoland and implies that it could all happen here if only we had enough faith or prayed more regularly or did some other worthy thing.

But the most common danger is that preachers who have become good story-tellers end up telling some fine tales which do not, as a matter of fact, illustrate what they purport to illustrate at all! The pious preacher tells a moving story of a man who was a drunkard, became converted, and now has risen to become the works manager. He suggests that this shows how, when you are converted, you become a success in life. It does no such thing. Many a converted Christian will not rise to become the works manager, and conversion is in no way the prelude to 'success'. Or the preacher tells how sick persons revived marvellously after a prayer group interceded for them, and says that this shows how God answers all believing prayer. It does not, because many believing Christians have prayed likewise and found that the sufferers did not recover; sickness is a deeper mystery than can be explained in one glib little anecdote. Or the preacher tells how the number of strikes in a local factory has increased lately, and that shows how everyone today is more and more greedy for money. It may mean nothing of the sort. It may well mean that the management at that factory is stupid, that the consultation procedures are a disgrace, that the workers are rightly beginning to stir after years of apathy or, of course, that plain greed or jealousy is at work. The matter is more complex than one naïve little com-

143

ment can do justice to. Preachers beware! For when we rush in with our bright little stories we may merely be lowering the authority of preaching for the more discerning of the listeners, and at the same time peddling superficial ideas.

The instance has to be one with which the congregation can fairly readily identify, or which easily comes within its range of imagination. It is probably better nowadays not to cite instances from Dickens, because very few listeners will know the story being referred to, or even from Shakespeare. You cannot assume that everyone has seen the same television programme as we have, or that all read the same daily or evening or Sunday paper. You cannot assume that everyone knows the basic moves in football, or cricket – or knitting, for that matter. So if you want to get apposite illustration from any such area, do some explaining as you go, or the point may be lost on half the listeners. That goes for the Bible too. You cannot assume that everyone has read and comprehended even the most famous of the biblical stories, so that again some background needs to be worked into the account. That brings us back sharply to the point raised above – beware of assuming too glibly that you know at once what a biblical story is meant to illustrate. As we have seen, the biblical material can be much more subtle than appears at first sight. Does the story of Daniel in the lion's den illustrate that prayer can tame hungry lions about to eat God's people? Assuredly not; for many a faithful Christian martyr has been devoured by hungry lions. It illustrates how God's people felt when, in a time of overwhelming oppression, they found God was mysteriously and surprisingly acting to save them.

This takes us back to where we started. The preacher needs to be the alert person who can see God at work all around and finds all of life to be full of the evidence of it. Out of that sensitivity to life you create a personal store of reflection and story. The Bible, the newspaper, the television programme, conversations, reading, all play their part. From that treasury you try to feed the appropriate matter into the sermon. But with care, for there are many pitfalls.

Beginnings and endings
Next, give some care to the opening and the conclusion of the

144

sermon. That initial opening minute of the sermon will determine whether or not many of the listeners will switch off and
resort to their own dreamings. It must arrest people's attention, making them feel that the whole matter is going to be
worthwhile attending. It must, as a general rule, begin where
the people are, expressing hopes and fears, ideas and questions
that are a constant part of their life experience. It needs to be as
vivid as possible.

But the conclusion is also important. It is the last thing cited,
so listeners will tend to remember that, and not the material
which preceded it. The conclusion, then, must be worth
remembering. It must not be limp. A limp conclusion is something like this: 'Well, friends, I'm sure we all ought to
remember these things a bit more', 'Those are just some of the
thoughts that come to me about this matter', 'I'm glad I've
been able to share this with you', 'I'm sure we're all going to try
harder in future', 'It all shows that we've got a lot to be thankful
for'.

The conclusion should be firm, not limp. It should capture
the point up to which the sermon has led and should express it
powerfully, so as to hammer it home. It should perhaps feature
a quick recapitulation on what has gone before, and then a
strong affirmation to round it off. If the sermon was built about
a specific text, that provides the finale, or some statement
derived from it. But there is a theological point to stress in this
connection. A Christian sermon should lead to Christ, should
lead to fresh light about him or from him, because he is the
centre of the faith and the climax of all Christian aspiration.
The conclusion of the sermon should therefore express some
note which is Christ-centred, Christ-affirming, Christ-full.

The levels of the sermon

Now do a check concerning the level at which the sermon is to
be pitched, and the assumptions made about the listeners. A
sermon to be delivered to Oxford University does not require
the same level as that for Little Grubbington on the Marsh. So
you must agonize over that projected material lying there on
the ideas sheet(s) on the table, asking the question 'Is all that
appropriate for *that* gathering of people?'. Consider first the

145

would one expect the listeners to know what it feels like when asked to conduct a morning family service attended by several children aged eight upwards you obviously cannot assume a personal experience of bereavement, nor of being unemployed, nor of being married. Instead of pitching it at that adult level which such experiences assume, you would have to pitch it at the maturity level of those aged 12 upwards. That is, pitch it slightly ahead of the youngest group present, for it is not bad for that group to be stretched and for the preacher to be helping them to look at life through the eyes of someone slightly older and more mature. But the gap must not be very big, or the preaching becomes unfair on the young.

Or consider the experience of the big wide world which the material assumes. In many a suburban congregation it is fair to assume that the majority of the listeners will have received some further education and will be accustomed to travel. They will regularly go on holiday in this country and possibly abroad. They will own cars. They will know what it is to be mobile, and may have lived in several different localities. But in some parts of the cities, in those 'urban villages' found in almost all industrial areas, and in many a rural village community, that will not be a common experience at all. Particularly if they are elderly they will be accustomed to a steady life bounded by much closer horizons. This is not to say that the village person is a dim yokel, for anyone who has lived in the country will know that the life experience there is different, but neither to be classed as better nor worse. It involves people of very high intelligence as well as low, as in the towns. There is a more profound awareness of the seasons, of the regularities of life, of sensitivity towards the natural order, of being bound up with creatures and crops in a mutual interdependence.

Thus in the village setting one would not make reference to the 'rat race' in modern industry and business, as if it were a shared experience to everyone present, nor assume many people with troubled consciences over joining a firm operating a closed shop policy. One would assume no knowledge of the effects of planning policy upon redevelopment areas, nor of the problems of life in high rise flats, nor of the need for community action in the inner city zone. Nor in a suburb or city

146

level of maturity which the projected material assumes. If the water supply fails, or whole herds have to be burnt because of foot and mouth disease, or good land goes derelict through a lazy person's neglect. Town and city dwellers do not know what it feels like to be tied, every day of the year, to the constant care of animals.

Again, consider the level of literacy in the congregation. That Oxford University audience will be decidedly sophisticated, used to complicated arguments and a precision with long words, able to appreciate references to Darwin, Marx and Freud. Not so at Little Grubbington, where God's people are not versed in the styles of the learned discourse, the use of sophisticated concepts, the quoting of erudite authorities. This is *not* to say that they are less intelligent, but that they are less articulate and less literate. They may well have a shrewdness denied to the Oxford don, and far more plain common sense about how to handle people and situations. One must *not* talk down to the people of Little Grubbington as if they were 'mere rustics'; instead one must use more pictorial speech, even fewer abstract concepts, even simpler sentences, and as always be humble in sharing the Christian faith with them.

Again, check the level of Christian experience which one is assuming. When the Youth Club is present that level is probably very elementary and introductory, but in a congregation made up of mainly elderly people, in town or country, it may be very advanced indeed. I remember a fine, wise devout old man nearing 80 who was a pillar of the little chapel and a source of ripe pastoral care to everyone in the village. His chapel had had a long succession of young local preachers, many of them on trial. He smiled rather sadly as he told how the last four Sunday evenings had all involved an earnest call to conversion and the new birth, yet he could not think of any member there who had not been a Christian for at least twenty years! Excessive evangelistic zeal can make us crassly insensitive.

This leads us to a thorny question – the place of provocative theological questions and assertions. Is the sermon the place to introduce disturbing doubts into the minds of secure old Christians? If everyone present is a fervent believer in the inerrancy of the scriptures should one try to undermine that simplistic

147

faith? If most of the people believe childishly that God answers every prayer and makes everything come out all right for us, should the preacher challenge it? Three comments must suffice. First, no preacher ought to imagine that doubts and challenges and questions are somehow unknown to these good people. They also have television sets at home, friends and relatives and neighbours who don't share the faith and don't want to. They also carry about all sorts of questionings within themselves every day. They cannot be protected from such reality, nor is it right for the Church to pretend to be an isolation hospital from the supposed germs of doubt and appraisal. A preacher who carries on blissfully presenting life in over-simple terms is trying to hide from reality, which is not where the Living God is to be found. Secondly, the preacher must be someone of integrity. If you believe that Jonah is an allegory it is dishonest to preach as if it is plain historical event. If you do not believe that Jesus raised Lazarus from the dead by revivifying a corpse, then it is manifestly wrong to preach from the account in John's gospel as if it is straightforward narrative. Instead it must be presented as highly significant theological reflection woven around a core of basic historical facts.

However, if you handle such items in an assertive manner, determined to shock, suggesting that the congregation's simple faith is ridiculous, you merely earn outrage. The listeners will not change their views, nor will they listen to anything that you say in future. Your authority has been thrown away, not because of the opinions expressed, but the manner in which it was done. There is no place in the pulpit for a person who treats the congregation with contempt. Of course not, for preaching is the occasion when one person is called to speak on behalf of all and with the authority of Christ. One does not preach *to* a congregation, but *for* it; not *at* a congregation, but *on behalf of* it. So the preacher must handle those questions and problems in a way which becomes a shared look at them and respects the different ways in which faithful Christians respond from their different viewpoints. You are not there to hector, lecture, harangue, correct the supposed idiot notions of the people, but to voice what it is like when we all together look at something which troubles us all, and seek the mind of Christ upon it.

All faithful preaching carries within it an implicit sympathy for, and awareness of, the massive range of the total Christian obedience to Christ from Paul to Archbishop Nikodim, from Peter to Martin Luther King, from the author of Hebrews to Karl Barth and Steve Biko and Helder Camara. Preaching does not happen on a soap box, but from the huge Christian witness by all the saints. So check, check those perspectives. Am I here being a narrow-minded pedant or the envoy for a vast army? Am I being aggressive, or courteous and gracious?

Lastly, consider the ability of the congregation to use technical theological terms. Not many can cope with them. To trot out the high falutin' references to transubstantiation, sanctification, utopianism, eschatology, substitutionary atonement, etc., is merely silly. Check every word that ends in -ation, -ism and -ology! The preacher, being an agent *for* the people, needs to be using the language which they normally use when reflecting upon life and its meaning, needs the signs, symbols, pictures, phrases, stories, concepts which are the stock in trade of their normal communication. Our common inability to express ourselves in the manner of most working-class folk is the most glaring of these failures in our own day. It is not totally our fault, however, for despite the way many idealize the working class cultures these are not very rich in language styles and can be very boring. This does not excuse our failures, for we must still use the appropriate language, even if it be limited.

So there is a lot of checking to do. Sometimes, when doing it, you wonder if preaching is ever possible! Who am I to attempt this dreadful task and make so many blunders? When in this state, God is calling you to prayer. There may not be need for elaborate requests, just for a resting upon God in the awareness that all Christian life happens by grace, and preaching is no exception. God accepts us, even in our feebleness and inadequacy, and somehow sustains us to draw out our best and to delight us with flashes of hope and promise. Just as God sustains us daily in the rich mystery of his love, so he will be

149

working ceaselessly to speak his Word through our feeble preaching. So we can keep going and keep growing.

Writing it out

By this time you should have available an ideas sheet covered with jottings of all sorts, comments upon the biblical material, ideas, stories, etc. There should also be a sheet which has a clear heading at the top, setting out the aim in a few words. It then carries an outline of the necessary structure, with hints concerning the beginning and the ending. Bear in mind a picture of the congregation, and a sense of what will be apt for it and what will not. The final task now is to write the sermon, word for word. Then check it for time, not by reading it through privately, but by speaking it out aloud at the pace you would normally use for public speaking. How long should it last? There are no immutable laws. It depends upon the setting, and your competence. When beginning, particularly if you do not have much flow of words in public, aim for it to last for about 15 minutes in normal situations, but shorter if the sermon is for a Family Service. Eight minutes is more appropriate in that case.

After a trial run it may become only too obvious that some parts need pruning altogether, that the whole thing is too long (the usual fault), that some parts involve repetition and can be cut without any real loss, that the balance between different points or features is wrong and needs adjustment, and so on. So more editorial work may be required before it can be put into its final form. Should you then preach from the full and finalized script? Only if you can do no other. To begin with, that may be necessary. But as soon as possible wean yourself away from having to read out every word. Learn to use notes which give an adequate outline of the material (e.g. the first three words or central word or words of each sentence). This gives far more freedom to look at the congregation, to move about slightly, to add in the occasional impromptu remark or happy inspiration, freedom to avoid being wooden.

That freedom can be abused. Some over-confident preachers use the bare minimum of notes and operate with a sublime sense of abandonment to the feel of the occasion. Such preachers often claim to have 'had a great time' and to have experienced 'great freedom'. The best judges are those who have had to listen, who may have found the sermon to be trivial, badly-constructed, wandering, repetitious or frankly boring. Preachers who sit very lightly to their notes, and who do very little hard work of preparation, are the most likely to end up as religious wind-bags. They often cannot stop. Their readiness of speech is a massive snare and delusion, which leads them to think that others enjoy listening to them as much as they personally enjoy preaching. Alas!

For this reason every preacher needs fairly regularly to write out complete sermons, word for word, even if by now that person is experienced and has the confidence to stand in a pulpit and speak with a fair measure of eloquence. So the general rules are: To begin with, write it out in full and speak from a full script; as soon as possible learn to use notes for the actual delivery, even though the whole was written in full beforehand; then, when you are confident and can always keep your public speech well ordered according to your previously-prepared outline and structure, prepare using full notes and not necessarily a full script; finally, never get into the habit of always preparing in note form, but make yourself write an occasional sermon out in full, so as to keep a close check upon what you are doing and saying.

151

Chapter 7

Preparing the service

(1) The order

IT is impossible to prepare a service without making use of one's theology of worship. The act of preparation is itself an answer to the question 'What is Christian worship? What is it for? What is it about? To what sort of God is it directed?' Every person who prepares an act of worship and then leads it is giving a personal answer to those awkward and massive questions. The preacher is not, of course, the only person who has to answer them. As was mentioned in the first chapter, the people who tell an architect what sort of church building he is to design for them are also giving an answer. In their case the result is perhaps even more important, since a building may be designed to last for two hundred years, whereas a single act of worship is planned for next Sunday and can be scrapped if it be shown to be poor.

In the first chapter various ways of understanding Christian worship were outlined, and some positive statements were made about the way in which the majority of us now answer these difficult questions mentioned above. 'Christian worship, whatever church it is held in, is God's people celebrating their faith, celebrating the gospel news, celebrating that all worth and truth belong in God. Worship is thus an ascribing of worthship to God.... It is a way of God's people saying that only God matters, only God is of supreme worth, only God is worthy of praise ... Moreover, God can be known through the story of his work amongst us, the history of the Jewish people,

152

the events of Jesus the Christ, so that a rehearsing of those events will be a major feature ...'

Let us reflect upon those comments and the theological affirmations that are being made within them, and the way that affects the task of preparing a service. It is obvious that the major focus of the act of worship is upon God, not man. The main concern is to glorify God, not to do good to man. One can almost detect a conviction, just under the surface of the words in the last paragraph, that if one sets out properly and gladly to praise God and adore him for being the sort of God he has been disclosed to be in Jesus then, and perhaps only then, will man get the most benefit from the experience. Put first things first (in this case, the ascription of worth and glory to God) and then the second derivative things (such as the improvement of man) will look after themselves. Concentrate upon the objective elements of the worship experience, those that are aimed solely towards God to glorify him, and then the subjective concerns of the worshippers will all in the end be more than satisfied. Christian worship is mainly a matter of what we offer to God, not a matter of what we receive back from him. The dominant mood of the occasion must not be that of a lot of needy people desperate for help and health, but of the reality of God, Father, Son and Holy Spirit, in whose hands we all find ourselves.

This leads on to a second reflection. It is because Christian worship is primarily an offering of celebration to the triune God that we lay quite heavy stress upon first-rate standards, meticulous attention to detail, careful preparation, sound theology. We are under total compulsion to offer our best, because the whole occasion is designed for God. Sometimes we are sorely tempted to say to ourselves 'I haven't much time to prepare for next Sunday, but it really doesn't matter all that much. The service is only at Little Backwater Street, hardly anyone will be there, and none of the congregation will be very experienced in theology or liturgy so I can get away with almost anything'. Woe, woe, woe to the preacher who has slithered into such sickly spiritual sloppiness! That preacher has been corrupted as badly as the person who tells blatant lies or commits the most brash of sins. The worship at Little

153

Backwater Street is mainly for God's sake, not ours. It needs as sound a theology and as appropriate a form and structure as does the service for ten thousand people in a mighty cathedral. It needs just as careful a preparation, and then it will please God just as much.

The third reflection concerns the phrase 'God's people'. Some persons lead Christian worship on the assumption that a few Christians are present but that the majority are all 'unsaved' or in need of conversion or sadly in default or otherwise estranged from the Gospel and the obedience of the Christian life. Nobody has any right whatever to make such assumptions. Instead the preacher is being asked to preside over the congregation's offering of its corporate life as the people of God, even though as a community of people it is all made up of justified sinners. It is a corporate offering, then, on behalf of *all* the people of God in that place and community. It is more significant than ten or ten thousand individuals gathered together out of common interest (as might happen if they were watching a football match) because it is bound to be a bigger affair than the mere numbers could ever indicate and to have greater worth than our human reckonings can assess. Just as a family gathering is a much more important occasion than a mere assembling of an identical number of people, because the family has a corporate value and character that is much bigger and richer than a mere gathering of bodies in the same place, so the congregation of God's people has deep importance. The whole body is reaffirming its character as the most remarkable family on earth.

A fourth reflection. God's people make a particular sort of celebration because of their unique history, a history to which the Bible and all the subsequent story of the Church bears witness. There is inevitably, then, a sense of history and the wealth of that past tradition apparent throughout the worship. God's people do not assemble brand new next Sunday as if they have been dropped from Mars or suddenly created out of the clouds. They assemble as people who are at this present moment within a centuries-long pilgrimage. Every stage of the journey has left some sort of impression upon them, has moulded their character and contributed to their culture and

154

their rich memory. They are a people fashioned by that history and carrying it along with them. Their speech is full of references to it, they repeat the stories of the crucial events of the past, they sing their marching songs, they teach the traditions to their children and their children's children. So it is inevitable that many of their words evoke especially strong response because of the weight of tradition and meaning which they conjure up, words like 'Zion', 'redemption', 'the promised land', 'the blood of the covenant', 'the thirty pieces of silver', 'the first-born from the dead', 'Pentecost', 'the new Jerusalem', for example. Those words and phrases will resound through their singing and praying. Christians are a special people, born out of a special history, aware of a special past and a special destiny. So Christian worship inevitably imparts that sense of the importance of past, present and future.

Finally, a reflection about the mood of Christian worship. It is not meant to be sombre nor muted nor cold. People on a long march towards a future that is full of promise are not meant to be thus. Nor are they meant to be flippant. The mood should be that of serious joy, of steady delight in God who has brought us safely through and will continue to do so. So pompous or ponderous solemnity is out of place, as is glib lightheartedness. Both of those extremes have their origin in something other than the Christian pilgrimage.

That takes us back to the basic question 'What is worship?' If it is to stress the otherness, awe (*mysterium tremendum*), then it needs a shape which gradually builds up that sense of mystery and depends less words and more on drama, aesthetic delight, the whole moving up to some great climax of wonder and ecstasy. If it is to focus upon the sudden mighty irruption of God into our lives it will again move to its climax towards the end (the appeal) and will leave everyone on that high note of challenge and expectancy. But if it be the normal act of God's people on their pilgrimage, it will have a different order and psychological character. It will be basically a three-fold shape, as follows:

(1) The approach to God (or the 'preparation')
(2) The message from God (or 'ministry of the word')
(3) The people's response

155

This means that for almost all the services which we conduct, including the Family Services which are becoming increasingly popular on Sunday mornings, we should assume that we ought to work with such a basic and simple pattern. It can be helpful to begin with a sheet of blank paper, to section it into three, and to prepare the service section by section. The sermon of course relates to the second section. It does not really matter whether or not you have begun by preparing the sermon first, and then will be preparing the complete order, or whether you have done the order first (having of course a good idea as to what the sermon is to be about) and then the final preparing of the sermon afterwards. What matters is that all the preparation is thorough and fitting.

The approach or preparation

Let us turn our attention to the first section, the preparation, the approach to God. What should happen? The focus should be upon God and his glory. There should perhaps be an introductory statement, a call to worship, that makes it plain that we are assembled before God. There should be the boldest of announcements of God's greatness and wonder and the marvel of his mighty acts amongst us. Some of the most appropriate means of making such a chorus of adoration is through singing, so a well-known hymn of adoration is especially suitable here. But the recitation of a psalm, or a hymn, or some statement of the massive truth that God is worthy of all praise, value, respect and honour is appropriate.

On the whole, Free Church worship is not skilled in the exercise of adoration, perhaps because we have relied too much upon extempore prayer and the most difficult matter of all is to put the praise of God into ready words. It is precisely at this point that words fail us and become such feeble vehicles for expressing the staggering wonder of telling God how marvellous he is. So most preachers tend to express prayers of thanksgiving at this point, thereby moving into a slightly easier but subtly different area. Adoration is directed 'straight' to God, an effort to say what you are aware of when fastening all attention upon him alone. It is an exercise in which you long for the imagination and artistry of the poet. But thanksgiving is

156

different, and easier. It is a matter of looking at the world's life, including your own, of seeing the power and grace of God at work within it, and telling God so with pleasure. It is easier because the attention can be focused again upon the familiar experiences of life where we feel more at home; we are often involved in thanking people, so we know the sort of words to use. We don't often use the language of enraptured love, only perhaps with one other person in our lives, and then only in private, yet here at the beginning of Christian worship we are called upon to use that language in public on behalf of a congregation of people. Maybe this is the hardest thing that a preacher has to do, that which requires the greatest care. For that reason it is this prayer above all others which probably needs to be written out thoroughly and meticulously beforehand (of which more will be suggested later in this chapter).

And then, possibly, thanksgiving. Thanksgiving for all that God has done and is doing, for creation and covenant, for the enormous events which have stamped Jesus into the world's life, for the gifts of the Holy Spirit and the existence of the Church, for saints and prophets, for the Bible and the creeds, for the whole tradition and heritage within which we stand, for the blessing of yesterday and today, for the things which we readily take for granted and those which need to be highlighted to stop us growing insensitive to God. The sky's the limit. But, inevitably, there are dangers. If the thanksgiving is all about the immediate things (the weather, the beauty of the scenery, the food we had for breakfast, the standard of living we enjoy) then we are in danger of making God into the one who cares only for us (does he not sustain the whole universe?) and of ignoring the whole pageantry of history as Christians see it. If we concentrate upon the mighty acts of God in the past we may not be acknowledging properly the purchase he has upon our lives *now*. We must hold the two together.

Most experts in liturgy suggest that thanksgiving does not necessarily pertain to our approach to God. It is more appropriate within the final section of the service, because after a hearing of God's word to us we should have even more to be thankful for. For example, the Response in 'The Sunday

157

Service without the Lord's Supper' (pp. B20–B21 in *The Methodist Service Book*) contains a prayer of thanksgiving. So too the final prayer after communion is a thanksgiving:

> We thank You, Lord,
> that You have fed us in this sacrament,
> united us with Christ,
> and given us a foretaste of the heavenly banquet
> prepared for all mankind.

So there is no necessity to include thanksgiving here as part of the approach. Yet it would be an odd service of Christian people if the language of thanks never passed our lips. Even the funeral service includes a great prayer of thanks, and would be grievously inadequate without it. So somewhere, in the approach, but preferably in the response (or else at both points) we must be thanking God.

But as we all know, when you become aware that you are in God's presence you immediately become aware of your own tawdriness, inadequacy, muddled and bungled style of life, failure and frailty. In short, you are aware of your sin and of your part in the huge sea of sinful, inadequate humanity. 'I am a man of unclean lips, and I dwell in the midst of a people of unclean lips.' We all must confess our sin to God. As in all things, good theology is our handmaid here to stop us saying things that are plain silly. We do not hold the doctrine of total depravity, in the sense that everything in us is evil and there is no good anywhere in mankind. Thus some prayers of confession become obsessively morbid and plain contrary to both Christian doctrine as well as common sense. The present state of the world is *not* like hell, nor am I a totally depraved sinner. As the little bit of doggerel puts it:

> Once in a state of passion
> I cried in desperate grief
> 'O Lord, my soul is black with guilt
> Of sinners I am chief!'
> Then stooped my guardian angel
> and whispered from behind
> 'Nonsense, you silly little man,
> You're nothing of the kind.'

Nor do we believe that sin is primarily a matter of doing wrong deeds. It is a state of one's being, a state of being out of line with God's holy purpose, of being askew. So in the prayer of confession do not focus upon naughty acts alone, on the telling of lies or the losing of temper or the grabbing of more for yourself. The emphasis should be upon our entire condition, our unhealth, our feelings and intentions and desires, all that makes us into the sort of confusion that we are. It is that muddle of humanity which we present in the prayer of confession, and upon it we ask God's startling mercy. The skilled preacher is the one who describes that condition most aptly, who makes everyone feel 'Yes, that's us all right'.

But then the gospel word must follow, for this is Christian worship, not just an occasion for accurate portrayal of humanity's fallen condition. Amazingly, few Christian preachers seem to realize that confession on its own is a depressing business that gets us hardly anywhere. In Christian worship there is a proclamation to be made. God in Christ forgives sins, accepts us just as we are, takes us on, stands with us, does not condemn, offers us pardon and a new beginning. He does this again and again, Sunday after Sunday, day by day, for ever and ever! So confession *must* be followed by pardon and the gracious sound of the Gospel news, It does not have to be done as if you were a High Priest dispensing absolution by divine decree, but clearly and unostentatiously by a strong recital of the amazing truth – God in Christ forgives our sins. Or you can use appropriate texts like 1 Timothy 1:15 or 1 John 1:9, or cite the Lord's words such as in John 8:11, or use the form in the Methodist Sunday Service: 'Jesus Christ came into the world to save sinners. Hear then the word of grace: Your sins are forgiven. Thanks be to God. Amen.' What matters is that every person has the chance to hear the plain word of the Gospel.

Many of those who lead Free Church worship choose to include here some prayers for the worship. They almost always end up as prayers for the worshippers' benefits, that we should 'feel God near', or be able to 'forget the world outside', or 'find a blessing for each one of us', or 'have our hearts lifted up', or some such sentiment. Thus they almost always betray our intense subjectivity, as if we come to worship mainly because

159

we want to get something out of it for ourselves, to have our emotional condition improved, or to be reassured that our lives are now better than before. But is that what Christian worship is for? Mutual improvement? Or is it the offering of homage and worth to God as he is in the mystery of the Trinity? For if Christian worship is primarily what we offer to God, then the opening prayers should be asking that we make an honest and acceptable offering, rather than concentrating on the personal benefits we are wanting. Those benefits are not the aim of the act of worship, but the product of it. Worship is not a disguised form of self-seeking, but something done for God.

It has been customary for the Lord's Prayer to be said or sung at the close of the opening prayers. There is no necessity for this, but by long tradition amongst us and by virtue of its nature as a classic summary of Christian prayer it has usually come here. However, in the Sunday Service it comes at the close of the intercessions, whereas in some Communion Services it comes just before the communion. There are good reasons for placing it at the close of a series of prayers, because it is so well-known as a summary; therefore place it either here or at the close of the intercessions later. The Collect of the Day expresses the day's theme in a succinct way, according to a well-developed style which makes it into both an affirmation and a petition. This means that it can come appropriately here in the beginning, thereby introducing the day's theme, or at the close of the lessons (since it pertains to them) or later in the closing prayers.

There is of course a rightful place for prayers of invocation in that opening section, prayers that God will take hold of our imperfect offering through the energy of his Holy Spirit and transform and perfect it. And so the elements which may all find a place within that opening section are those that relate to:

The call to worship
Adoration and praise
(Thanksgiving)
Confession and declaration of forgiveness
(Collect of the Day)
Invocation and prayer for the worship
(The Lord's Prayer)

160

and the task of preparation is to see that these are appropriate for that particular congregation, well ordered, theologically healthy and clearly expressed.

The Message

Planning the second section of the service is not merely a matter of preparing a sermon and attaching some convenient bible reading to it, although a sermon will probably feature here. It is primarily a matter of ensuring that the Word of God can be heard as clearly as possible. That is a very daunting task, for it is precisely when we claim to speak on behalf of God that we are most exposed to that sin which in the New Testament is regarded as one of the most damnable of all – the sin of arrant self-righteousness, of presuming that we especially are in possession of God's final truth. So the only mood in which to prepare this section of the service is that of 'fear and trembling'.

The first problem is a very practical one. Should the offering and announcements be sited here, immediately after the 'approach' has been made, or as an interval between some of the readings? Theoretically the best place for the offering is in the final section, as part of the people's response to God, since that is what the giving of money is meant to be. But we should not be too pernickety about this, for sometimes there are sufficient reasons why it should come earlier. In the morning service especially there may be need for it early because the children and their teachers can then share in this act with the whole congregation before proceeding to Sunday School or Junior Church. The announcements have a legitimate part in the service, for they outline the life of the congregation and, rightly handled, need not be an intrusion nor nuisance. If they precede the offering, then the prayer with which the money is offered to God can also be one in which the ongoing weekly life of the Church can be offered. Ideally then this should feature later, but the ideal liturgical considerations do not over-ride plain common sense. What we should not do is to intrude the offering between the lessons and the sermon, for these belong together and need to be linked by a suitable hymn, not divided by notices and money.

161

The next consideration pertains to the sermon. What sort of sermon is it? In the previous chapter five main types were outlined. Each has its rightful place within the total preaching programme of the Church. Every preacher should attempt to keep a rough balance between them all, or the preaching becomes stereotyped and monotonous. But clearly the way in which the central part of the service is designed will depend to a considerable extent on the nature of the sermon. Likewise this section will be influenced by your use or otherwise of the lectionary, and preferences for one translation rather than another (both discussed in chapter five). Suppose it is an expository sermon. Then it will be necessary for the particular passage to be read beforehand, and helpful – if it be in a church which duplicates the notices – for it to be set out there, so that all can refer to the text. It might also be helpful for the same passage to be read again after the sermon, by which time it should carry far more light and power than before. But if the sermon comes within the other categories there is always the temptation for the preacher to think 'I've got the sermon sorted out. I'll have to put some Bible readings in. What can I remember that has some connection with the theme?' That is plainly wrong. Whatever sort of sermon it be, it should make clear reference to some of the central affirmations of the Christian faith, and its arguments should be dependent upon them. What is likely to be most apt, then, is such reading from the Bible as is directly dealing with one or more of those central affirmations. To be true, there are some important themes with which this procedure is inherently difficult. The doctrine of the Trinity is a case in point, for it was only formulated long after the New Testament books were written and so is virtually unknown in its pages. But that is an exceptional example.

Must you have an Old Testament reading? This was considered in chapter four. Normally, yes. Is it permissible to have one or two readings from the New Testament only? There are no *laws* here. The compilers of the lectionary indicate three passages to be read, one from the Old Testament, one from the gospels, one from the epistles. That is an appropriate balance. But you are not chained to such an arrangement, and should

162

feel able to adapt the number and type of reading to the particular situation.

Should you plan to supply an introduction to the biblical readings? Generally speaking, yes, but with brevity. Here we are somewhat put off by the mystique with which we surround the words of scripture. Many people assume that because God 'speaks' somehow through them we must merely read the selected words with care and awe, and God will mysteriously make it all plain to the hearers. But that is a very clumsy way of understanding how God speaks. His capacity to get through to us is not improved when the people of God start off in ignorance of the passage, its setting, its style, its intentions. How on earth can we grasp the significance of many a prophetic passage unless we first enter into the situation by an act of historical imagination? And how can we do that without some preliminary assistance? Or again, how can we grasp the profundities of many a New Testament passage without previous hints? But we must be balanced. It is scripture that matters most, not some preliminary digressions about it. A couple of carefully-prepared sentences should be enough to set the stage, as suggested in David Calvert and John Stacey: *Prefaces to the Lessons* (Epworth). And then do not make the readings too long, unless they are narratives that are easy to follow. Normally about 15 verses are enough, but of course the passage chosen should make a coherent whole.

Is it permissible to use readings from other sources than scripture? Of course! Other sources may be of value even if they lack the tested authority of scripture. What is the sermon itself, but a string of words from another source than scripture? We are usually too unimaginative here. There are often good reasons why such readings are needed. Suppose, for example, that the sermon is apologetic and is about the problem of pain and suffering. The meditations of someone who has experienced such an agony are obviously relevant. Suppose the sermon is about the plight of the poor, or the curse of racism, of the problems of abortion, then some vivid reading from the newspaper, or a contemporary comment, or a report from some relevant agency can obviously illuminate the theme. Especially when we remind ourselves that preaching is the art

163

of building bridges between the Christian tradition and contemporary Christian experience can we see that discriminating reading from contemporary sources may be invaluable to us. To cite a few books at random, here are some which aim to supply us with ideas: *Word Alive*, Edmund Banyard (Galliard 1969), *Let the Bible Live*, Peter White (Galliard 1973), *Words to Share*, Donald Hilton (Denholme House 1974), and the biographies of Christians, such as John Newton's *The Fruit of the Spirit in the lives of great Christians* (Epworth), or their current reflections, should be used by us as a mine or treasury. There is also much useful help in materials designed originally for use in school assemblies, e.g. *Exploration in Worship*: Sheila Hobden (Lutterworth 1969) or *Assembly Workshop*: Ronald Dingwall (Darton 1972).

Is there a place for the creed here? A creed such as the Apostle's is, after all, a means of linking our faith today with that of the Church down through the ages. The sermon too should have been attempting this. Whenever a congregation recites the creed it is saying that it stands within that long tradition, holding that area of belief, so there is some point in its being used here. However, there is little traditional place for such recitation at the normal Sunday services within the Free Churches. Instead we have used hymns to express our convictions. This means that the creed should occasionally be used, since it is a good thing for the congregation to be accustomed to its affirmations. Which creed? Normally the Apostles, which is shorter; the Nicene is longer, enters into more complex concepts concerning the person of Christ, and is by tradition associated with the eucharist.

You may be getting restive as you read this chapter, for all the discussion so far has been about books and passages to read, words to use, the type of sermon to preach. It is the old Protestant obsession with *words* all over again. Does not God communicate to us through film, pageantry, drama, symbol, poetry, dance, song, the visual, the ecstatic, the work of the creative artist as much as the orator? Indeed he does, and our stress upon preaching and reading has meant a sad neglect of these other media. We are simply not good at their use, nor have we seriously attempted to master them in the practice of

164

worship. We should all share in a general confession at this point. In the next chapter we look at the opportunities of presenting the message in other ways.

So the second part of the worship is prepared – lessons, readings perhaps, possibly notices and offering and prayer, sermon, creed, a hymn or hymns that help to develop the theme being explored, some words of introduction to the scriptures, and maybe, if you are lucky, some chance to utilize the skills and talents of others and make the word 'come alive' in fresh ways.

The order of service sketched out on your preparatory sheet has now become something like this:

Approach:	Call to worship
	Adoration and praise
	(Thanksgiving)
	Confession and declaration of forgiveness
	(Collect of the Day)
	Invocation and prayer for the worship
	(The Lord's Prayer)
Message:	Lessons
	(Collect of the Day)
	(Readings)
	Sermon
	(Creed)

and into this outline some hymns or psalms have been fitted. Possibly, if it is a morning service, the notices and offering have had to be added at the end of the Approach.

The Response

The final section should enable the congregation to express an adequate response to the message just experienced, and to the whole goodness of God as set forth in the Gospel news and the Christian tradition. It should of course utilize the singing of hymns or songs (of which more will be said later) but in particular it should issue in prayer. There may well be three elements in this prayer.

First, there will be intercessions. As we have seen, the early Church based the first major part of its main weekly service upon the tradition it had inherited from the Jews in the regular

165

pattern of synagogue worship. This too was in three fairly simple, but not equal, parts: a very brief introduction to worship, then a series of up to seven readings from the Old Testament, then a sermon which was an exposition of one of these. The final act was mainly one of intercession, praying for the people of God. The early Church developed this so that the message was followed by a series of prayers for the Church and the world, for the poor and needy, for the rulers and authorities. In effect, the first thing that Christians did after having heard the gospel was to direct their attention to other people and away from themselves. The catechumens (that is, those under preparation for baptism and Church membership) would leave before these prayers were begun, because intercession was supremely the action of the believing Church.

When the Church is devoting itself to intercession it is acting as priest to the world, standing before God on behalf of the world and speaking for it to him. It is 'the priesthood of all believers' at work, so that the famous phrase would be much better applied to such praying than in being used as a party battle cry about ministries within the Church. To be caught up in that costly priesthood is the privilege of every believer, and matters far more than seeking or refusing ministerial status within the body of Christian people. No Sunday service should be completed until that priesthood has been exercised. It is one of the most significant ways in which the Christian can be rescued from self-concern and the Church from introversion. It is the summons to live on a bigger map, to make the wide world our parish. Everyone knows that this element in the service can become a rambling tour of all the good causes in existence, or a string of rather vague platitudes. It can lack shape and form, or it can be generalized to the point of ineptitude: 'Lord, please bless all the sick.' It requires very careful preparation. The outlines suggested in the Methodist Sunday Service and U.R.C. Communion Order are good clear ones which avoid banality, give a good scope, have a sequence which makes obvious good sense (the world, Church, the nations, our own country, our neighbours, those in sorrow and sickness, ending with thanksgiving for all the saints), and leave opportunity for inserting specific persons and causes. But of course they can

166

become flat if used over and over again with wooden mono-
tony. For that reason four other forms are provided in the
appendix (pages B24–B31 in *The Methodist Service Book*).
Few preachers seem to utilize these forms, but they provide a
much more satisfactory scheme of praying than the old-
fashioned 'long prayer'. That tended to become an emotional
Cook's Tour round the universe, pausing at every trouble spot
until it got back to home base, by which time most of the
worshippers were pretty well winded or their attention had
wandered away as far as the prayer, but in opposite directions.

Intercessions should take up some of the themes handled
during the sermon. The one immediate thing we can do
together about issues raised in the preaching is to pray about
them. But they need to have a clear pattern and preferably to
include regular opportunity for the congregation to join in
some sort of response, otherwise it becomes extremely difficult
for the average worshipper to keep attention focused on the
preacher's words. The ability to shut one's eyes and keep one's
attention on someone else's speech is not nurtured within
modern culture, nor our current educational system, and very
few people possess it. The mind goes wandering off at a tangent
all to easily, so the leader needs to incorporate devices that
help to hold everyone's attention. These also help to affirm
that this is the prayer of everyone involved, not just the individual praying of the leader. For these reasons – one practical
and one more theological – it is good for an intercessory prayer
to be broken up into a sequence which actively involves the
congregation. The forms in the Sunday Service do this, so
do litanies, but you can also construct simple forms which
are appropriate to the occasion. The people can be asked
to respond with a brief phrase after a standard bidding (or
'versicle'), thus:

Bidding: Lord, in your mercy
Response: Hear our prayer

Bidding: Lord, have mercy
Response: Christ, have mercy

Bidding: Lord, this is our prayer
Response: Help us to know and to do your will

167

Bidding: The Lord hears our prayer
Response: Thanks be to God

Bidding: Lord, hear us
Response: Lord, graciously hear us

Bidding: Lord, show your mercy
Response: Lord, show your mercy

Bidding: Lord, may your kingdom come
Response: Lord, may your will be done

If you want this to be slightly more elaborate it may be necessary to have the form set out on the notice sheet. But if the church does not duplicate such a sheet every week, it may then be necessary to supply a special one. If you know the congregation well and can make the appropriate preparations beforehand it is even better for the intercessions to be led by individuals in the congregation and from the places where they usually sit. In that case especially the prayers need to be short and to the point, clearly audible, and again utilizing some standard response.

The second feature of the final prayers is thanksgiving, mentioned earlier in the chapter. Again the Methodist Sunday Service makes provision for a variety of forms and four additional ones are set out on pages B32–B37. If the congregation has sufficient service books for each member, then everyone can easily share in such acts and every preacher can know that the people will be able to follow the course of the prayers closely. A careful study of these forms will show that thanksgiving is meant to be on behalf of the whole Church and meant to be trying to outline the whole range of God's goodness towards us in creation, in salvation, in offering us holiness, in blessing the Church, and in offering the final hope of completion. There is a limited place for those thanksgivings in which only one or two people can share, or which only apply to that immediate locality. Thanksgiving is on behalf of the Church both militant and triumphant, here and everywhere, so it is not particularly apt to thank God for good weather when it is pelting with rain ten miles away, nor to be thanking him for the sunshine when every local farmer is longing for rain. It is not meant to be an intensely individualistic act, but a corporate one.

168

As was mentioned earlier, it is meant to reflect the vast scope of God's mercy towards us. To put the same matter in a different way, it is meant to reflect the trinitarian God. Thus thanksgivings which always extol the wonders of creation and get no further are poor truncated things, however expressive the language and magnificent their enunciation. Thanksgivings which rehearse the deeds of Jesus and get no further are tolerable, yet too limited. They will be restricted to the past, to the first century. Those which go into ecstatic raptures over the work of the Spirit in our own day are similarly exciting, yet limited. They do not set a big enough canvas against which God's glory can be sketched, for they show no proper sense of the whole sweep of human history from the primal beginnings and the initial creation of time itself on the final consummation of all things and all universes, when time will be no more. That is the sort of backcloth against which the great thanksgivings of the Church must be painted.

The final thanksgivings are meant too to pick up some of the notes sounded in the message, putting them in their appropriate context. For that reason the standard forms referred to above can have special items inserted, and all except form A in the Methodist book make that abundantly clear.

The third feature of the prayers should be some form of commitment and possibly petition. We need God to equip us to serve him in the world, we need to make some explicit promising of our lives to him. It is usually not enough for the preacher to end the sermon on some note of exhortation, for we need some means of saying that we pledge ourselves to living out that summons. Thus if you close a sermon by calling on us to practise forgiveness towards each other, or to care for the poor in the Third World, or to be more zealous in our daily witness for Christ, or to give more money to God's work, you leave us high and dry if that is all that you say and do. Such a call merely leaves the congregation with a slightly embarrassed sense of wanting to do better but being only vaguely committed. A call to forgiveness is best followed by everyone sharing together in the peace, for that means that we have to do something simple which can be made the means of our expressing a deep intention to be forgiving. The plea for the Third World is better if

169

afterwards there are ways and means of effecting such an intention (petitions, study courses to commence, activity outlined, etc.). The call to more effective witness might be best followed by a guided prayer in which each person is asked to think of someone who constantly challenges them about their faith, or whom we constantly meet but with whom we can never share something of our own spiritual objectives, with help in how to pray for that relationship. If we should give more money, then the Finance Steward should be on hand somehow.

But the outcome of the sermon may perhaps be a new confidence amongst us. In that event, some sort of credal statement may be the most appropriate (after all, in the Sunday Service the Creed follows after the sermon and intercessions). It may utilize the great creeds of the Church, or it may be a simple pledge such as the following:

We put our trust in God the Father, The future belongs to him.

We put our trust in God the Son. Nothing can separate us from his love.

We put our trust in God the Holy Spirit. He is remaking all things by his power.

We will serve him in the world

We will praise him in the Church

Until the Lord comes.

Amen.

This example may seem to some people not to be specific enough. We could have sung a hymn which expresses the same sentiments. That is true, but we are so used to singing hymns vigorously that to speak a brief statement sometimes means very much more. If you want to make the pledging more specific than the above, you may well need to consult others in the congregation beforehand.

If you want people to make a rather special prayer, then it is best if it is set out on the order sheet of the notices, and people can be encouraged to take it home afterwards and live and pray with it throughout the coming week. Suppose the sermon has been on faith and doubt, and at the end you wanted to use material read in the diary of Daniel Berrigan (the American

Jesuit who roused so much conscientious objection to the Vietnam War). Then Berrigan's reflection could well be put into the form of a prayer and be reproduced on the sheet and commended for further use during the coming week, thus:

> Grant to me, Lord, enough doubt to keep faith on the move
> > enough faith so that doubt may have a direction
> > enough doubt so that faith may be marked by intellectual passion
> > enough faith so that doubt may be contained
> > enough doubt so that faith may not be housebound or castrated or forbidden the real world

Or if this seems sophisticated you may wish to use a vow such as this (taken from Douglas Rhymes: *Prayer in the Secular City*, p. 135):

> So in the freedom of the Son, the Perfect Man
> We shall make money honestly
> We shall make love honourably
> We shall make time for those who need us
> We shall make friends of our enemies
> We shall make amends straightaway
> We shall make Him supreme
> For his service in the world is perfect freedom.

or the famous prayer of St Francis:

> Where there is hatred, let us give love
> Where there is injury, let us give pardon
> Where there is doubt, let us give faith
> Where there is despair, let us give hope
> Where there is sadness, let us give joy
> Where there is darkness, let us give light
> For your name's sake. Amen

or a prayer designed for the close of worship, such as this (taken

171

from *Contemporary Prayers for Church and School*, edited by
Caryl Micklem, p. 84):

> Here we stand, Father, ready to go.
> May all our going be at your behest, all our arriving be in your
> name.
> May the gifts you have committed to us return to honour you
> And may all that we are become filled with your Being
> Through Jesus Christ our Lord.

or the Collect of the Day, or the words from a hymn such as
MHB 382 or 385, or the fifth and last verses of 392 (CP 753) or
many other verses available in the regular hymn-books we use.
A preacher who often provides the congregation with such
material on the order sheet is offering each worshipper the
chance to gather together a small treasury of prayers.

There is an important place in congregational prayer for
silence. At this point in the service you may wish to suggest that
persons meditate quietly about some special point, or that
people offer their own personal petitions and intercessions.
Quiet meditation should not be long. Two minutes is about the
maximum. You should always give some hints as to how to use
the time. Individual prayer can well be suggested for issues
which will confront each individual differently during the coming week – crises to be coped with, decisions to be taken,
problems to be resolved – to be concluded by your offering
some general summary petition and maybe all saying the
Lord's Prayer.

It is most appropriate for the offering to be included in the
final portion of the service. It too is a response to the goodness
of God, who enables us to maintain life and to have the
necessary means. When money is being presented at the communion table it symbolizes the ongoing life of service of the
whole people, it is both a gift of money and a sign of discipleship. It is therefore a very important act, and should not be
trivialized. If it is the custom for everyone to stand at that point,
thereby associating themselves with the importance of the act,
so much the better. But the prayer with which the money (and
all else that it signifies) is received should be worthy of the

172

moment. It is not merely the occasion when we hope that the bills can be met; it is the symbolizing of the offering of ourselves to God for service in his world and Church.

The hymn or hymns which are included here should, of course, reflect the mood and meaning of this portion of the service. It is fitting to sing hymns which express our commitments to world and Church, our desire to carry further the matters about which we have been listening and praying, hymns of commitment and affirmation. We can easily become too sentimental about the closing hymn, especially if it be in the evening. Those hymns which imply that we are going out into a bleak dark world of sin and savagery are highly coloured and probably false to most members of the congregation. Many of them also are extremely banal. The most apt hymns will be those that sing of the resurrection, of the confidence that it is Christ who prevails throughout his universe, of God who is able to keep that which we have committed to him.

The dismissal and benediction are significant statements, since we best remember that we last heard, especially if it was expressed powerfully. Until recently it was held to be peculiarly the prerogative of the minister or preacher to pronounce the benediction, as if it were a specially sacred rite. That merely shows how readily we were inclined to accept false priestly notions into our midst. If it be equally practicable for the congregation to say it themselves, then so much the better. Short statements, built up from brief phrases which are easily memorable, such as the traditional trinitarian grace, are much better said by everyone than by a single voice, whereas a dismissal tends to be better spoken by one person because it is a command. So as a general rule it is best for one voice (the preacher's) to speak a dismissal command, and then for everyone to share in the benediction. There are of course exceptions to such a rule, as when the most apt benediction may well be a text such as Ephesians 3:20, 21 which the congregation may not know off by heart.

Summary

The order of service will thus be in three sections, and together the form will be something like this:

173

Call to worship
Adoration and praise
(Thanksgiving)
Confession and declaration of forgiveness
(Collect of the Day)
Invocation and prayer for the worship
(The Lord's Prayer)
Lessons
(Collect of the Day)
(Readings)
Sermon
(Creed)
Thanksgiving and dedication/commitment
Intercessions and petition
(Affirmation of faith)
(The Lord's Prayer)
Offering and prayer
Dismissal and Benediction

together with hymns or songs or psalms or maybe an anthem or choral item. If however the service was a communion or eucharist, the third section would of course have a different form in which the focus would be on the four acts of Jesus at the Last Supper, yet the character of that section would not be essentially different. The 'Bible service' outlined here has a general shape which is the same as that of the Eucharist. It should be compared with 'The Sunday Service without the Lord's Supper' in *The Methodist Service Book*, pp. B19–21.

Chapter 8

Preparing the service

(2) The prayers and hymns*

Preparing the prayers

SOME of the difficulties in leading the prayers of the congregation have already been mentioned. Adoration involves the language of enraptured love. Thanksgiving must not be set upon too petty a basis, thanking God just for those benefits we presume to have been received by our circle during the previous week. Confession should not be vague and generalized, and should be followed with the Gospel word of forgiveness and the promise of new life. Intercession should not be a long ramble, and should be regularly interspersed with opportunity for the congregation to share audibly in it.

All these warning sounds are a reminder that the preparation of the prayers is just as important, and just as difficult, as the preparation of the sermon. It is a skill that demands a keen sense of the use and value of words and phrases, an ability to put an idea into clear language, and a good working theology. Like the sermon, it is a point in the service at which theology is coming prominently into notice. But it needs to be stated even more cogently than in the sermon, because in prayer there is no opportunity to say that there are different points of view on this matter, or to raise questions, or to cite various authorities, or to use illustrations. The language of prayer is as far as possible the

* In this chapter four hymn-books are constantly referred to by abbreviations. They are *Congregational Praise* (CP), *Hymns and Songs* (HS), *Methodist Hymn Book* (MHB) and *New Church Praise* (NCP).

language of precise conviction. There is little place for speculation. So it is more difficult and demanding to lead congregational prayer than to preach.

The major theological problems occur in adoration and
intercession. Adoration is wrapped in mystery, for how can we
talk about God towards him? Or how can we construct some
sort of mental picture of God which will hold meaning for all
the congregation? The theologians say that God can only be
known by analogy, that we can only think of what he may be
like (e.g. he is like a father or governor); others have said that
he can only be known through people, through the relationships we all share with others, and that modern man simply
cannot conceive of God as transcendent over and through the
whole universe. Here we note that the secular theologians who
argued that nobody today has a sense of transcendence have
gone out of fashion, mainly because the vast majority of Christians do indeed have the *feeling* that God is supreme over all,
whatever the intellectual posers this produces. Thus almost all
of us feel the need to adore, to reach out hopefully, trustingly,
towards that which is outside ourselves, to God. So adoration is
desired by virtually everyone in a church. Your task is to
express that 'reaching out' worthily. It is by no means impossible. Here, for example, is a simple offering of adoration (from
Prayers for Todays Church: ed. Dick Williams, No. 449):

O God
Greater in majesty than we can imagine
Mightier in power than we can comprehend
More beautiful in holiness than we can perceive
More humble in love than we can ever hope
Further beyond our thinking than we can ever know
Closer to our hearts than we can ever sense
God eternal, known to us in Jesus
We worship and adore you in humility and love
For ever and ever. Amen

Or here is another couched in more traditional language which
could of course be adapted into contemporary idiom if you
wished (from *My God, My Glory:* ed. Milner-White, p. 95):

176

Blessed be Thou, O Lord God,
  in the thousand mysteries of thy Word and will
  in the thousand thousand wonders of thy love
Let all mortal flesh keep silence
  and lift itself above all earthly thought,
  kneel and adore.

Or here is one cast in a different style (from *Contemporary Prayers for Public Worship*: ed. Caryl Micklem, p. 17):

People ought to praise you, God of earth and heaven
All of us ought to praise you
  You are always there, never growing old, fresh as each new day
  You were in Jesus, showing us your love by his death
  and by his resurrection giving us hope of living with you for
  ever ...
To God the Father, God the Son, God the Holy Spirit let all the
  world give praise today, and every day, and for ever and ever.

Thus the prayers of others can be a guide, inspiration and stimulus to us in framing prayers of adoration. So too can poetry. So, of course, can the psalms. Many psalms are the ecstatic delight of some remarkable Jewish genius pouring out his sense of wonder towards the God of Israel. That genius can be our teacher too, especially if we nourish our spirits upon some of the recent translations of the psalms listed at the end of this book. Many an effective Christian prayer of adoration can be built from our meditation upon those psalms and our development of them to express the wonder felt by Christians.

Other major problems occur with intercession. What happens when we pray for the Church in Fernando Po? Anything? Is it all a mental exercise which pious Christians enjoy and which may encourage them to feel good, or does the prayer have an immediate beneficial effect upon Fernando Po? Does the prayer enable God to do something which otherwise he would not have done? Here Christians are divided. Many believe devoutly that there is a mysterious effectiveness about intercessory prayer which cannot be explained in any scientific manner at all. It is a means whereby God opens up situations for good and changes them. At times, as we all know, that belief can degenerate into naïveté, with believers expecting

177

responses to their prayers as if they had put a coin into a slot machine and the desired result should pop out quickly at the other end. Sometimes it can produce elaborate heart-searchings as to why the desired result did not happen. Was it because we were not sincere enough in the prayer? Should we try again, but harder this time? Sometimes believers can be wrapped up in endless worry and concern over whether or not the responses were obvious, whether or not God was hinting that we should wait a bit, or repudiating the request, or wanting its nature altered. Sometimes the querying and worrying which attends this simplistic approach to intercessory prayer can be destructive of tender faith ('If that's what Christian belief is all about, it's a wash-out, and I'm not trying it any more').

For these reasons many Christians adopt a different under-standing of what is happening when we pray for others. They believe in intercessory prayer as a means of looking at the world 'through God's eyes', and thus as a way of communing with him. That alone is its justification, and all speculation about its effects or its potency is irrelevant. We pray for others because God is concerned about them, and we wish to be caught up in that concern. That's what Christian living is all about. That's all there is to be said about it. 'Christians pray for others because this is part of the Christian way of living and loving', as Neville Ward puts it.

Whatever our view of intercession we must see to it that we pray for those purposes which we are utterly assured represent the will of God. We try to express these with precision and not vagueness ('O God, bless them all'). We know that God wills man's dignity as a child of God, man's value, man's corporate life being one in which justice and righteousness prevails, man having his daily bread and his basic rights as a person but, supremely, man growing up into the stature of Christ. That gives point and direction to our prayers of intercession. When it comes to sickness and disease we cannot tread so firmly. Clearly death is part of God's will for us, otherwise the world would be cluttered up in no time with millions of antiquated and ever-more-fragile human beings. Intercession for the sick and dying is thus inescapably caught up into mystery and paradox, praying for wholeness and total health whilst know-

178

ing that there is a time for each one of us to experience the collapse of this body, to die. Dust thou art ... Which means that prayer for the sick should not be cast in the mould of glib assurance that we know exactly what God wills, or that our praying is bound to improve the sufferer's health at once.

The problem here has become our self-confidence that we know exactly and precisely what God wants. Do we ever know that? Can we ever be so presumptuous as to claim to know it, except in the general sense outlined in the last paragraph? Our awareness of the almightiness of God and the tiny little size of man ought to warn us not to be brash. The two things of which we can be utterly sure are that God's purposes are far beyond our ability to imagine or understand, and that they are totally loving. So intercessory prayer has a style about it of surrender to the will of God in confidence, rather than an assertion that God ought at once to do such-and-such a thing which we personally want.

So, here is a prayer which is dubious theologically: 'Lord, we pray for our chapel here. Bring in the people, Lord. Fill our place here with hundreds of Christian people seeking you and finding you. Restore to us the days that have passed. Show again that the Church is the strongest force in our land, the greatest power in this neighbourhood.' Such a prayer assumes that we know what God wants, our chapel to be full. Perhaps God does. Perhaps he does not. Perhaps a better prayer would be: 'Lord, speak to this age in your loving power. Speak to all people in this neighbourhood. Make us, and all our brothers and sisters in Christ who worship in other Churches in this locality, fit to sound and carry that Word, fit to be nurturing new Christians. But at all times, however hard or easy they are, keep us trusting you.'

Again, this prayer is doubtful: 'Lord, restore old Mrs A to health and strength again. Revive her. Heal her from all her infirmities and sicknesses, just as you raised Lazarus. Show us your power, Lord.' Perhaps a better prayer would be: 'Lord, we pray that all your healing grace may be at work in Mrs A's life. May she be strengthened in body, mind and spirit. Whatever she has to face, may your grace sustain her in courage and serenity and keep her in the faith.'

179

We can also intrude our self-interest into prayers of intercession unless we are careful. Perhaps this point becomes clearest when we look at a parody of Christian prayers (from David Head: *He Sent Leanness*, p. 22):

> We citizens of the world do beseech You that the standard of living of our country may approximate more and more closely to that of the United States
> *You can do all things, O God*

> We pray that the down-trodden may take it patiently, that nations with empty larders may prefer starvation to communism, and that all who have been deeply insulted and despised may have short memories
> *You can do all things, O God*

Intercession is not a way of wangling our wishes out of God, nor of gaining his support for our pet projects. It is the humbling attempt of trying to see situations as God sees them and, since we can only fumble our way, to be surrendering ourselves to that almighty Will which in infinite love is already at work in all places to effect its perfect fulfilment in ways beyond our imagining. It is always tinged with adoration.

Gifts required for leading prayer

There are four gifts which we all need to cultivate in leading prayer. First, a wide knowledge of the prayers and hymns of the Church down through the centuries. To put it crudely, the preacher must be a sanctified scrounger from every possible area of Christian history and experience. Or, to express that more nobly, the preacher should aim to open up the vast treasures of Christian spirituality to the congregation. It means collecting many books of prayer, and using them in private devotion first so as to find what is most authentic and helpful. It means knowledge of hymnody, for most hymns are prayers put into verse form. If you use a traditional prayer, tell the people its source. Thus if you are praying for the renewal of the Church you may feel it quite impossible to improve upon this ancient prayer, but should say that it comes from Archbishop

180

Laud in the seventeenth century (from Milner-White: *Daily Prayer*, p. 73):

> Most gracious Father, we humbly beseech thee for thy holy catholic Church. Fill it with all truth; in all truth with all peace. Where it is corrupt, purge it; where it is in error, direct it; where anything is amiss, reform it; where it is right, strengthen and confirm it; where it is in want, furnish it; where it is divided and rent asunder, make up the breaches of it, O thou Holy one of Israel.

But you will also want to use prayers that have freshness and sparkle about them, that put the yearnings of our times into bright clear words and phrases, so you need a good library of today's prayers. Use them for inspiration, and then adapt them. Why not? You may find yourself praying (from Catherine Marshall: *The Prayers of Peter Marshall*, p. 123):

> In the name of Jesus Christ, who was never in a hurry, slow us down O Lord, for we live too fast. If we are to burn ourselves out, may it be in causes worth dying for. With all eternity before us, teach us to take time to live, to know You and to know each other, to see the long views as well as the short.

Secondly, we need the gift of a big mind, a large imagination, a wide range of interests, otherwise our prayers operate in the same little restricted areas again and again. Some people argue that we should use the daily newspaper to provide the substance for the intercessory prayers especially. That is not a bad idea, but you soon find that intercession becomes confined to the limits of the daily paper, that the same subjects crop up with monotonous regularity – crime and violence, tragedy (earthquakes, etc.), violence between nations, hunger and deprivation. Like all good ideas, it needs to be used sparingly. The people themselves can of course supply all sorts of themes, so that you can ask them for prayer items. You soon discover however that they suggest prayers within a fairly narrow range of concerns. All the time the alert preacher struggles to extend that range.

181

Thirdly, we need the gift of brevity, neatness and precision. God is not honoured by long-winded waffle. The great masters of the spiritual life are our constant guides here. Consider this exquisite prayer (from George Appleton: *Jerusalem Prayers*, No. 15):

> Dear Lord
>   Unfaltering faith
>   Imperturbable patience
>   Unfailing love
>   Discerning wisdom
>   Quiet serenity
>   today, dear Lord

Not a word is superfluous. The petition is crystal clear. In 15 words he asks for the graces of the Christian life, yet in no demanding nor bombastic manner. It is good to remember that when the disciples asked Jesus how to pray, he gave a model consisting of a mere 64 words spoken in a minute (i.e. the Lord's Prayer in the version of the latest agreed text).

Fourthly, we need to utilize fairly thorough or complete notes, without sounding wooden and cramped. At this point some readers may feel irked because the whole of this article seems to have proceeded on the assumption that extempore prayer should now be ruled out, and only written and carefully-prepared prayers be used. No, but nobody ought to indulge in extempore prayer until having first mastered the task of assembling prayers properly. The right places to begin the experience of extempore prayer are in personal devotion and in the prayer meeting. If you begin to lead public worship by relying solely upon immediate 'inspiration' the dangers of becoming monotonous, verbose, cliché-ridden and narrow are overwhelming. In leading worship you should *first* learn to prepare in great detail, then to use fairly full notes, and only then to practise the extempore. It is a most advanced art, in other words, and is not dependent upon the ability to gush out words towards God and to feel powerful religious emotion. The preacher is not praying on his or her own behalf, but as agent for the immediate congregation and the whole Church

182

catholic. Therefore it is not an exercise in individualism requiring ardent faith plus a fluency with words. It involves the responsible handling of many people's yearnings, for it involves *congregations* in praying.

Finally a few simple warnings. Prayer is not a matter of relaying information to God. He knows it all before we open our mouths. So beware of the informative style, which seems at times to be as much directed to the congregation as to the Lord. 'Lord, here we are. Some of us have come grudgingly. Some of us have come out of duty. Some have come to be with friends. Some have come out of routine. But, Lord, make us all feel your presence with us' makes one wonder to whom the preacher is really talking. To God? Or maybe directing a sally or two at certain people in the congregation? And, moreover, is the purpose of Christian worship to make us 'feel God's presence', or to be offering ourselves to God? The nature of the petition makes one sense that the preacher is more concerned with us humans than with God in his glory.

Beware too of those semi-intercessory prayers which don't quite manage to be prayer but come near it. A preacher will say something like 'Lord, today we think of all the poor, the unemployed, the destitute, the starving, the hungry. Help us never to forget them, Lord.' That is only on the edges of prayer, because intercession is more than merely 'thinking about' others. It is a matter of linking ourselves and others with the whole purpose of God. Another device often used for semi-intercession is that of 'commending' people to God. 'Lord, we commend to you those who keep law and order in our country, the police, the magistrates, the probation service, etc. . . .' What does it mean to 'commend' such worthy persons? We do not really know and are not told. It would be more helpful if the prayer was more specific, praying that magistrates may be able to exercise justice impartially and with a flavour of mercy, that the police should be firm, courteous and scrupulously fair, and so on. The artifice of 'commending' people to God has enabled the person leading the prayer to avoid the hard work of making the prayers specific and linking them into God's will.

Beware of course of antiquated religious jargon, a stilted

183

language which you would never use in normal speech. 'O Thou great Redeemer of Zion, send now thine almighty redemption upon all Thy disciples....' Beware of mixing the styles, as in 'Father, we adore you and pray Thee to grant us peace....' Beware of the religious cliché. One preacher I vividly remember from my childhood talked repeatedly about 'boundless blessings', which then became his nickname throughout the Circuit. Beware of the constant reiteration of 'Lord' at the beginning of every sentence. Christian prayer is offered to the Father through the Son and in the power of the Holy Spirit.

Psalms, hymns and songs

Now we look at the task of selecting the hymns and songs and perhaps psalms to be sung by the congregation. Psalms have never featured very prominently in Free Church worship and especially so today. They are not particularly difficult to sing once the basic principles have been mastered, and many a parish church congregation can sing them with vigour and accuracy. On the whole we have not taken enthusiastically to them, nor have the recent translations and styles of singing them (as with the Gelineau settings) caught on amongst us. Unless there is a strong tradition of singing psalms well, we are best advised to speak them. This can be done by everyone saying the whole or, more interestingly, the preacher and people reading alternate verses or sections of verses. Hymns and songs are, however, immensely popular. There has been an explosion of new ones in the last 20 years, so that there is a very large storehouse from which to select, and every preacher needs to have a working knowledge of the contents of the major hymnals and song books. This requires access to the standard hymn-books of the main denominations and the many supplements that have appeared recently, as mentioned in chapter three. Hymn-books for use in family worship have also been appearing – most notably the recent *Partners in Praise* (Methodist Youth Department) – and those especially for young people such as *Youth Praise*, or those which capture the current evangelical mood, such as *Living Waters*. There are also one or two good collections of the work of individual hymn-writers, of which by far the best is Pratt Green's *26 Hymns*, and a huge number of song books of which the *One World Songs* (Methodist Division of Social Responsibility) is one of the best.

You may feel daunted by all this material, and tempted to retreat into the presumed safety of the standard traditional hymnology. Much of the new material is, inevitably, poor and ephemeral. We should not make the slightest effort to encourage its use. Yet much of it is eminently suitable for worship today and has caught the mood and language of this generation effectively. It is the preacher's task to try to choose the most appropriate items from this large store and to blend them into the congregation's diet without too much fuss. In a normal service at which there will be four or five hymns it is sensible to try to sing one new hymn or song, depending on the situation. In many cases this may entail the use of a duplicated sheet setting out the words, but congregations are becoming accustomed to this sort of provision.

It is more important to concentrate upon new *hymns* than new *songs*. There is a clear difference between them, as indicated in chapter three. A hymn is intended to be sung by the whole Church, by Christians with a wide range of theology and experience, and to last a good time. It needs a strict metre, so as to be free from odd lines or verses that require difficult adaptation to the tune. It needs to be set within the central area of Christian theology. But a song can be much freer in its style and metre and theology. It can be much more of a personal statement and even somewhat eccentric, as are some of Sydney Carter's. It is not meant to last for centuries, but may catch vividly the challenge to the Christian conscience of some issue in the immediate present. For that reason song books soon go out of fashion, and most churches are well advised to be careful before spending money in buying large stocks of them; but every church needs hymn-books, and preferably at least two different ones. Songs, then, make for satisfactory solos or group or choir items. Congregations need to concentrate more upon hymns. Preachers have a large responsibility for introducing them to the best, in consultation with choir masters and organists.

Hymns assessed

The Free Churches have made a remarkable contribution to all Church life by encouraging the writing and singing of good hymns. Preachers who complain that they can never find suitable hymns must be woefully unaware of the extensive resources available today, especially within our traditions. But what is a good hymn? Here are some brief guidelines.

(1) A good hymn is good poetry. It is controlled by a firm, tight metre, rhymes well, the stresses in the words fall correctly so as to preserve both the sense and rhythm. It can be sung and memorized with ease. Look at Wesley or Watts or Doddridge when at their normally high standard; there is a deceptive simplicity about their verses, thus:

> Come, Thou long-expected Jesus,
>   Born to set Thy people free,
> From our fears and sins release us,
>   Let us find our rest in Thee.
>
> (Wesley, MHB 242, CP 59)

> The Lord pours eyesight on the blind;
> The Lord supports the fainting mind;
>   He send the labouring conscience peace;
> He helps the stranger in distress,
> The widow, and the fatherless,
>   And grants the prisoner sweet release.
>
> (Watts, MHB 428, CP 8)

> Hark the glad sound! The Saviour comes,
>   The Saviour promised long;
> Let every heart prepare a throne,
>   And every voice a song.
>
> (Doddridge, MHB 82, CP 74)

Good poetry is not an art that has been lost; it is present in many modern hymns, as this tiny extract shows:

186

We have not loved you: far and wide
The wreckage of our hatred spreads,
And evils wrought by human pride
Recoil on unrepentant heads.

(Donald Hughes, HS 15, NCP 17)

(2) A good hymn is both good religion and good theology. It is about God and his work for man, and not about less important matters. It is based on strong convictions of the Church universal, not on dubious assertion or muddled doctrine. It is therefore a means of leading the singers to God and of enabling God to speak to them. It could almost as well be prayed as sung, so that John Wesley could rightly say of it as he did about his famous 1780 collection: 'This ... is a little body of experimental and practical divinity.' It will move to a high climax at the end, so that the final verse is a good test of the hymn's value. Consider this fine example of a high conclusion:

Love, like death, hath all destroyed,
Rendered all distinctions void;
Names, and sects, and parties fall:
Thou, O Christ, art all in all.

(Wesley, MHB 720, CP 241)

or this from a modern hymn:

Glorious the day when Christ fulfils
What man rejects yet feebly wills;
When that strong light puts out the sun
And all is ended, all begun.

(F. Pratt Green, HS20, NCP 28)

(3) As a development of the previous point, a good hymn makes the singer feel that our experience of God is being expressed most powerfully, better than we could possibly do it for ourselves, using the strong imagery of the Christian tradition in such a way that it 'fits' and appears to be vividly contemporary. The best hymns achieve this, again, in an apparently effortless way:

187

See, from His head, His hands, His feet,
  Sorrow and love flow mingled down:
Did e'er such love and sorrow meet,
  Or thorns compose so rich a crown?

(Watts, MHB 182, CP 131)

or a similar effect comes from a modern hymn:

In blazing light your Cross reveals
  The truth we dimly know,
How small the debts men owe to us,
  How great our debt to you!

(Rosamond Herklots, HS 18, NCP 25)

(4) Finally, a good hymn has an elusive quality which is best termed 'flair'. It uses language in an exciting, vivid, original way. Its phrases linger in the mind and demand to be pondered over again and again. It hints at depth, a rich store of spiritual wisdom. This quality is soon recognized in the Wesleys, Watts, Doddridge, Montgomery, Keble, Paul Gerhart, or the translations by Neale or Catherine Winkworth. It is to be found in modern writers also. Seek, and ye shall find. . . .

These guidelines help us too to see what hymns we should avoid. Here then are five further negative guidelines, followed by three other practical points:

(1) Avoid hymns cast in archaic language or concepts or whose symbolism is now obscure, except for those few which have established themselves in a very significant way within the Church universal. Thus a hymn like 'O safe to the Rock that is higher than I' (MHB 499) is virtually impossible to sing any more. It uses analogies for the Christian life which are too remote from our experience. Worse, it muddles up several such analogies in a sentimental fog. However, some fine hymns are likewise almost unusable, which is a matter for profound regret. It is an inevitable result of the way our thought-forms and imagery are changing rapidly. Thus 'Guide me, O thou great Jehovah' (MHB 615, CP 500) has now become almost too archaic for normal use, relying so extensively on the imagery of the settlement into the promised land, whereas contemporary imagery focuses much more upon the theme of

liberation from slavery. Such a hymn has to have acquired an exceptional place in the tradition if it is still to be used. John Bunyan's 'Who would true valour see' (MHB 620, CP 486) is an obvious example of just such an exceptional hymn. It can still be used, just, despite reference to 'hobgoblins' and 'foul friends.' Martin Luther's 'A safe stronghold our God is still' is another which is just usable, because of the place it has forged for itself in the Church's history.

(2) Avoid hymns which rely heavily upon flowery language and which appeal to the most sentimental and uncritical tastes and moods. Sometimes these seem designed to make us wallow in the most indulgent and self-satisfied emotions, as if religious experience be a matter of trying to create as much feeling of smug unruffled pleasure as possible. In this connection the second half of the last century was a shallow period for hymn-writing, with a few honourable exceptions, and we now have a legacy of very poor material from that era. You have to be a religious ice-cream merchant to be able to cope with something as sickly and sugary as 'Still, still with Thee, when purple morning breaketh' (MHB 474). Sometimes these hymns became absurd and even resorted to such nonsense as 'In the beauty of the lilies Christ was born across the sea' (MHB 260, CP 170). Alas, that is religious trash.

(3) Beware of hymns that are too intensely individualistic, singing all the time about my state, my needs, my help, my re-assurance. Strictly speaking, as indicated above, these should be classed as songs. As such they were popular in the revivalist crusades of the Victorian era. That does not qualify them to be sung by the corporate body of Christian believers today. Thus a hymn like 'Pass me not, O gentle Saviour' (MHB 335) reeks of self-concern and is utterly indifferent to anyone else. It is too selfish for the modern congregation. Such favourites as 'Blessed Assurance' (MHB 422) are also questionable for this reason.

(4) This leads to another feature to avoid. Many hymns are built round a religious experience which is expressed in ways and terms which are unreal for contemporary Christians. Such experiences were genuine and marvellous to the believers of the day. To sing in such terms then would have been wholly

189

fitting, but not for us nowadays. Thus those hymns which describe people writhing under colossal burdens of sin and dreading the gaping grave are unsuitable (such as 'Rescue the perishing', MHB 338), whilst those that describe the saving grace of Jesus as being an experience akin to being 'washed in blood' are usually too repulsive to our generation for normal use (e.g. William Cowper's 'There is a fountain filled with blood', MHB 201, CP 265). This poses acute problems today, because much of the most exuberant and passionate hymnody of the evangelical revival was of this type. If we treasure our heritage we want to handle such hymns with deep respect. We know that they meant a very great deal to former generations. They expressed the intensity of religious emotion that trans-formed so many people into sturdy Christians. Yet neverthe-less they cannot be the staple diet for today's believers. We do not believe that sin is something like a rotten tooth that has to be pulled out from the depths of our personalities. We can't express the freedom Jesus gives us by using the language of being washed in a purifying bath of blood. Yet both of these notions appear again and again in many of the most glorious traditional hymns, as in such verses of Charles Wesley (taken from Hymns 105 and 559 in MHB):

> Jesus, the First and Last,
> On Thee my soul is cast:
> Thou didst the work begin
> By blotting out my sin;
> Thou wilt the root remove,
> And perfect me in love.

> Anger and sloth, desire and pride,
> This moment be subdued;
> Be cast into the crimson tide
> Of my Redeemer's blood!

The ecstatic language of the previous Christian generations has to be replaced by the ecstatic language of today's Christians, not because the old language was bad or inadequate, but because the full glory of our contemporary experience of

190

Christ can only be conveyed by adequate contemporary language and imagery.

(5) Finally, avoid bad theology. This is not a reference to some subtle theological points about which scholars might stage great arguments, such as whether or not Charles Wesley should have written the line 'Veiled in flesh the Godhead see' as part of his great carol 'Hark! the herald angels sing', but of those affirmations which ordinary Christians find to be untrue to their experience. Thus a verse like the following is suspect:

> Not a shadow can rise,
> Not a cloud in the skies,
> But his smile quickly drives it away;
> Not a doubt nor a fear,
> Not a sigh nor a tear,
> Can abide while we trust and obey.

Such a verse makes the hymn (MHB 516) unsuitable, because it is untrue. So are hymns which reduce the most profound mysteries to simplistic proportions, such as those which suggest that God puts everything right for us and we need have no more fears or doubts (MHB 536 comes very near to this, too near). Then there are the hymns which are sodden with uncritical nationalism, such as MHB 900, CP 756 ('I vow to Thee, my country, all earthly things above') or, much more terrible, those that reduce Jesus to the kind and amiable do-gooder in a world where everyone is going to be nice to everyone else (as in 'It fell upon a summer day', MHB 166, CP 111).

Many of these adverse comments may make the reader feel that too much stress is being placed upon the words of hymns. They are not, after all, credal statements, so why be so concerned? The answer is that hymns convey the Church's theology in a very profound way, gently and almost unconsciously. People remember hymns much better than sermons because they *sing* them, and the singing engraves them in the memory. Thus hymns and liturgy are probably more important in passing on the faith from generation to generation than are the Church Membership Classes, the creeds, the manuals, the confessions of faith. You can test that out very easily. Ask the

191

average Christian to repeat a few verses from 'The Lord's my shepherd' or 'Hark, the herald angels' or 'Praise, my soul, the King of Heaven' and it is readily done. Ask that average Christian to repeat the Apostles Creed, and he or she is lost. For that reason you want Christians to sing hymns that will become deeply engraved in the subconscious and will nourish faith. You do not want the Christian subconscious to be awash with religious trivia, nor to be offering banalities to God in song. So you bother about the words of hymns.

Now there are three other simple practical principles to consider when choosing hymns. First and obviously, choose the hymn which is fitting for that point in the service and which assists the worship of the congregation in its aims at that stage. In the first part of the worship we come to God with praise, with ringing affirmations that he exists as the supreme reality of the whole of existence, worthy of all honour. We come with thanksgiving and joy, but also with a sense of the sheer almightiness of God, the ultimate overwhelming mystery of the Trinity, the awe at his surpassing glory, the astonishing wonder that he cares for us and pours out his love throughout his universe. Inevitably we look to the great hymns of praise that have inspired the Church catholic, to writers like Wesley and Watts, to the opening sections of most of the hymn-books. If you seek for a hymn of invocation, after the opening prayers perhaps, turn to those on worship in the Church, or to the sections on the Holy Spirit. If you want a hymn of confession you are hard pressed. There are remarkably few such hymns available (18 HS, 25 NCP being a welcome exception). Within the section of the service dealing with God's message choose hymns about the Bible and God's word, or about the theme of the readings and sermon. The former are not easy to discover; there are few good hymns in the traditional books and the theme has not inspired modern writers. One magnificent exception is George Caird's 'Not far beyond the sea' (49 HS, 67 NCP). When you look for hymns relating to the sermon theme there may again be a great gap in the hymnody available. There are almost no hymns on the fall, on the myths of the Flood or Babel, on the deliverance from Egypt (one has to go to the negro spirituals here), on the work of the prophets, on

192

baptism, the teaching ministry of Jesus, or the calling of Christians to discover their place in the world Church. Perhaps some preachers will see these gaps as a challenge for new hymns and songs to be written? Then the final part of the service should feature hymns of commitment and dedication, of affirming the faith, of trust and confidence.

Secondly, aim to vary the style and metre of the hymns as well as their mood. You do not want four or five common metre hymns each with five verses, nor a string of hymns with choruses, nor a series of solemn ones, or bustly, marching songs, or quiet, reflective ones. After the first choosing, check carefully to make sure that you have selected a range of metres, lengths, styles and moods, that you have drawn upon the great catholic tradition as well as hymns of today.

Thirdly, bear in mind the particular congregation involved, the facility it has for making music and the musical tradition it has developed. It is absurd to expect a tiny rural congregation equipped with a harmonium to be able to offer Luther's 'A safe stronghold our God is still' or Addison's 'The spacious firmament on high'. This raises the question of the matching of tunes and words, and the roles of preacher and organist and choirmaster. There is a longstanding etiquette that preachers choose hymns and then organists or choirmasters choose the music. Basically it is right, since an organist knows more about that congregation's musical ability and tradition than the preacher does. What you aim to do is to establish a good working relationship with those who lead the music-making, so that together you can select what music is most adequate and suitable for the words chosen. All parties should try to avoid being doctrinaire and rigid. There is no very special virtue in always singing the tunes that are set in the hymnals, especially if they are extremely difficult for the people – as are many tunes, unfortunately, in *Hymns and Songs*. Nor is there especial virtue in the new and novel, in the use of guitars or, for that matter, in the exclusive use of organs. All preachers know that every hymn or song has to have music to convey and express it, so should consciously avoid those set to highly unusual metres for which there is only one known tune, which are virtually impossible for the congregation to manage. For the rest, there

193

is probably one standard tune that fits the words uniquely well, or else a range of possible alternatives. You can normally trust everyone's good sense to find the most fitting music. (On the matter of choosing hymns, see also the Local Preacher's leaflet: *The Local Preacher chooses his hymns*.)

But what should you do if told just before the service that you must fit in two anthems, a solo, two items from the young people's folk group, and that Mrs Smith always likes 'Abide with me' on this date because it is the anniversary of her husband's death? You should keep cool! Try to relate as much of this material as seems suitable for worship to those times in the order where it is most appropriate. You cannot alter a congregation's musical and worship tastes by an argument in the vestry five minutes before the service begins. Moreover, in the end, it is the congregation's worship and not your particular brainchild to which the people have been invited (i.e. Christian worship is not like a skilled artiste putting on a special programme to which the general public is invited). Thus you do your best to harness that material, and only reject any if the representatives of the congregation can see with you that there are good and valid reasons for doing so. Then, afterwards, ask that such a difficult situation never arise again, and plead for responsible consultation beforehand.

Chapter 9

Various worship occasions
and styles

Experimental services

THIS is a most unsatisfactory term, and many a reader will doubtless cringe at it and comment that there is nothing 'experimental' about the Gospel news, about Christian belief, about the worship of the Triune God, or about Christian prayer. It is a makeshift and unfortunate term, yet we know the vague feeling of unease that lies somewhere in the background and leads to its widespread use. Amongst many of the most sensitive Christians there is the feeling that much of our traditional worship pattern is dull, predictable, stiff and inflexible, that we are too unimaginative in our use of music or styles of presentation, or that we are only using the leadership potentials of the one sole person, the preacher or minister. So when we try to break out from some of the crusty old moulds, we claim to be 'experimental', for want of a better word.

The intention behind the pressure for unusual acts of worship may be a very creative one. It may be the pressure of the Spirit wanting to burst the old wine skins. It may on the other hand be unworthy, a desire by some pressure group to come to the fore and insist on being noticed, or to 'have a crack' at the congregation, or to get the organist or choir out of their customary positions to show them that others can do their jobs better. It may simply be to shock everyone else, or to pander to the latest *avante garde* fad from the teaching profession, or the world of pop music, or the hi-fi electronic whizz-kids, or the social conscience. The task of the preacher is first of all to act as a purifying agent for all those muddled feelings and intentions, so that the dominant motive that emerges is that of glorifying God more fully. To the extent that people are genuinely saying 'We can present the call and purpose of God much more effectively', there is something valuable and positive upon which you can build. If people are also saying 'We can make a better and more thorough offering to God if we introduce such-and-such a style of worship', there too are positive resources.

In both such cases your role is bound to change from the traditional one of being the sole author of the worship pattern and sole dominant voice throughout the service. The pressure is now upon you to become more like the leader of a worship team or, to change the illustration, to becoming the conductor of an orchestra. Many preachers have fundamental objections to this, preferring to feel that everything is always totally in their hands, preferring to be the traditional king pins who makes all the decisions and keep the prime position for themselves. That objection needs to be strongly challenged. You do not stand over the Church, to tell it how to order its worship life, and to assume a position of total primacy in that ordering. You are the *servant* of Christ through and in the Church, to share in the ordering of the worship of the congregation, and to act on behalf of the whole Church. So you should never resent the offers from groups or individuals to share in that leadership, but should encourage such sharing even if you feel, rightly or wrongly, that you could do better on your own without such assistance. That smacks of your pride.

In such a situation your task as leader of the team or group is to try to see that it is a worthy act of Christian worship, fulfilling its basic canons and principles as much as any other service does. It should not give vent to plain bad theology, to a distortion of the Christian faith, to the worship of man and his skills, to the exaltation of any individual participants, to sloppy thinking and praying, to banal utterance, to slovenly behaviour, to triviality, to a wallowing in sentimentality or bathos, and so on. Many of these dangers are especially present when youth groups are asked to share the conduct and preparation of the service. This is not surprising. Young people are bound to be

196

less experienced in leading corporate worship and are more open to the fads of the moment. But to ask that youth group to spend much time and thought in making adequate preparation along with a more skilled leader is a most effective means for their own education into the nature of Christian worship. In that case, your task begins a very long while before the service is due and is even more important than usual.

There are in particular three things which you will try to help such a group to avoid. First, that the worship becomes an educational session in which the congregation is bombarded with facts and information. You go to the Harvest Festival and find that it is a constant recital of data about world hunger, and that the leader justifies all this by assuring everyone that it is an 'experimental' Harvest because we all need to get away from the sentimentality and irrelevance of the old-fashioned occasions. Maybe we do, but Christian worship is intended primarily to be an occasion when we are directed to God and his truth and commit ourselves to his obedience through his grace. It is not mainly an educational session to alleviate our ignorance about any of the great world problems, however important they may be. The educational role of Christian worship is very much a secondary one. The whole event becomes distorted when in effect the preacher or leader has become the lecturer, or teacher, or even bully, and the congregation have become pupils back at day school.

Secondly, guard against the worst forms of superficial emotional indulgence. A nearby parish church once outraged me by a huge placard advertising as a special series of services some pitiful banality which it called 'Rainbow Services'. The smaller lettering indicated that we were invited to 'enjoy the rainbow of memory, and sing the hymns grandmother used to love!'. I confess to some relief when they tried it only twice and then abandoned the experiment. But emotional indulgence can occur in other forms. A pressure group in the Church may promote a service which only serves the purpose of producing a very bad conscience in everyone – about the appalling housing in the inner city, about the incipient racism lurking beneath all English life, about the awfulness of being utterly lonely (with a folk group singing plaintive songs *ad nauseam*). Merely to

197

promote a bad conscience achieves nothing. The Christian Church lives not by making people feel wretched, but by promoting forgiveness in the name of God, and by offering the means to the new life through the grace of Christ and fellowship of the Holy Spirit. Thus any act of worship which leaves us with a confused and murky conscience and nothing else is woefully far short of Christian worship. The Gospel has not been sounded.

Thirdly, the new types of experience into which the congregation is being invited to enter must not be too far from its expectation or ability. Theologically, worship is offered by the congregation, by the people of God. It is not the worship formulated for the satisfaction of the preacher, or a group working with the preacher, to suit their tastes. An earnest preacher wants to startle a prim middle-class congregation to consider how much waste we produce in our affluent life-style, and arranges for some dustbins to be emptied of piles of litter into the aisles. The outrage is such that from that moment everyone in the congregation has switched off and will hear and receive nothing that the preacher then says. No amount of justifying patter about the need for the 'experimental' will rescue the event. Or again, the sermon is being introduced when, by design, a crowd of young people surge in carrying banners and shouting slogans. It terrifies the elderly who think that a riot is about to erupt, scandalizes the middle-aged who regard their Church as the house of God, and disgusts many of the younger people who see it as a cheap gimmick to get attention. All of them will treat the rest of the sermon with sullen suspicion, and everyone will afterwards demand that there be no more 'experiments'. Or again the Youth Choir is going to sing, but substitutes a popular local Rock Group who turn up their amplifiers to the maximum and make the chapel roof rock, deafening most of the worshippers. There are bitter and furious complaints afterwards, directed at all things young and modern and musical, and the Youth Choir has almost sealed its fate. In such cases it is useless for the preacher and helpers to argue afterwards that we need demonstration as well as exhortation, that nowadays banners are a common means of saying your piece, that rock music speaks deeply to this genera-

198

tion. All in vain. The experimenters went too far outside the congregation's area of known common experience and expression. Their efforts were indeed gimmickry and, therefore, useless.

The moral of all this is that all preachers must understand their role as servant of Christ through and in the Church, should be able to make others see that role if they are to share in leading the worship experience, and should never let that leadership be set at irritating cross-purposes with the congregation's aims and expectations.

Yet these remarks sound negative and too full of foreboding. On the positive side, try over and over again to obtain help from members of the congregation in both the ascertaining of what God's word has to say to us all, and in trying to communicate it as effectively as possible. To consider the first need, is there not something slightly absurd about a preacher who aims to expound, say, the meaning of a biblical passage and does it by sitting brooding in a study, relying solely on individual insight and inspiration? Is there not something far more authoritative about a preacher who first asks a group to wrestle with that passage – maybe a fellowship group, women's meeting, house group, or one gathered specially for the purpose – and then prepares the sermon out of that group's shared reflection and debate? Or suppose that the sermon is going to begin with some troubling problem such as the morality of Christian involvement in strike action. You may not know all that much about it, may not have been deeply involved in it, may not have wrestled urgently in your own conscience about the matter. It is manifestly easy to get all sorts of prejudiced and ill-informed opinion on such an emotive issue. First call together a group of Christians who have had experience of this problem, let them talk openly about it, tease out with them the most difficult aspects, and then prepare a sermon from that corporate reflection. Many minds are better than one. Many viewpoints can prevent the sermon from becoming highly individualistic and distorted, and can draw out perspectives that you alone would never have perceived.

Or consider the presentation of the message. A preacher acting as a solo voice in the pulpit is using one very limited way

199

of communicating God's truth, the monologue. Sometimes that truth may have at least two facets and these may appear almost contradictory so that no one voice could present them. The sermon cries out to be a dialogue, not a monologue. Take, for example, the awkward problem of whether or not Christians should be willing to serve in the armed forces or take part in armed violence against others. It is so awkward that it is rarely preached about. If the pacifist were to present that case, it could easily cause offence. If the non-pacifist were to present the case, it could equally cause offence, since Christian opinion is deeply divided on this issue. That being so, the whole matter is handled much more responsibly if it be a dialogue in which one participant holds one viewpoint and the other speaker holds the other. That enables both to speak with integrity, and nobody in the congregation to suggest that a partial Christian judgement was being propogated. The dialogue is not to be designed as a sort of verbal tennis match which the congregation watches, but an event in which each of the two participants tries to offer God's will and purpose as seen by someone with that perspective, so that it challenges the congregation to decision. It is not a tame version of the discussions seen on some television programmes. It is far more serious. It is aimed to clarify the commitments of the congregation, not to be an entertainment to people sitting in armchairs.

There are very many other ways of expressing the message. The use of simple drama is an obvious one, strangely neglected by the Churches. Many a bible reading is much better presented by more than one voice, for example, and is very much more powerful if linked to some simple actions by the speakers, or illustrated by a group using mime. But also many a sermon is vastly more memorable, gripping, effective, if illumined by a vivid piece of drama. Take a simple example. Suppose you want to present the fundamental Christian duty to seek reconciliation between rival or quarrelling parties. One of the major points to be stressed, let us say, is that whenever quarrels are seen in different perspectives, when they are set out on a bigger scene, they immediately begin to look different. Especially does this apply when seen in the light of God's action in Jesus, his cross and resurrection. But how can that

200

insight be *spoken* in a sermon? It is not likely to get across. But stage a simple drama. Let two persons stand facing each other across the front of the Church and to stage a quarrel, each of them suffused in self-righteousness and utterly convinced that their cause is just. It is a stalemate. Let someone be standing in the centre underneath a cross. Let that person address each belligerent in turn, calling upon both to look at their cases in the terrifying light of the cross, prising open the self-interest and distortion on each side. Let the rivals slowly move towards each other as their positions in the argument begin to shift. That slight physical movement of the actors illustrates the point more powerfully than any preaching could. And, of course, if the drama could end with both parties kneeling beside each other, more effective still, as long as it did not appear to be artificial or contrived.

It is not the aim of this book to describe all the ways in which drama and other styles of presentation may be used in worship, but to encourage you to thank God when there are people in a congregation who are glad to help in leading the worship, who have skills and talents which can be harnessed. Regard such people as precious allies and, like the conductor of an orchestra, bring them in at all the suitable times. Some can act, some can mime, some can manage choral speech, some can dance, some can paint, some can present ideas or visions or pictures through all sorts of audio and visual aids. Thank God for that! All of those talented people are your allies.

There are also talented people who would not dream of coming forward and saying 'Here am I, use me'. They may be too shy, too unsure of themselves, unaware of the value they can be to others, or inarticulate. The thought that they have something useful to offer may simply never have occurred to them. Some of them may be Christians in very unusual circumstances, or in responsible positions. Be on the look-out for people like this, because they can be asked to give their testimony during the worship, or they can be interviewed as an element within the sermon. Interviews are normally more interesting than monologues. The interviewer can ask those questions which most concern the congregation at that moment, can exercise some sort of control upon the way the

201

thinking is going, and can effect a more lively interchange of voices and personalities than is possible when a sole voice is doing all the communicating. Other possibilities are outlined in the leaflet *Changes in Worship* (L.P. Office). See too the bibliography at the end of this book.

Family services

Many preachers are frightened by the presence of children in worship. Children fidget, lose their collection money so that it rolls under the nearby pews, get easily bored, chatter with each other, and are generally a disturbing influence. So you may be only too glad to see them disappear after the opening 15 minutes of morning worship. Sometimes there will have been a plea beforehand that there be a children's 'address'. You then feel under obligation to tell them some sort of tale and to tack some sort of Christian 'moral' on to the end of it. Is that satisfactory?

We should be delighted when there are children in the congregation, if proper provision is made for them by the Church concerned. It is wholly to the good that they are growing up within the regular worship life of the Church. They will learn a great deal simply from the atmosphere of the service, from the sense of importance and perhaps solemnity that it evokes, from the exuberance of the hymn singing, from the deportment of the preacher, from the hush that accompanies the prayers, from the rituals that are being enacted (such as the presentation of the gifts of money during the offering). They will learn from merely looking round them and seeing a special table at the front, special symbols, special features like the prominent Bible and the raised pulpit.

Your task in those opening few minutes is to help all persons present to realize that they belong together, and that this is a preparation for our waiting upon God. The children belong just as essentially as do the veteran Christian adults sitting in the back pews. It is the Church of the children just as much as it is the Church of the adults. It is the children's worship time just as much as it is that of the adults, even if the children will soon depart and experience it in another part of the building. So your attitude should be a glad acceptance of the children. Try to make that opening act of worship as fitting as possible for such a family, covering a wide range of age and experience.

To give a children's address may not be very satisfactory, unless it will illuminate the theme that the children will later be considering in their own sessions. Nor does an entertainment have to be provided for them. If, however, a story can be briefly put across, which happens to be both illuminating and entertaining, so much the better. It is not your task to function as a special comic for the young, even though many of the adults would enjoy such light relief, but to facilitate Christian worship for everyone. Often some straightforward explanations of some aspect of the worship will help the children to participate more fully, but your aim should not be to single out a few moments as those which must be peculiarly for the children. It is primarily to make an adequate offering to God from the whole assembly. The special considerations which apply because of the presence of children are those which apply within Family Worship in general, so we will now concentrate upon those.

The structure of Family Worship is no different from that of normal Sunday worship. The purpose is the same, to give glory to God, hear his word and make a fitting response. The one difference, which should not be unduly exaggerated, is that the range of experience represented by the congregation is much wider. You must be alert to that range. Note three things as a result.

First, that the youngest end of the age range cannot be expected to concentrate on any one theme, or in any one posture, for very long. The different elements of the service need to be briefer than usual. The mood needs to change more frequently, the body needs to be in different positions, standing to sing or make the offering, sitting to listen, bowing for prayer, clapping or linking arms for some other part of the service, the style of the activity needs to vary. More than ever, the communication media need to be many, so that less weight is placed upon the spoken word and more given to pictures, drama and simple pageantry, chanting or speaking or singing together, and especially the use of symbols or demonstrations. We all know that it means little to be told that we consume on

203

average about 3,400 calories of food per day whereas elsewhere in the world poor people are lucky to get 1,200. It is another of those solemn statistics that bombard us all the time in the modern world and which regularly bounce off us again. But put an average English person's daily food supply on one plate in a prominent place at the front, and nearby put an average Indian peasant's. The effect of that contrast is shattering. That demonstration is unforgettable. The bare statistics are however a bore. We all learn more deeply from demonstration, from seeing with our eyes, but children need such help even more than adults.

A Family Service should not last long. About 50 minutes are adequate. The prayers cannot be of normal length, since young people find it even more difficult than adults to concentrate with the eyes closed; there may be more times of prayer, but each one very short and to the point. The hymns should not be long either, unless they accompany a procession or some movement which can capture the attention of the youngest. If there is a large congregation, let there be some action during the reception of the collection, or it can become a time for useless fidgeting. There should be a sermon of course, for this is the worship of the whole people of God, but it should be especially brief – maybe eight minutes long.

Secondly, there is even greater need for there to be wholesale participation in as much of the service as possible. If it is at all practicable for everyone to share in the prayers through some simple liturgy using, for example, the orders offered in *Together in Church*, or liturgies devised on the spot, so much the better. Let nothing be done by one voice or instrument that can be done as well by all, or several. There needs to be a leader, a central and controlling voice and person, but let that role be as minimal as possible. Let the worship involve young and old in every possible manner.

Thirdly, there is even more need than usual for clarity. This definitely does not mean that everything has to be so simplified that a toddler can understand it, but that everything is made as clear as possible. Many of our central beliefs and affirmations must of necessity be full of mystery to the most enlightened adult and will therefore defy total explanation and simplicity.

204

Christian people of all ages only grow by wrestling on and on with those glorious mysteries, whilst never comprehending them fully. So this is not a plea for complete comprehension of the massive themes that echo throughout Christian worship, but for the clearest possible expression of them. Elaborate, or archaic, or technical wording and phraseology should be avoided like the plague. The prayer that begins 'O thou ineffable ground of our being and predicate of our existence' is pompous and confusing at the best of times, but downright absurd in the context of Family Worship. The sermon about 'the essential paradox of the Saviour in his God-manhood' expresses the preacher's utter insensitivity. If a creed should be recited, better to use the Apostles than the Nicene, or the short one in the Baptism of Infants:

> We believe in God the Father
> who made the world;
> And in his Son, Jesus Christ,
> who redeemed mankind;
> And in the Holy Spirit,
> who sanctifies the people of God.

Clarity does not involve reducing deep and difficult themes or issues to such an elemtnary level that they become trite, but in expressing them as accurately as possible using the simplest words, but without that air of condescension whereby sometimes the pompous try to patronize the young. It is not, of course, a bad thing if some members of the congregation find themselves stretched by the material of the worship experience and the ideas that are involved. For every person worship should expand our abilities, enlarge our experience, broaden our knowledge, develop our imagination and our talents, stimulate our minds, challenge us to a bigger life, and help us to grow, however old or young we are. We should not claim nor believe that this is only possible when we are worshipping alongside others of roughly the same age and maturity. It happens in many subtle but significant ways when we are together in a community embracing all sorts of ages, types of person and ranges of ability. Some sorts of growth are only possible in the midst of such diversity. Thus Family Worship is not to be seen as a concession to the needs of children, who will benefit from being alongside the adults. Nor is it to be seen as a means of increasing the size of the congregation. It is a means of expressing the family character of the Christian community,' and enables everyone within that community to be enriched, both the strong and the weak, the young and the old, the rich and the poor, the learned and the unlearned, the men and the women. For we are all members of each other, all need each other, all contribute to each other's growth in Christ.

Special seasons and occasions

In chapter three the various strengths and weaknesses of the Liturgical Movement were discussed. Amongst the former was the renewed stress upon the importance of the Christian Year. The great festivals of Christian celebration should become the highlights of the Sunday worship. Of course, every preacher who follows the lectionary themes closely will be celebrating those festivals, since the lectionary is designed to enable that to happen. Every preacher who does not follow the lectionary themes ought nevertheless to make the major festivals of Advent, Christmas, Lent and Passion, Easter, Ascension and Pentecost into major celebrations of Christian truth built round the original events being rehearsed at that season. To fail to do this would be to falter very seriously in our basic duty to God's people.

In some cases the local congregation has made quite elaborate preparations and then wants you as preacher to fit in. The Youth Fellowship has prepared a nativity play for the Sunday before Christmas. The choir has obtained help from far and wide and will be offering an oratorio on Palm Sunday. The Sunday School will be mounting a display and doing playlets and special singing at the Harvest Festival. So be it. Your task, as always, is not to show resentment at what might be personally unsatisfying or which will reduce your significance within the worship. Rejoice, and work as constructively as possible with those others who are bringing their special contribution, aiming as always for a wholesome offering of worship to God.

But what about those great seasons for which you feel sadly

ill-fitted? You may have some difficulty in conceiving of the Holy Spirit and therefore in preaching about him, and even more problems with the doctrine of the Trinity on the Sunday after Pentecost. Aim, nevertheless, to help the people of God celebrate that aspect of its faith on that special day. Long beforehand, talk about the issue on every possible occasion to others and especially within fellowship groups, prayer circles, women's meetings. Share maybe the basic problem – 'I am due to preach here on Pentecost Sunday. I am not quite sure what to say or how to put it across. Can you help me.' It is likely to be an extremely valuable service if it springs from a tremendous tussle which has gone on in your heart and mind for weeks. The sermon is likely to be of great help to the many others who also have that travail in themselves. To be resolute about tackling the matters which are forbidding, difficult and surrounded by masses of questions, is to be growing in one's own faith and also offering the chance for others to travel the same road. So unless the time is too short or the difficulties insuperable, don't evade the awkward themes. This goes equally for preaching on the atonement during the preparation for Easter, and on the resurrection on Easter Day and Low Sunday. Great struggling is likely to make for better preaching.

There are other special occasions which have a more national origin, such as Remembrance Sunday, Education Sunday, Mothering Sunday, etc. It is wrong to ignore them, since the members of the congregation will come on that Sunday expecting some elements in the service to reflect that theme. You may well feel that such a theme should not be completely dominant on that day, but even so should express some helpful responses to it. Then there are special Sundays which the Christian Churches nationally or denominationally want remembered – the Week of Prayer for Christian Unity, Christian Aid week, Sundays for the Church Overseas or Home Mission or Christian Citizenship. Of course you should try to make those themes central and dominant in the worship, for each congregation is part of this larger national or denominational whole. Finally, there are the local occasions – Church Anniversary, Women's Sunday, and so on. The former is a magnificent opportunity to concentrate worship upon some

207

central aspect of the Church's life and mission. But those other occasions, geared to the interests of smaller groups within the congregation, should not be pooh-poohed. They offer the chance for the contribution of that group to the whole to be acknowledged gladly, the insights from that group to be shared more widely and, quite often, the participation of members of that group in the conduct of the service. There is much opportunity for good in such occasions.

But suppose you are asked to lead an act of worship and are told that it must be totally 'free'? That is, that particular Christian community may have developed a style of worship that is relaxed, participatory and unstructured. This may be due to the influence of the 'charismatic movement' as it is loosely called, or it may be because of the venue (e.g. in a student hostel). Enquiry usually shows that the worship is not so totally unstructured, but that there is an anticipated form (albeit, much less definable than the standard Free Church communion service). It may turn out to be something like this:

Singing and hymns
Praying, especially featuring invocation and thanksgiving
Scripture reading
Sharing of insights that have come to members during the week or of texts that have spoken with especial power
Sermon and, perhaps, comments
Praying, especially intercessions
Singing and hymns

or it may have even less predictability about it. So be it. It is not your task to dictate to a congregation what exactly the form of its customary worship is to be. There is a rightful place within the Christian tradition for a much more flexible shape, one in which it is much easier for everyone to make a contribution, one in which there may be far more stress than usual upon the gifts of the Holy Spirit. Then concur, unless it will be too difficult for your personality to cope with such a situation, or impossible to act with integrity because of deeply-held convictions. Most of us have a great deal to learn from the happy spontaneity of some such Christian groups, just as it is quite possible that they too have a lot to learn from more developed styles and our more orthodox allegiance to the whole corpus of

208

Christian belief. You are not called upon to be a liturgical snob, but to be sensitive to Christians of all sorts everywhere and at all times, so as to be better able to represent the Church catholic in the leadership of worship.

Evangelistic services

Within the worship of most congregations there is a place for the service in which the Gospel news will be offered and the members of the congregation given appropriate ways of responding to it in repentance, faith and commitment. There is an especial obligation upon the preacher to handle such an occasion with sensitivity and a basic respect for persons. Their intelligence should not be by-passed by the recitation of texts as if they are slogans which resolve all problems. Sweeping half-truths should not be paraded as the will of God. Music evoking a nostalgic sleepiness should be avoided. The pyrotechnics and exhibitionism of the great crowd manipulators are not at home within the Christian Church. Sunday worship is not an occasion for the flamboyance of the mass orator. The normal canons of Christian worship apply and deserve respect; bad theology is as abhorrent here as it ever is. There are particular dangers which the faithful preacher avoids.

First, it is disrespectful and inaccurate to treat the whole congregation as if it is made up of outrageous sinners who all need to be converted. It will consist of many devout, experienced and graceful saints who have tasted more of the mercy of God, in all likelihood, than many preachers. There will be old veterans who have held the faith through all sorts of personal tragedies and testings, others who have made enormous personal sacrifices for the will of God and the life of the Church, others who have profound mystic awareness of the reality of God, and some who are at that moment engaged in small but quite heroic efforts to maintain a Christian witness. How dare someone treat those choice saints as if they were pagans estranged from God, all needing to take the first steps in discipleship!

Secondly, it is quite unhelpful and crassly unimaginative to imply that every Christian has the same pattern of religious

209

experience whereby the same stages are gone through in the same predictable succession. It is naïve to assume, for instance, that one basic sequence through which all must pass is that of awareness of personal sin and guilt, desire to be saved from them both, commitment to Christ in faith, then discovery of forgiveness and renewal. Some persons undoubtedly have an experience of that shape and order. Many others don't. Some have an experience of a sense of purposelessness, then a steady discovery of the value and aim of life as it is in Christ, then a growing sense of commitment and, perhaps last, a growing sense of personal unworthiness or sin. Others do not experience that last stage in any powerful way at all. Some fortunate people grow up in a world which has always been God's, and have never ever known what it is like seriously to doubt him. Others have never had any sort of background belief in God whatever, and only begin to develop one after their commitment to Christ, however logically odd that may seem. There is thus no standard person, no standard series of religious stages to be gone through, no formal pattern to which all must adhere. Any evangelism which assumes such a standard pattern is out of touch with reality, and may bruise and bewilder those persons whose growth in Christ doesn't follow that pattern at all.

Thirdly, there is the constant danger of urging people to be committed to 'Christ' without spelling out its possible meanings, so that the word 'Christ' acts as a blanket title to an unknown package. Often this is done as if there is one supreme moment of commitment, the central and traumatic one, and that the consequences are self-evident. But the consequences are not obvious at all, and in practice every person goes on discovering what commitment to Christ means right through life and then beyond death. At every point of my pilgrimage Christ has new commitments, discoveries, challenges, reassurances, resources and visions for me. Thus, as an example, here is a decision sheet used at an evangelistic service, designed to enable each worshipper to make an appropriate commitment to Christ whatever the circumstances, experience, situation.

I will:
Begin a new pattern of personal devotion . . . .

210

Make my financial giving to Church and charity
  more realistic   ......
Become a member of the Church   ......
Do my Church job(s) better by being more diligent
  and/or seeking extra training   ......
Offer to work for the Church in
  fellowship/house groups   ......
  Sunday School or youth work   ......
  Visiting or acting as a steward   ......
  Local preaching or ministry   ......
Offer to give up a Church job I am not doing well
  or should pass on to others   ......
Do serious study of the Christian faith   ......
Give up habits and attitudes I know to be wrong   ......
Make all my personal relationships more loving   ......
Change my work for something more worthwhile   ......
Commit myself to social or community or political
  work in the field of ....
Commit my life wholly to Christ and his Church   ......

This sheet is not ideal. It focuses much attention on Church life and little upon life in the world, but it attempts to facilitate new commitment for every member of the congregation, which is what evangelism in the context of Christian worship should do. Some Christians, of course, would find the use of any such sheet unpalatable.

The preceding warnings may sound excessively negative. Is there not a vital place within the normal worshipping life of the congregation for the challenge to repentance, the new birth, commitment and surrender? Manifestly there is, and within a healthy Church life that challenge will recur constantly, but not monotonously, and will be geared to every Christian person and not just to the youngsters who have not explicitly made a Christian commitment and confession. Because at this point we are talking about the heart of the Church's life, it is especially important for preachers to be in touch with the congregation's pastors (minister, youth leaders, elders, stewards, pastoral committees) before acting independently and out of a conviction that it is time for some envangelistic note to be

211

sounded next Sunday. Evangelism too should spring out of the Church's life, not be imposed upon it by someone who feels that it will do that congregation good to experience it for a change.

Planning and consultation

Constantly during these recent chapters we have been returning to the same themes – consulting people beforehand, planning well ahead, sharing the preparation of the sermon and service with others. The preacher has been presented as a person who has to act along with many others for the sake of the congregation, not as a person who acts over against the congregation. Many churches have now developed formal channels through which such consultation can take place. In Methodist churches, for example, there is now provision for the Consultation on Worship, which is more likely to function effectively in the larger congregations. Other churches have similar bodies, or may appoint an ad hoc group from members of the Church Council or Deacons or Elders. Whenever this happens it is likely to be a good sign. It indicates a church trying to take its worship-life much more seriously, trying to work out more satisfactory forms of worship, trying to bring about a more thorough sharing of skills and resources. Let every preacher co-operate with such bodies as constructively as possible.

At first sight it seems simple to suggest that a special service should be designed by, say, you as preacher and a small group with particular talents. As mentioned before, it is in practice a very big task involving hours and hours of preparation, discussion, suggestions being amended then tried out again, and maybe rehearsals in the church concerned. Such time is usually very well spent indeed. It has the same sort of richness as a good fellowship meeting plus the added advantage of a goal to work towards. For the group concerned, it is likely to be an experience of genuine Christian growth. Although special services often need an inordinate amount of time to prepare, they provide fine opportunity for this growth and should not be scorned.

There are other ways in which preachers may make more

212

thorough and detailed shared preparation. A group of preachers can plan to share the conduct of worship together, or to prepare a sequence of services which will develop a particular theme. This is usually called 'team preaching' and is outlined in the leaflet *Team Preaching and Planned Preaching* (L.P. Office). The team of preachers becomes in effect a specific fellowship called together for this purpose, and can be an important means of support and training to each member. Join such a group if you can. If there is none, but a desire for one, then start it yourself. Remember that such groups often function best when they have a short life, long enough to accomplish one project. Then disband, but try to start a fresh one with perhaps a different membership soon afterwards and for a similarly short time.

Chapter 10

More practical matters

Preparation

A GREAT deal of the previous chapters has been devoted to the tasks of preparing services and sermons, but there are some final stages. To repeat the end of chapter six, it is almost always necessary to work right through the sermon after its initial completion and to check its language carefully. It is at first somewhat depressing to discover how many times you can do this exercise and still find ways of improving the previous drafts. The glib phrases need to be ironed out; the religious clichés need to be replaced; the technical theological terms which only the few will understand need to be simplified (a process which may not alter their meaning – it may actually improve it). The grammatical errors need to be corrected. So you may find phrases like 'In the providential mercy of God', which probably needs to be changed into something like 'Thanks to God's care ...'; 'those who are washed in the blood of the Lamb' needs to be replaced by something like 'Converted persons'; 'righteousness' can be simplified to 'being put right with God' (which is an accurate rendering of the New Testament term in most of its usages); sentences like 'The troubles in Ireland makes religion look divisive' needs to be corrected to 'The troubles in Ireland make ...'.

Long sentences with many subordinate clauses need to be changed into several short and sharp ones, which make it much easier for the listener to be gripped by the subject. Thus a sentence like 'Whenever you think about the cross you must not think of it as ordinary, although lots of people were killed by that method in Jesus' day, because of the cruelty of the Romans who used it to deter the rebels amongst the Jews and

214

valued it as a gruesome sort of spectacle, but you must think of it as having a sense of religious disgrace about it also because the Jews had a horror of a corpse being on show, probably based upon the Old Testament text which says 'Cursed be he who hangs upon a tree' and, of course, the sense of awe that everyone has in the presence of death, which is really something we all share in ...'. Such a long-winded ramble needs to be split up into something like this: 'When you think about the cross, don't just regard it as something ordinary. True, the Romans killed off lots of enemies in that cruel way. They thought it a fine deterrent against rebels. It made a gruesome enough spectacle. But remember that there was a religious horror about it too. Jews had a sense of awe in the presence of a corpse, as do we. They also had a command in the Old Testament which reads 'Cursed be he who hangs upon a tree''.' That meandering sentence has been turned into seven sentences. Nothing has been lost, but a noticeable crispness has been gained. It will now make for much more interesting and arresting speech from the pulpit. So, work through the sermon yet again, looking for the cumbrous sentences which have umpteen subordinate clauses, and re-write them.

Similarly, watch out for every chance to get in a vivid phrase, a word or two with a touch of originality that will jog the listener and then stick in the memory afterwards. Thus, you are telling the story of Zaccheus and you find yourself writing something like 'Zaccheus was short, so he climbed up a sycamore tree to see Jesus better. When the Lord passed he noticed him there and stopped and said "Zaccheus, come down. I want to come to your house".' It is all ordinary, predictable stuff, the speech being as drab as a Lancashire slum. Try re-writing it, and it may turn into something like this – 'Zaccheus was a tiny fellow, the sort we would have called "a titch" at school. He'd scrambled up a sycamore tree to get a better view of Jesus. How absurd for the richest racketeer in town! Jesus saw him stuck up there and shouted out "Hey, Zaccheus! Come on down and throw me a party".' The drabness has all gone, and the account now has some sparkle in it. It's that sparkle that we are after in our preaching. Some people seem to have a natural flair for it. They are lucky. They will easily get people's attention. The rest of us have to keep working away at it by constant practice.

The same sort of checking is needed with the prayers. They too need to be direct, to utilize a minimum of words, to get to the point boldly and clearly. Sometimes we are especially shy of using bright or cheerful language in prayers, feeling that it is irreverent. But what does that mean? It means that we feel that perhaps God is not really pleased with it. But why not? Why should God be considered to be a serious Professor of Medieval English totally lacking in any sense of humour or fun? The more you think about it, the more you must acknowledge that that is not the picture of God we are given in the New Testament, nor the sort whom Jesus told us to address as 'Daddy'. (*Abba*). Let the language of prayer flash with streaks of originality and poetry as much as the rest of the public speech in the service. God does not want us to be even more boring when speaking to him than when speaking to each other.

The other sort of checking and re-checking concerns time. It is extremely difficult to estimate how long a sermon will take. There is only one reasonably satisfactory way – to speak it out loud at the sort of pace and volume which will be required in the church building for the service. All sorts of surprises then await us. Some sermons which we had confidently expected to be short turn out to be just right; some we thought to be ideal turn out to be far too long or (sometimes) far too short. Some passages now seem to be tedious or even turgid; others seem to skip their way through important matters far too quickly. It is only the preliminary run-through that can make some of these imbalances clear. Thus you set out to take a service having already spoken through (in your own bedroom or study) those parts that depend upon your own speaking and composition. As a very rough guide, expect to speak 100 words a minute.

Time and dress

Try to get to an appointment 15 minutes before the service is to begin. You need that time to take a preliminary look at the building and its layout, to consult the stewards about the details of the service, to consult with the organist or choirmaster about

216

the music, and to be suitably composed in yourself. It simply does not matter if you arrive half an hour early, but it matters greatly if you arrive at the last minute and everything is rushed in order to propel you into the pulpit on time.

In our culture you should aim to be dressed well, as if going to a wedding or similar function. We are not meant to be dressed casually, since this is no casual occurrence, but the worship of Almighty God. We are not meant to be dressed in formal black either, since this is no funeral. We are meant to be at our best, in such a way as to add dignity and a slightly formal touch of joyousness to the proceedings. Some churches expect the preachers to wear a gown. The right response is to do whatever the local church expects unless there is overwhelming conscientious reason for not doing so. After all, the worship is that of the Church, not an event when the individual desires or foibles of the particular preacher require meek subservience from everyone else. On the other hand there are some churches, especially smaller rural ones, where there is a long-standing dislike of gowns and anything else that could be construed to be 'churchy' or 'liturgical' or 'priestly' or (horror of horrors) 'catholic'. If that be so it is not the calling of the preacher to defy such scruples, nor to attack them head-on and force a confrontation with such a 'foolish' crowd. Your task is to lead worship in such a way that, as far as possible, everyone present is indeed led to God and enabled to offer God his due. So meet the congregation's wishes as long as these do not threaten personal integrity. When in churches that prefer gowns, wear one. When in those that abhor gowns, don't wear one. After all, this issue is trivial and not worth getting too heated about.

In the vestry beforehand

The 15 minutes before the service spent in the vestry is precious time. It helps you to get attuned to the place and people, to get the feel of the congregation. It is a halfway stage between an ordinary journey through the ordinary world and the special worship of God, who is Lord of the extraordinary. Use the time to find out as much as possible about the service, about the way things are done here, about the life of this congrega-

217

tion, about their expectations, about whether or not everyone will be singing or saying the Lord's Prayer, about the taking of the collection, the reading of notices, special features this week, special considerations. Is anyone seriously sick or in need of special prayer? Are there any special items for our thanksgiving or confesson or intercession? Is there special music to be used at the most fitting time in the worship? Is there anything in particular which the preacher will be expected to do? As always, the rule is to do what is asked of one unless there is very grave reason for refusing.

Sometimes the stewards enquire tentatively whether or not you will read the notices. As a normal rule, it is better for the steward to do so. This involves a change of voice, and there is absolutely no reason why the preacher should be expected to do it, but many reasons why it is more suitable to be done by the appointed person of the local congregation. Sometimes the stewards or elders greet you with an outline form of service, mention that this is 'the order', and then ask for the details of hymns and lessons to be entered into the appropriate slots in the standardized sequence. If this order seems quite all right to the preacher, so be it. If it appears to be unsuitable, ask first if it can be changed, say why, and then try to proceed with changes if the stewards or elders are in support. They are there to represent that congregation, so their views are significant and their co-operation is necessary. In the vast majority of cases nowadays they are quite willing for changes to be made in a routine order provided that they can see the sense in doing so. There has grown up a much more flexible attitude towards the ordering of worship during the last 30 to 40 years. But in all such discussion courtesy is not merely an old-world virtue; it is a permanent part of the Christian character. Let it be exercised in the vestry, and the ordering of the service be determined finally by that grace.

Before going into the church you hope that there will be a prayer for the worship. That is not really the preacher's job, but for those who have received the preacher on behalf of the congregation. You may be asked to lead a prayer with the choir, in which case make it brief and to the point. Then, when going into the church, check that the notes for the service and sermon are to hand, that the necessary hymn-books and Bibles and perhaps other books (for prayers or readings) are available.

In the church

Expensive girls' schools used to lay great stress on 'deportment'. They probably still do. They regarded it as very important for girls to be taught how to walk with dignity, how to smile and shake hands without drooping the shoulders and imitating the jelly-fish, how to bow and curtsy, how to sit so as to look both relaxed and alert, how to walk out of a room. It sounds old-fashioned to us today, yet preachers need 'deportment' and, when you think of it, so do teachers and Lord Mayors and concert pianists and anyone else on public show. Preachers should not droop their shoulders, or shamble into the church, or trip on the pulpit stairs, or gaze fixedly at their shoes. Preachers should be grateful to God for their bodies (as should all Christians), and then want to honour God with the way they use them during the service. Stand *up*, O men (or women) of God, the Church for you doth wait. Leading worship is bound to mean being upright for all to see as clearly as possible, since all have to take a lead from the preacher. So stand up clearly, for all to both see and hear. Walk uprightly, for nobody need be ashamed to be a preacher.

If it be a church featuring both a lectern as well as pulpit, it may be normal for the first part of the worship to be conducted from the former, only the sermon to be preached from the pulpit, and maybe the subsequent closing prayers to be taken again from the lectern or the communion table. That is something you should find out beforehand. There is no over-riding necessity for such movement in the service, but it is not a bad thing. Movement adds to interest. The reservation of the pulpit for the preaching alone is one way of making visible how important the preaching is, so it is placed 'high over all'. Common sense tells us that the offering prayer should be spoken from the communion table and that the gifts should be received there, so again some simple movements are required of the preacher. Let them be done with dignity and head held high, but do not be too solemn.

Every person has distinctive mannerisms. That is one of the many little things that makes each person so unique and interesting. Most of us are quite unaware of our pet oddities at this point. They can become very irritating to others since, being preachers, we are on show for an hour. The preacher who is for ever scratching his head, stroking the chin, twiddling her curls, fondling the wrist, fiddling with glasses, can drive some listeners to distraction, and can become a household joke. For this reason every preacher needs a honest critic (husband or wives are often useful in this connection) who will keep a close eye on the eccentricities and point out when they are becoming an annoyance or absurdity.

Almost every person accompanies speech with some sort of gesture; very few of us remain utterly motionless when talking to others. The gestures help to illustrate our speech, help to give it a sense of urgency, help to make it appeal both to the ear and the eye, give it some visible focus which moves along with the movement of the speech and thought. So you are not meant to stand like a sentry, impassive and inscrutable. Your speech should come from a moving, living, throbbing body. But the gestures should assist the speech. They should not be so extravagant that people's attention is captured by your antics rather than speech; they should not appear to be contrived, as if you are a clockwork toy wound up for the occasion and now going through the requisite jerks; they should appear to be natural and true to the subject matter. If you are referring to the 'wideness of God's mercy' of course it is right for your hands to be held out as widely as possible. If the reference is to pleading, or praying, or embracing, or threatening, or welcoming, or triumphing, your hands and body should demonstrate that theme, that emotion. The expression, the stance, the tension of your body, all help to express the message. What matters is that they do indeed help to express the message, and not divert from it. But God deliver us from statues in the pulpit, even if they are speaking ones.

However, the major worry with most preachers occurs over the use of the voice. All sorts of things can go wrong, and the average congregation has within it several people who are much quicker to reprove a preacher over a bad voice than over bad theology. It depends greatly upon the setting. In small churches there is a great temptation to relax into a conversational style and level; it is almost always wrong, because the building is not quite small enough for that (it would have to be the size of the average living-room). In medium-sized buildings there is no alternative but constantly to throw the voice to the back of the church (where the deaf people usually sit) and to regard the back door as the target for each word spoken. In large churches there is probably a microphone and the technique is totally different. You need to stand in front of it and not to stray too far on either side, then to speak clearly as if in a large room. The clarity of the speech will matter much more than the volume, and if you want to woo the congregation with a strong whisper let it be from very close indeed to the microphone and then, when the speech level is returning to normal, stand back again or the people will get a great booming bellowing noise from the apparatus. Do not sing loudly into it, either.

The commonest faults occur with our tendency to drop the voice at the end of sentences, or to miss the final consonants of words so that their endings are slurred into the beginnings of the next ones. Then again, it is all too easy to 'go stiff' in the pulpit so that the voice is kept at one level all the time. It then sounds weary and monotonous. We need to develop the full range of the voice, the deep power at the bass levels, the light soaring of the soprano levels, and all the ranges in between. We need too to vary the pace of delivery, to use pauses, and then rapid spurts, and then a steady run, and so on. It is impossible to teach this by writing about it here. You need that honest critic who has been specially asked to watch out for all these points. Quite often there are skilled people available in the life of the church – speech therapists, dramatists, teachers, elocutionists – who can be asked for help if necessary. If you genuinely want to fulfil this difficult vocation well, be perfectly willing to gain the advice and help of such experts. In most cases only one or two simple lessons suffice to iron out the major faults.

The constant use of 'um' is really a matter of nervousness. 'Jesus went up – um – to the mount – um – and his three

221

disciples – um – with him and – um – he went aside to pray and – um – then there shone – um – a light from heaven'. Usually the preacher is quite unaware that this is actually the sound being made. The remedy is in constant practice, on learning to *face* the congregation and look each one in the eye, of acquiring confidence. It takes time, of course. One of the most useful exercises for such a nervous person is to use some period early in the service, such as the opening hymn, to look carefully round at every face present, to take in the features, and to be quietly thanking God for every such person. That exercise helps to establish rapport, check nerves and create mutual strength. The other way of monitoring your pulpit speech is to use a tape recorder and record those parts of the service which depend upon your spoken voice – prayers, lessons, sermon – and play it back afterwards. It is of course a bewildering experience at first. Does my voice really sound like *that*? I can't believe it! I never realized that I speak so fast, or so slow, or at such high pitch, or in such solemn tones. We ourselves are the worst possible judges of our own speaking unless we have heard it as other persons have to hear it. At first it is slightly weird, but the obvious faults are much more likely now to be obvious to us too. Soon you get accustomed to your own speech and, just as in the Christian life as a whole we have to learn to accept our basic selves and then work steadily at their growth in Christ, so we learn to accept that peculiar voice and to set about its improvement. In this task, draw upon the resources of the more skilled whenever possible. But also listen to the really skilled people, especially when they are appearing on television or radio, and notice the way they control pace and pitch, put music into their sentences, lay stress upon certain phrases and syllables so as to bring interesting light and shade, how they use pauses to great effect, how they sometimes build up the intensity within a sentence until it reaches a climax upon the concluding and crucial word.

Don't worry about accent or dialect unless it is so thick or extreme that no normal person can understand it. A slight amount of dialect in your speech makes it far more interesting. Worry however if your speech sounds so high falutin or sophisticated or 'upper class' that the average person in the congregation will be put off by it; worry too if it sounds so rough and ready and uncultured that that average listener will again be put off or tempted to smile condescendingly. Watch out for the standard faults, and if you hear yourself saying 'Hi think this imm his evenly, heven if it as a igh tune, friends', then get your honest critic or some other mentor to teach you the place of 'h' in English speech.

Few services proceed without some sort of distraction or other. Babies cry. Children snigger or shuffle about. Somebody drops a hymn-book, and someone else drops their glasses. A bird flutters in through an open window and cannot get out again. An elderly person turns up a hearing aid by mistake and it emits loud crackling noises. Don't worry, that's a normal part of life. Just keep going as if nothing untoward has happened, because if you are put off then everyone else will definitely get distracted. If you can act as a centre of steady interest, that helps to hold the general attention. This applies if a toddler escapes from the parents and goes wandering about in the aisles or up in the front, or if there is someone who is mentally handicapped and keeps doing odd things, or if something unfortunate occurs which makes everyone turn to stare (e.g. if someone faints). Keep going as if nothing has happened. Do not rebuke naughty children or giggly teenagers or anyone else being a slight nuisance, but it may be right to have a private word with such people afterwards. As for the people that rustle sweet paper the moment the sermon begins, one can do little about them except ignore the disturbance. Those people who like to help the preacher along with the occasional grunt, or the 'Amen', or even 'Hallelujah', thank God in your own heart for them. Black preaching carries tremendous power in the black congregation because this support for the preacher is highly developed. It is a powerful way of participation and of urging the preacher along, and was once very popular in many Free Church congregations. There is nothing wrong with it whatever, but it is most likely to be found today in the countryside or in small inner-city congregations.

After the service

None of us can manage a difficult and exposed task like that of

223

leading public worship unless we can be given regular reassurance. Most members of the congregation know this only too well. The remarks at the end of the service are usually not very significant beyond their saying 'Thank you for being a preacher. Keep going'. Many people do not know how to say that, so will merely offer something like 'I enjoyed your service' or something slightly banal. There is no point in getting worried because people mentioned 'enjoying' the service. The remark is not meant as a careful theological reflection upon the nature of Christian worship, but as a polite encouragement. If all that was said was 'I enjoyed those hymns' there is no need to take offence. It is meant as an encouragement, and not as a subtle way of saying 'Your preaching is appalling'.

However, we are all human flesh and blood and we crave for as much psychological support as we can get. We tend to depend upon our own feelings and our sense of atmosphere in order to get the needed reassurance. We tell our friends afterwards that we had 'a great time' or 'a great feeling of fellowship' or 'tremendous freedom' or something of the sort. Beware. Don't build up your confidence as a preacher by relying upon what you presume to have been the emotional tone of the services you have conducted. Christians especially ought to know how deceptive our own feelings are, and how great is the capacity of the self to be deluded about its own condition. Christians should be firm believers in the remarkable ability of all men to suffer self-delusion when it suits their egos. But Christians especially should know that, in the profoundest sense, we are not justified by what we *feel* nor, of course, by what we say or what others say about us, nor, for that matter, by the intrinsic excellence or otherwise of the service. We are only justified by grace through faith. What 'justifies' the worship we lead is whether or not we do indeed offer it trustingly to God and begin and end it in that trusting sense of 'This is my offering, Lord. In your mercy perfect it'.

Christian worship has all sorts of peculiar and unpredictable results. A friend was serving in the army and wandered into a chapel one Sunday evening because it had started to rain. He remembers it as an artless service, with a small elderly congregation and a dull preacher. But that event transformed his life, initiated his conversion, and it may well be that the preacher still doesn't know. People are 'spoken to' in many an act of Christian worship, and nobody else may ever know anything whatever about it. A woman whose marriage is a hell receives from the reading a sentence that enables her to hold her life together; a man living in dread that his wife is mortally ill is arrested by a line in a hymn and is given the access to remarkable spiritual resources; a young person follows the prayers and emerges from the church convinced that a whole new career must be embarked upon at once, before it is too late; a person feels that a passage or sentence in the sermon was directly spoken into his or her heart and may even say to the preacher afterwards 'How did you know about me in order to say what you did?'. It is all, in the best sense of the word, mysterious. Christians try to grope towards that mystery by saying that God's Holy Spirit is at work within Christian worship, or may express it by saying that the worship conveys God's 'Word'. Those terms are merely religious symbols, tokens, pointing to that sublime and almighty mystery which is the Being and Work of the Living God. We believe profoundly in the Holy Spirit, and rejoice in all this quiet and often secretive work of his. But do not constantly look out for these tokens and signs, as if we are flops unless such things are for ever happening to us or within our experience. That smacks of unfaith, of wanting to be justified by evident results, of wanting to make our own personal religion into a success story with ourselves at the centre. We should never seek our reassurance from such quarters; but we should be full of gratitude and joy whenever such encouragements come our way. They are a bonus. The regular reward from God is simply the knowledge that we are doing His will and Making the sort of offering which His Church needs from us.

So you go home after the service, not too elated because someone said some nice things, not too depressed if nobody did. If however you know in your heart that things went badly, that you muffed the sermon or bored the row of young people at the back or chose all the wrong hymns or tackled the wrong sort of subject, what then? Pray for forgiveness, and try to learn as much as possible from the experience. In the end, in the hard

225

school of life into which God in his mercy has tipped us, we actually learn as much (or even more) from our failures as from our successes – if we want to, that is. If you prefer instead to nurse hurt pride, or to feel bitter towards that horrible congregation, or to wallow in self-pity, nothing whatever that is good will come out of it. Sin will have a field day. You can choose to turn even the most unpleasant incidents into material for growth, and in that event you will be asking yourself what went wrong, how it can be averted in future, whether or not the preparation was a fault or you had misjudged something. If you are baffled, share the experience with others. Never let it remain as a guilty secret locked up inside you, for there it will fester unless it can be opened up and released.

Preachers should keep records of what they do, and where and when. Nothing very elaborate is needed, just a good notebook and a discipline of using it every time you conduct a service. The record should contain details of sermons preached, order of service and lessons and hymns and prayers used. Should you use a sermon twice, or more? Of course. John Wesley is reputed to have said that a sermon wasn't much good until it had been preached 20 times. There is some point in that remark. After you have preached a sermon you reflect and find all sorts of ways of improving it. Then, next time round, it should be a better offering, and an even better one the next time after that, and so on. There comes a time however when it begins to get stale and too well worn. At that point, put it away into storage, and maybe in a few years' time go back to it and find material for a completely fresh start at that theme. Moreover, you find that constant preaching makes your theology develop, expand, change. After a year or so you find that you can no longer preach the same sort of statement again. It seems inadequate. You want to get at the issue in a different way, using different sets of ideas. So the old sermon must go into a limbo, to be totally recast, perhaps much later, after it has had a decent rest.

Much of this notion, of using and re-using sermons until they are played out, assumes that there will be opportunity for such repetition. If however you adopt a strict practice of only preaching upon the lectionary passages and themes this will

226

not be so. You can only preach that first-time sermon again in two years' time when the lectionary cycle has come round again. This is a reason for not necessarily sticking with inflexible determination to the lectionary themes; another reason is of course that the average preacher cannot be expected to make a new sermon every time there is another appointment to be honoured. If you have six appointments to fill in a quarter it would be hard work to prepare six new sermons. The congregations might be better served if one new sermon were prepared and used three times, and two older ones were repeated. In all of this, there are no immutable laws laid down in heaven, or even in the headquarters of the denominations, thank God.

Training never ends

No Christian will ever claim to be perfect. Most will find it hard to admit that they have made much progress upon the long road to such a goal. Those who do not think about the Christian life in terms of perfection, or movement towards a goal, will confess to profound unease if ever asked 'Are you fulfilling God's will for your life?' or 'Do you believe that you are whole as a Christian?' or, to use the popular way of putting it in modern theology, 'Are you truly human?'. We can never give a plain and satisfied answer to that sort of question. The Christian life is for ever a matter of pressing on, growing, discovering new wholeness, finding new dimensions to human life under God. It is for ever a matter of being intensely dissatisfied with where you are and what sort of person you are and what sort of offering you make to God by living like this. There are often, in addition, those very dark periods in which your experience seems to be under grave threat or in deep shadows. The preacher is no exception to this, but may indeed be even more aware than others of the ongoing muddle of faith and doubt, glory and tragedy, grace and sin, that is the stuff of our Christian existence. So preachers in particular know that Christian life is a matter of perpetual movement. We never stand still in the Christian life, but God is for ever calling us on.

In addition to this basic Christian factor in our existence it is also obvious that preaching is a matter of skills, of technique. A preacher is a special sort of artist. No artist ever imagines that

227

he has perfected his art. No craftsman who has any ability whatever will ever pretend that the craft is mastered. So the preacher has to live both as a growing Christian, but also as a craftsman or artist for ever trying to improve his skills. Thus the faithful preacher does not say with relief when the exams are all passed and the Church's commission has been received 'Ah, what a relief! Now I can stop having to learn and be trained. I have arrived at the destination. The Church says so, and I have a Bible plate from someone in Westminster to prove it.' The training for all of us merely enters into a new phase when the initial period of apprenticeship is over and the 'qualified work' has commenced. We are never in a position to stop in our tracks and freeze our development. Preachers should know what it is to be always growing, always searching, always probing into things, always wrestling with theology and the Bible, always trying to become more alert to God and man. If we cannot be like that we cannot help other Christians. We cannot speak for the Church, which is God's people on pilgrimage. We cannot quite know what it is to live by faith.

So this chapter has to end with a simple plea to the reader to grasp at every possible opportunity for further growth and training. Prize the fellowship of other Christians through which you can grow in understanding and ability as a theologian. Prize the chances offered by all sorts of agencies today whereby you can master more of the Bible, the Christian tradition, Christian thinking, whether those agencies be from within your local church or through your denomination and its facilities, whether from other Churches or secular agencies like a University extra-mural department. Prize every opportunity to build up a library of Christian knowledge and reflection, every opportunity to develop the skills of communication by which you have to express this craft. In the end, prize every opportunity for your life to be used by God.

Check list for the sermon

HERE is a suggested check list to apply to your sermons, or to be given to an honest critic who listens to them. The list is only a suggested one; you may feel that other questions should also be posed, or some of these may be dropped. In that case build up your own check list, using this one as a basis.

(1) What is the aim?
    Is this aim simple and clear?
    Is this aim realistic?
    What type of sermon is it?
    Is there a clear structure?
    Does the sermon attempt to convey or achieve too much?
                                                    too little?

(2) Is the introduction an arresting one?
    What are the main affirmations?
    Are these true to the Christian tradition?
    Are they satisfactorily related to the biblical material used?
    Is the Bible being misused at all?
    Is the conclusion an appropriate climax?
    Does it enhance our appreciation of Christ?

(3) Is there some imaginative material here? Or useless fantasy?
    Are the language and concepts too technical or scholarly?
                                  too old-fashioned?
                                  too dependent on religious clichés?
                                  too colloquial?

229

Are the sentences short and crisp?
Is the grammar correct?

(4) Is this sermon interesting?
Does it raise major problems and then avoid them?
Are there sufficient illustrations and stories?
Do these actually illuminate the issues being presented?
What is the most memorable section?
Is this profound enough to be worth remembering?
Is the sermon worth hearing again?

Check list for the service

AGAIN, this is only a suggested check list and different readers may wish to add to or subtract from it. Because this is more likely to be used by your 'honest critic' than by you it is cast in the past tense, so as to be shared later with you.

(1) Were the major stages of the service clear?
Was the approach to God effective?
Was there a satisfactory offering of praise and adoration? confession and forgiveness?
Were the prayers expressing good Christian theology?
Was their language fresh, clear, helpful?

(2) Were the biblical passages integral to the main theme?
Which translation(s) was used and was this the most suitable?
Were the readings so introduced as best to convey their meaning?
Was there any effort to convey the message by other means than Bible reading and preaching?
Could other means (e.g. drama, symbolism, visual aids) have been used profitably?
If such means were used, were they effective?

(3) Was the sermon's conclusion followed up adequately?
Were the intercessions and petitions suitable?
Were these prayers expressing good Christian theology?
Was their language fresh, clear, helpful?
Was there an appropriate time given to thanksgiving?
silence?
commitment?

Was the congregation helped to be involved in the prayers?

Were the prayers of the right length?

(4) Were the hymns right for that stage of the service?
Were they satisfactory in their theology?
Were they sufficiently varied in length, mood and metre?
Did they prove suitable for that congregation to sing?

(5) Did the preacher have annoying mannerisms?
Did the preacher use appropriate movements and gestures?
Was the preacher's deportment good?
Did the preacher convey the impression of excessive
nervousness?
over-confidence?
carelessness?
Was the preacher's voice range well utilized?
Did the preacher vary the pace of delivery well?
Were the readings and sermon made interesting by the stresses being well placed on some sentences, phrases, words?
Was the preacher always audible?

(6) Was the whole order satisfactory?
Have you any further comments to help the preacher?

Bibliography

Chapter One
An interesting introduction to the need for worship as a joyous celebration of God is in Harvey Cox: *The Feast of Fools* (SCM). A very thorough and readable introduction to all the major forces at work upon the Churches today is David Edwards: *Religion and Change* (Hodder), or a study from a journalist's standpoint is available in David Perman: *Change and the Churches* (Bodley Head). A more serious theological study is in J. G. Davies: *Everyday God* (SCM) of which the second part is especially useful. J. G. Davies also edited *A Dictionary of Liturgy and Worship* (SCM) which is a major reference work.

Chapter Two
A clear introduction to the theme of the opening section of this chapter is in G. F. D. Moule: *Worship in the New Testament* (Lutterworth). For the Methodist background see Henry Bett: *The Spirit of Methodism* (Epworth, but long out of print) or Gordon Wakefield: *Methodist Devotion* and John Bowmer: *The Lord's Supper in early Methodism* (Dacre). For the wider background see also Horton Davies: *The Worship of the English Puritans* (Dacre), and if at all possible see the classic little study by Bernard Manning: *The Hymns of Wesley and Watts* (Epworth, but again long out of print). See too Arnold Clay: *What is the Lord's Supper?* (Epworth).

Chapter Three
The major work which goes into elaborate detail is Gregory Dix: *The Shape of the Liturgy* (Dacre), but the ground is

233

covered well and the implications for contemporary worship are neatly sketched out in Michael Taylor: *Variations on a Theme* (Galliard). The teaching of the Liturgical Movement concerning both the worship and mission of the Church is interestingly outlined in A. Shands: *The Liturgical Movement and the Local Church* (SCM) although the examples are mainly American. See also, if you can borrow it, or obtain it in a library, R. J. Billington *The Liturgical Movement and Methodism* (Epworth). The most fascinating study of the worship, art, preaching, and theology within all the English Churches in this century is Horton Davies: *Worship and Theology in England*, vol. v, 1900–1965 (Oxford). A small but lively book expressing criticism of some recent trends is T. G. A. Baker: *Concerning Worship* (SCM). See also *The Daily Office*, by the Joint Liturgical Group (Epworth and SPCK), and for morning and evening offices, a daily lectionary and other prayers see *The Daily Office Revised* (SPCK).

Chapter Four
See first David Stacey: *Interpreting the Bible* (Sheldon) and, of course, the same author's *Groundwork of Biblical Studies* (Epworth). The best discussion on the place of the Old Testament is in John Bowker: *What about the Old Testament?* (SCM). There is a longer scholarly work which deals especially with preaching from the Old Testament in John Bright: *The Authority of the Old Testament* (SCM). The whole range of serious questions about the role of the Bible is tackled by James Barr in *The Bible in the modern World* (SCM). A more extreme position is taken up by Dennis Nineham: *The Use and Abuse of the Bible* (SPCK).

Chapter Five
Several books are referred to in the text of the chapter. In addition, one of the classics which should be consulted is James Stewart: *Preaching* ('Teach Yourself' series, but previously titled *The Heralds of God*). Colin Morris: *The Word and the Words* (Epworth) makes a vigorous defence of preaching. The standard work on the New Testament is C. H. Dodd: *The Apostolic Preaching and its developments* (Hodder). Other

234

recent works which are valuable to consult are Ian Pitt Watson: *A Kind of Folly* (St Andrew's) and Cleverley Ford: *The Ministry of the Word* (Hodder). But do these writers and the theologians make too grandiose claims? Here consult John Stacey: *Preaching Re-assessed* (Epworth).

Chapter Six
John Gunstone's two volume *Commentary on the New Lectionary* (SPCK) is a useful background work. On the problems of preparing the sermon consult Ernest Best: *From Text to Sermon* (St Andrew's), but on the whole issue of sermon construction there is much help in the standard work of W. E. Sangster entitled *The Craft of the Sermon* (originally Epworth; parts recently republished by Pickering and Inglis). Other works which are helpful (but which overlap slightly with the previous chapter) include David Francis: *The ABC of Preaching* (Epworth) and the extensive book by R. H. Fuller: *What is liturgical preaching?* (SCM)

Chapter Seven
There are few books which deal solely with the concerns of this chapter, but it would be helpful to see the opening chapters of Neil Dixon: *At your service* (Epworth).

Chapter Eight
For the psalms, refer to the Grail version published by Collins as a Fontana entitled *The Psalms: a new translation*. On hymns see K. L. Parry: *Christian Hymns* (SCM) and on how to choose the most appropriate see Erik Routley: *Hymns today and Tomorrow* (Darton). Hymn-books are discussed in Norman Goldhawk: *On Hymns and Hymn-books* (Epworth). The most profound work on the nature and forms of prayer is Neville Ward's *The Use of Praying* (Epworth). There are very many books of prayers for use in public worship, many having been cited in the text of the chapter; useful additions are *New Prayers for Public Worship* (John Paul Press) and *Prayers for the Church Community* (NCEC) compiled by Donald Hilton and Roy Chapman.

235

Chapter Nine
For family worship consult *Together in Church* and *Partners in Learning* (Methodist Division of Education and Youth), *All Generations* (Church Information Office) and *Worship and the Child* (Joint Liturgical Group, published by SPCK). For guidelines on new experimentation, together with some examples, see Alec Gilmore: *Tomorrow's Pulpit* (Lutterworth) and J. G. Davies: *New Perspectives on Worship Today* (SCM)

Chapter Ten
Now read R. E. C. Browne: *The Ministry of the Word* (SCM), a series of profound reflections upon the whole task of preaching seen as the work of the artist.

Other aids

Available on subscription from the **Methodist Publishing House**, Wellington Road, Wimbledon, London SW19 8EU: the magazine *Worship and Preaching*
Available from the **Local Preachers' Office**, Room 195, 1 Central Buildings, London SW1H 9NR:
  Basic Documents: An Introduction to Worship
                  An Introduction to Preaching
                  The Use of the Bible
                  Practical Points for Preachers
  Refresher Courses: The Enrichment of Worship
                  The Modern Use of the Bible
                  The Improvement of Preaching
                  Family Worship
  Leaflets: New Preachers – Note!
                  The Local Preacher Leads in Prayer
                  The Local Preacher Reads his Lessons
                  The Local Preacher Chooses his Hymns
                  Changes in Worship
                  Team Preaching and Planned Preaching
                  Commentaries on the Bible
                  Reading and Study for Local Preachers

Local Preachers' Studies

Worship and Preaching
Study Scheme

Text-book: Richard G. Jones, *Groundwork of Worship and Preaching*

(1) A six-month course is envisaged, taking a fortnight over each study. Students working by correspondence course should send the answers to two questions, save in Studies 11 and 12, every fortnight to the appointed tutor, beginning as soon as possible, and without further notification, after receiving the tutor's name and address. Other students may wish to use the questions for discussion in groups or for examination practice.

(2) The attention of students is drawn to the bibliography.

Study 1
Chapter 1. *Christian Worship*
1. Send your tutor a sermon and order of service for his comments.
2. Which of the five buildings described seems to you best fitted for Christian worship as you understand it? Argue your case.
3. How could you make a Methodist service more of a celebration?

Study 2
Chapter 2. *Worship in the early Church and the Free Churches*
Be sure to look up all the biblical references in this chapter.
1. What elements of early Christian worship is it important for us to preserve?

2. What features of Methodist worship would you wish to keep at all cost?

Study 3
Chapter 3. *The Liturgical Movement and many reforms*
1. Write out the order of service you normally use and compare it with *The Sunday Service without the Lord's Supper* (*Methodist Service Book* pp. B18–B21). To what conclusions do you come?
2. What can the Liturgical Movement as here described do for a village chapel?

Study 4
Chapter 4. *Handling the Bible*
1. Justify your own view of the Bible and say whether or not it has had to be modified as a result of reading this chapter.
2. Put up to your tutor a sermon outline that avoids the errors listed in this chapter.

Study 5
Chapter 5. *Preaching and the Bible*
1. Answer the question, 'Who are you to stand up there and say that?'
2. State any problems you may have in reading in church the lessons in the Lectionary and in preaching from them. Can these problems be resolved?
3. In the light of the second half of this chapter, submit a sermon outline on one of the following texts: Gen. 2:15–17; Isa. 10:20; Matt. 25:29; 1 Cor. 8:9.

Study 6
Chapter 6. *Preparing the Sermon*
   Sections: Introduction
                  What sermons cannot do well
                  What sermons can achieve
                  Types of sermon, types of structure
1. Discuss what you hope to achieve by preaching.
2. Submit to your tutor an outline of an expository sermon, or an 'argument' sermon or a doctrinal sermon.

238

Study 7

Chapter 6. *Preparing the Sermon*
  Sections: Texts and pretexts
            Illustrations and alertness
            Beginnings and endings
            Writing it out

1. What can be done to ensure that a sermon is always interesting?
2. Send to your tutor for comment the opening and concluding paragraph of your last sermon.

Study 8

Chapter 7. *Preparing the Service (1) The Order*
  Sections: Introduction
            The Approach
            The Message
            The Response
            Summary

1. 'The main concern (of an act of worship) is to glorify God, not to do good to man.' How can this truth be made plain to a congregation?
2. It is sometimes said that the reason for the three-fold order of service suggested in this chapter is that it reflects the nature of the Gospel i.e. God speaks before we respond; the initiative is always with him. Comment upon this argument.

Study 9

Chapter 8. *Preparing the Service (2) The Prayers and Hymns*
  Sections: Preparing the Prayers
            Choosing the hymns and songs

1. Write out (a) a responsive prayer of thanksgiving, (b) a prayer of confession and acceptance of forgiveness and (c) a responsive prayer of intercession.
2. Choose three of your favourite hymns. Now look at them in the light of (a) the belief that worship should be corporate rather than individual, (b) the belief that worship should be relevant to the daily life of the congregation, and (c) the belief that worship should be intelligible – in the thought-

forms and language of the actual people worshipping. Send your conclusions to your tutor.

Study 10

Chapter 9. *Various Worship Occasions and Styles*
1. What are the characteristics of children, and the practical problems we should remember when planning church worship with children present?
2. Discuss the merits and demerits of the 'Children's Address'.
3. Write out the outline of a sermon for a Family Service in which visual aids are to be used, giving precise details of the latter.

Study 11

Chapter 10 *More Practical matters*
   Check List for the Sermon
Send the full text of a sermon to your tutor. With it send a self-assessment exercise: your own answers to the questions on the Check List.

Study 12

Chapter 10. *More Practical Matters*
   Check List for the Service
Send an order of service to your tutor with the prayers written out in full. With it send a self-assessment exercise: your own answers to sections 1–4 of the Check List.

240

Index